WHY DEVELOPING COUNTRIES FAIL TO DEVELOP

International Economic Framework and Economic Subordination

Why Developing Countries Fail to Develop

**International Economic Framework and
Economic Subordination**

Purushottam Narayan Mathur
Emeritus Professor
University College of Wales, Aberystwyth

Preface by Wassily Leontief
New York University

Foreword by Yoshimasa Kurabayashi
Hitotsubashi University

MACMILLAN

First published 1991

Published by
MACMILLAN ACADEMIC AND PROFESSIONAL LTD
Houndmills, Basingstoke, Hampshire RG21 2XS
and London
Companies and representatives
throughout the world

Printed in Hong Kong

British Library Cataloguing in Publication Data
Mathur, Purushottam Narayan
Why developing countries fail to develop.
1. Developing countries. Economic conditions
I. Title
330.91724
ISBN 0–333–47634–4

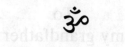

श्री कृष्णार्पणम्

To
my grandfather
B. Brij Behari Mathur

who stopped the cultivation of the cash crop (Indigo), realising it as one of the causes of famine of 1890s and started informal rationing as well as mango tree plantation work in the village

And To
my dear wife
Mrs Sushila Rani Mathur

who not only made this book possible with constant help and encouragement, but also freed the author from the other chores of daily living

Contents

PART VI STRATEGIES FOR DEVELOPMENT

List of Figures

List of Tables

Acknowledgements

The ideas contained here have been developed in book form at the instigation of Professor I.F. Pearce, who encouraged the author to collect the various threads of his ideas into this volume; the author is grateful to him for his continuous help and encouragement. Part of the text was reproduced in University College London, Discussion papers in Economics.

Quite a few colleagues have also helped me at various stages. It is not possible to acknowledge all of them by name, but I would like to mention in particular Messrs David Law, Michael Cain, and Nicholas Perdikis, all my colleagues at the University College of Wales, at Aberystwyth. Dr M. Mahdi, post–doctoral fellow at University College of London, and Dr Mushtaq Ahmed, Associate Professor at University of Multan in Pakistan.

Parts of the text were delivered at seminars at various research institutions, and I am grateful to the participants in these for their comments. Prominent among these were the University of Puerto Rico, at San Juan and MayaGuez Campuses; the Government Development Bank, Puerto Rico; the ESRC/Development Study Group, United Kingdom; North–East Hill University, Shillong, India; Jawaharlal Nehru University, New Delhi; the Institute of Growth, Delhi; the University of Bombay; the Institute of Social Sciences, Ahmedabad; the Institute of Social and Economic Research, Trivandrum; the Maharashtra Association for Cultivation of Sciences, Poona; the University of Baroda, Baroda; the 1986 Tokyo Conference of the World University. Also discussions with Dr M. AL Eigailly and Dr Y. M. Sulaiman of the UN Economic Commission for Africa during the author's consultancy with UNECA were very helpful. I am also obliged to Prof Yoshimasa Kurabayashi for writing such a perceptive foreword.

I am particularly beholden to Nobel Laureate Professor Wassily Leontief, whose theoretical point of view was an inspiration for the development of the ideas expressed in this book. He has been a constant support in my long quest for understanding, the sinews of the workings of the economic system. He was also kind enough to write a few lines for the preface.

P.N. MATHUR

Preface

Forty-five years ago Professor Arthur Lewis made a path-breaking contribution to the understanding of the less developed economies that later earned him a Noble prize.

Mathur – who also comes from a less developed country, India – while teaching in England has centred his research on the fundamental analytical study of underdevelopment in the third world.

His conclusions presented in this volume deserve as much attention as Professor Lewis's observations attracted half a century ago.

WASSILY LEONTIEF

Foreword

In this volume Professor Mathur develops a system of equations which enables one to determine the internal price structure of goods and services for a given level of value added by industry in a country on the basis of the Leontief type of input–output relations. It is shown by the system of equations that the wages in one country should be less than and the value of imported commodity more than those in the partner developed country to which the commodities are exported. It naturally follows from this theoretical framework that the goods having higher import content will be more than proportionately costly. Nontradable services are likely to contain a small portion of commodity input, so it is more inclined to be on the cheap side. In contrast, transport equipment, producers durables, etc., are likely to have large direct and indirect import content, and here they should be more than proportionately costly.

Based upon this theoretical framework and with the help of statistical evidence, the author observes that five groups of developing countries are distinguished. They are:

(a) labour–constrained dual economies, traditional sectors being almost self sufficient;
(b) land–constrained dual economies, traditional sectors being almost self–sufficient;
(c) foreign–exchange–constrained new economies, some sectors having international trade–dependent wage goods technology;
(d) sovereign entities working as locations for offshore assembly plant;
(e) oil exporters.

Those developing countries which fall into the category (a) are characterised as a dualism between a self–sufficient and traditional society and commercialised segments. It is notable to see in the dualism that commercialised segments hardly interact with their stagnant counterpart. The author observes that the illustration of the developing economies of category (a) seems to be sufficiently appropriate for explaining the characteristics of those developing economies in sub–Saharan Africa. By contrast, in the developing countries which belong to the category (b) it is not labour but the land which causes the bottleneck of production. It is implied by the constraint of land that, with the current technique of production, agricultural production is not sufficient to reach the full employment of the whole labour force. In such circumstances, the only way to move towards better standards of living for the people is to increase land productivity. However, the increase of agricultural productivity requires the application of fertilisers and other chemicals to crops and the extensive use of more advanced agricultural instruments and machinery. Thus, it naturally follows that the supply price of wage goods is greatly dependent on international prices of the required imports. The rise of export prices which results from increasing the supply of wage goods tends to reduce the exports and this becomes a major bottleneck for the development of those countries which are classified as this type. The author suggests that some big developing countries like India and Pakistan might fall into this category.

Category (c) is essentially directed towards identifying former colonial economies of Latin America. As a result of historical development in these economies, they are crucially dependent on the imports of intermediate inputs. Any lack of foreign exchange will immediately lead to a shortage of imported intermediate goods. This will force the agriculture sector in the economies to leave the land either uncultivated or starved of the necessary inputs, thus resulting in the decline of economic activity. It is most likely with the wide fluctuations in the prices of internationally traded commodities that the foreign exchange availability of these economies will be changing fast from relative abundance to relative scarcity. Professor Mathur's new work provides a crystal–clear, sharp–edged and bright explanation of why most developing economies have been forced to stay at a standstill in the 1980s and suffer from the collapse of commodity prices in the developed countries. This volume is a valuable contribution to the discussion of a new international economic order which both economists and politicians in the world have sought in recent years.

YOSHIMASA KURABAYASHI

Introduction

After the Second World War, a consistent and conscious international effort was made to develop the economically underdeveloped majority of the world. This effort has been coordinated by the World Bank and the IMF. The developed countries, headed by the USA, were in the forefront of offering profligate advice and 'aid' to achieve that purpose; whole new academic disciplines grew up; quite a few development institutes were founded; the teaching of the theory and art of development to the academics and bureaucrats of the developing world became one of the major exports of the Western universities. However, during the years 1945–90 not a single country graduated from the 'under-developed' to the 'developed' category, and whatever illusions of slow progress towards the goal there were, were shattered by the debt crisis and its aftermath in the 1980s. The only stars remaining in the firmament were the economies of the offshore assembly and distribution centres of city states like Hong Kong and Singapore, and even they could boast an industrial wage level of only about a third or a quarter of that of the industrialised world. If one takes a similar time period before the First World War, one finds quite a few countries graduating into the industrialised world – France, Germany, Japan, and the USSR, for example: something has obviously gone wrong.

NON-APPLICABILITY OF RECEIVED ECONOMIC DOCTRINES

To perceptive economists working in the development field, the irrelevance of existing economic theory to the problems of the developing countries became obvious quite early on. Dudley Seers argued that 'economics' as practised was largely the Anglo-Saxon economics of advanced, industrial, private enterprise economies. He argued that the economics of this 'special case' could not apply to the under-developed countries because their institutions and social structures were different, and that an understanding of the international relationships between rich and poor countries was crucially important for appreciating their problems. He emphasised the need to study the world economy, which he contrasted with the theory of international

1

trade (Seers, 1962; 1963). Subsequent efforts in instituting interdisciplinary studies that were supposed to yield relevant theories for guiding development policies also failed to produce any fruitful results: a major theoretical understanding of the economics of under-development cannot be attained through an uncoordinated application of disparate theoretical prescriptions.

TOWARDS A NEW PERSPECTIVE

The basic macroeconomics for analysing the problems of under-development had been developed in the 1880s by the Indian economist and politician Dada Bhai Naoroji (1988). Naoroji's Drain Theory inspired and became the bedrock of the economic justification of Mahatma Gandhi's movement for Indian Independence. But it was completely ignored by the Western academic community, which was preoccupied in trying to discover 'universal' principles governing long-run economic behaviour. The absence of a suitable microeconomic theory congruous with Naoroji's macro vision precluded any understanding of the mechanics of the detailed operation of the economic system, so a total system on that base could not be constructed. That had to wait until the development of Leontief's (1936, 1951) input–output analysis, a technique which enables the analyst to trace the repercussions of 'unequal' colonial trade from one sector to another. Programming techniques, both linear and non-linear, enable the implications of various constraints under which the economy of an under-developed country works to be examined.

These techniques liberate us from the tyranny of the neoclassical assumptions about smooth production and consumption functions imposed on an analysis by the technique of calculus of which they are integral part. These assumptions are not strictly true for developed countries themselves; they are definitely misleading for the economies of under-developed countries. These economies have only a few techniques of commodity production available – usually only either traditional or modern – and these production techniques are quite distinct, making the assumption of a smooth production function fallacious. This makes the availability of individual factors of production bottlenecks to possible production, rather than mere signals of a need to change production technique. And such change of any technique is not a costless process but requires capital accumulation, using scarce factors such as foreign exchange. An individual's consumption function is truncated from below, as there is a subsistence level of consumption below which it is difficult to reduce the wage level. In the developed countries, this level may never be reached and so it is not necessary to include this limiting condition when developing a theory for them. However, at the margin this subsistence level itself can be influenced by harsh or more relaxed institutional conditions; it may thus be possible to lower this subsistence level further in dictatorial regimes than is possible in a democracy.

THE INTERNATIONAL FRAMEWORK AND THE PROBLEM OF PRICE RELATIVES

Apart from the internal conditions vitiating the assumptions of neoclassical economic theory, the economy of under-developed countries is dominated and constrained by the international health of the markets for commodities that they export. The marginal cost of production of these commodities is determined mainly by the country which produces such export commodities at the lowest wage rate in terms of international currency unit. If the wage goods in the country are produced by the traditional methods of production which do not use modern inputs, the price of wage goods in general and foodgrains in particular can be reduced as much as necessary. But this price level makes the use of modern production techniques, with imported chemicals and other inputs, economically infeasible. As there are strict physical limits to traditional production, this tends to lead to famine conditions in these under-developed countries.

This price structural problem, basic to the status of under-developed economies and their economic relations with the developed world, became evident only after the publication in 1982 of UN studies on the purchasing power parities of a sample of countries. These studies, *inter alia*, gave the relative prices of a large number of commodities in both developed and under-developed countries. These, combined with the characteristics of the under-developed countries distinct from those assumed in the foundations of the neoclassical economics, gave an insight into the real working of the microeconomics of these countries parallel to the macro insights of Dada Bhai Naoroji. The economic system so developed is the subject matter of this book. To fix ideas only bold outline is presented.

FAILURE OF DEVELOPMENT

This perspective helps to elucidate the historical experience of the under-developed countries' economies; it explains how 'unequal' trading relations lead to the distortions in the price structure of the underdeveloped country, making balanced development of the country impossible and facilitating the 'economic drain' that kept the country permanently under-developed. Any change in the commodity prices favourable to the under-developed world was inevitably followed by a reaction that left their situation worse off than the one they had started with. The so-called 'debt problem' of the under-developed world promises to become a 'debt trap' unless the rules of international economic game are changed. Under-developed countries seem to be trapped in providing 'unrequited exports'; this will not only keep the living standard of the employed population low, but also perpetuate the hunger of the increasingly large unemployed segment of the population. And the only advice the development experts seem able to give is to cut down the population, so that reduced resources may suffice to feed it.

This analysis makes it clear that such pessimistic conclusions will prevail, irrespective of any tinkering with the structure of the 'debt problem'. Reduction of debt, or increasing the period for payment, are not going to deal with the underlying problem: the basic structure of current international economic relations itself requires to be overhauled. The understanding gained by relating economic theory to the actual conditions of the under-developed countries will help to improve the situation as and when the political opportunity to do so presents itself. Meanwhile, we need carefully to evaluate the economic consequences of any self-help scheme that these under-developed countries may themselves devise, either singly or jointly.

STRUCTURE OF THE BOOK

The book is divided into seven parts. Part I gives the central argument in simple terms. Part II discusses the relevance of various economic theories in relation to the prevailing economic environment and constraints; it further gives a background synoptic view of these countries' economic history. Part III develops the theory of the determination of commodity price in international markets and shows how this provides a framework in which both developed and under-developed economies operate. Parts IV and V develop a macro and microeconomic system for under-developed economies. Part VI examines the consequences of some possible strategies for development. Part VII is mathematical and deals with the precise delineation of the theory of international trade when Say's law of equal exchange is not satisfied in every period. It also develops, *inter alia*, the structure of the resulting prices as well as the production possibility curve for the under-developed country in such a situation.

The book is written for students and practitioners interested in development who wish to comprehend the working of the economy of under-developed countries participating in international trade. It is, therefore, primarily non-mathematical. Except for Part VII, which is in the nature of a mathematical Appendix, most of the book does not employ mathematics at a higher level than that of school algebra, and even that can be skipped without much loss of the argument. Most of the propositions are illustrated by empirical examples taken from the experience of India as an under-developed country, and of the United Kingdom as a developed one; these are countries whose economies have been closely followed by the author over the last forty years. However, for special conditions examples from the experience of other countries have been readily used. Comprehensiveness in the empirical part was not attempted as the aim was to give scholars and practitioners an appropriate perspective view. The author would consider himself amply rewarded if this helps to increase even slightly the understanding of the stark dilemma being faced by the under-developed majority of mankind.

Part I
The Central Argument

1 The Development Dilemma

COLLAPSE OF DEVELOPMENT IN THE 1980s: AN UNEXPLAINED PHENOMENON

In the years after 1945, developing market economies made respectable economic progress; hardly any of them entered the category of the industrialised market economies, however. And in the 1980s many of them, especially those in Sub-Saharan Africa, Latin America and the Middle East became burdened with negative growth of per capita income; in some cases, decades of development efforts were wiped out. No development theory had predicted this result; conjectured causes of this phenomenon, as well as the solutions proposed, have been of an ad hoc nature. But unless a theoretical understanding of the nature of the malady is achieved, we will not know whether the solutions proposed by the World Bank and others will not in fact make the situation worse, especially as most of the solutions proposed address the problem of repaying the debts rather than how to continue on the road to development.

This book is written in an attempt theoretically to elucidate this peculiar phenomenon. We want to examine in depth whether the current country-centric theories of economic development need be recast so as to incorporate the causes of the changes in the world commodity prices as an integral part. Analysis carried out by World Bank experts and others take commodity prices and their changes as almost given; this leaves the developing countries as helpless sufferers of the crisis. We have to discuss how this incorporation is to be done, and how it will affect the development strategies.

The effects on development processes of low price levels and substantially different price structures in developing countries, as revealed by UN studies on purchasing power parities, have also not been appreciated. This made the results of project analyses at micro level and development plans at the macro level quite inappropriate, leading to failures of individual projects and frustration of development efforts. The debt crisis of the Third World countries in the 1980s is just one symptom of a deep-rooted malady. The best laid development plans, that seemed so promising in the 1960s and 1970s, could

9

not withstand the chill winds of the international economic order of the 1980s, and those chill winds could not be withstood, since the implications of the differing price structures for development theory have not been appreciated.

The process of price determination in different situations becomes crucial to appreciating the growth process, and so is a relevant topic for discussion. The mainstream economic analysis completely fails in this task. Samuelson (1984), for instance, ascribes these differences in structure of prices to the distinction between tradeable and non-tradeable goods. While prices of tradeable goods were supposed to be similar, the differences in non-tradeables prices were more extreme. The reason adduced was that different productivities in tradeables lead to differences in wage rates, while the local prices of the non-tradeables depended on the local wage rates. However, this explanation is found to be insufficient when we note that the price structural differences within tradeables themselves were also found to be of a significantly high order (see Table 1.1 below for a summary presentation of price structures).

It seems that, in the short run, the general assumptions on which neoclassical economic theory is based are not satisfied in the developing countries, nor is there any tendency for the economy to move in the direction of the long-run equilibrium envisaged by neoclassical economic analysis. This implies that to understand the economies of the developing countries we have to look to the economic consequences of the constraints, both national and international, under which they are operating at the present time. For this purpose we will have to explore the position of developing countries in the context of world economic growth, and how such countries are able to respond to changes in the international economic climate within their own local constraints. This we shall now proceed to do.

DIFFERENT PARADIGMS IN ECONOMIC ANALYSIS

It is thus clear that to understand the current economic situation of developing countries the neoclassical paradigm is unhelpful. However, that is not the only paradigm in economics, though it is theoretically the most sophisticated. However, mathematical sophistication is no recommendation for use if it does not help in elucidating experience on the ground. Any appropriate paradigm can easily be cast into a mathematically sophisticated framework that will help to bring background assumptions and implications into relief. The real problem is its applicability in the actual situation. Modern macroeconomics depends on a different paradigm of economic reality, as is evident from the fact that all attempts to construct 'microfoundations' of macroeconomics have failed (Weintraub, 1979). The commercial revolution that was the harbinger of the industrial revolution had its economic paradigm in Mercantilism with its emphasis on the freedom of merchants. The industrial revolution saw the development of classical economic thought advocating the freedom of the producer; as the economy was working under the constraint of availability of land, and there was an army of unemployed labour, the paradigm of the wage fund became the anchor of employment theory, with labour's demand being relegated to the subsistence level. After the resistance of English landowners to the imports of corn from the colonies was overcome with the abolition of the corn laws, the land constraint on the British economy was removed. With economic growth the standard of living of common people also rose above subsistence level. The necessity for a new paradigm for economics not based on land constraint and incorporating a theory of demand became apparent. The neoclassical paradigm filled the need.

These paradigms were, however, not found useful in understanding the economic plight of workers as well as that of colonies and dependencies. In the terminology of Toynbee,[1] we can say that while they helped in understanding the economic issues being faced by the 'creative-cum-dominant' minority of the modern commercial–industrial civilisation, the internal and external proletariat did not find in them a satisfactory explanation of their plight.

These proletariats created their own systems. Marxian economics developed as an attempt by the internal proletariat to understand the working of this economic system; while Dada Bhai Naoroji's 'Drain Theory' (1888)[2] was developing a paradigm to elucidate the economic situation of an economic dependency. Both works proved to be potent forces in political developments. While the communist revolutions got economic inspiration from Marx, the Indian freedom movement of Gandhi used Naoroji's theory to emphasise the economic harm being inflicted by British rule in India. But while Marxism, being the intellectual tool of the internal proletariat, could get to the attention of the world academic community, the drain theory remained external to mainstream economics. However, when we look at the current economic predicament of the developing countries, we find that the paradigm developed by Naoroji can significantly help us to analyse the situation. What follows is an attempt to adapt the theory to present-day problems.

THE PATTERNS OF DEVELOPMENT

The developing countries have largely been producers of agricultural and mining products. Their manufacturing has largely consisted of the output from traditional industries and some modern industries processing such things as agricultural products and textiles, primarily for local consumption. The development process has so far mainly consisted in transferring the technical know-how of developed countries in creating modern production facilities to developing countries by the installation of suitable capital equipment, as well as by the creation of an industrial infrastructure. This has been accomplished in no small measure by the granting of loans, mostly by the governments, banks and other institutions of the equipment supplier countries, supplemented by financing from the World Bank. Simultaneously a significant amount of investment was carried out by multinational firms.

These investments were of two kinds. One was to produce in developing countries goods primarily meant for the developed countries, the other was designed for the economic growth of developing countries themselves. Usually a loan provided for starting a business is repaid with interest from the earnings from that business. This should have worked well for the first type of loan, as the product of the business was supposed to provide not only the income, but also the hard currency in which the loan (together with its interest) was to be returned. However, the earnings from the second type were in the local currency; there were not even any identifiable earnings from the loans provided for strengthening infrastructure. Payments on account of the second type of loans had thus to be from the usual export earnings of the country rather, than from the earnings of the production capabilities created by its use.

WAGE LEVELS FOR DEVELOPING COUNTRIES AND LOAN REPAYMENT

The manufacturing industries which export to developed countries are producers of products which could in fact be produced within the developed countries themselves. The feasibility of these exports thus primarily depends on low labour costs. The basic technology of production is by and large the same as that established in the developing countries through technological transfer rather than new fundamental research incorporating an intermediate technology. Further, with 'technological transfer', more often than not, the appropriate machinery and other equipment is also exported to the developing country and ordinarily comes from the same production line as the one established in the developed country. So the production technique is largely the same except for that required for subsidiary activities like transport of material, etc. As the products of the industry thus established are primarily meant to be exported to the developed country itself, the developing country should provide a substantial saving in labour costs.

PRICE STRUCTURE IN LOW-WAGE COUNTRIES

But how can low wages in developing countries sustain their labour force? The answer to this can be gleaned from the UN studies on international comparisons of real product and purchasing power parities. These studies, though meant for comparing the total real gross product of different countries shown of the distorting effects of exchange rates, give, *inter alia*, the price structure of the consumption and investment goods of the countries studied.

Table 1.1 gives these price comparisons for three groups of developing countries. Group 1 consisted of countries having real GDP per capita less than 15 per cent of that of the USA, Group II between 15 to 30% and Group III between 30 to 45% in 1975. The sample for Group I countries consisted of Malawi, Kenya, India, Pakistan, Sri Lanka, Zambia, Thailand, and Philippines; that for Group II of Korea, Malaysia, Colombia, Jamaica, Syria, and Brazil. Group III was represented in the UN sample by Romania, Mexico, Yugoslavia, Iran, Uruguay and Ireland.

Table 1.1 shows that low-wage countries also have lower prices of essential consumer goods, though not proportionately so. Though the average wage rate in Group I countries is only 8.4% of that of the USA, their real wage rate works out at 21%. For Group II and Group III it is 22% and 44% respectively instead of 11% and 26%. It may be noted that for Group I and II the real wage rate is the same, the apparent difference being completely compensated by higher

Table 1.1   Average price indices for groups of countries (1975)[1]

	Real income group					
	I	II	III	IV	V	VI
Real GDP per capita (USA = 100)						
Range	< 15	15–30	30–45	45–60	60–90	>90
Mean	9.01	23.1	37.3	52.4	76.0	100
Price indexes (USA = 100)						
Tradeables	60.0	70.7	86.6	97.9	118.5	100
Of which						
Food	49.8	62.9	68.2	82.2	107.2	100
Of which						
Bread and cereals	35.3	56.7	55.0	58.1	97.2	100
Meat	44.4	67.3	72.7	93.2	127.2	100
Coffee, tea, cocoa	81.8	118.5	167.7	285.1	192.8	100
Tobacco	73.2	66.2	130.4	78.5	147.8	100
Clothing and footwear	55.7	59.0	79.8	100.5	126.0	100
Furniture, appliances	77.6	91.4	96.3	94.9	93.8	100
Transport equipment	168.4	163.5	226.2	162.4	149.1	100
Producer durables	130.1	105.6	135.8	116.4	125.8	100
Fuel and Power*	64.4	82.1	81.9	99.1	151.7	100
Of which						
Liquid fuel	123.4	118.4	113.7	166.0	166.5	100
Non-tradeables	24.9	37.2	46.5	53.4	96.7	100
Of which						
Construction	46.0	52.2	72.8	78.5	115.8	100
Services	20.7	34.1	41.2	46.3	94.6	100
Of which						
Education	11.0	17.7	32.2	38.0	100.7	100
Medical Care	27.5	29.7	35.9	33.2	62.0	100
Total consumption (including government)	40.1	50.1	59.2	69.1	102.8	100
Non-residential capital formation	109.0	95.6	118.7	107.4	131.5	100
Av. industrial wage rate**	8.4	11.0	26.0	36.9	77.5	100
Av. real consumption of industrial worker	20.9	22.0	43.9	53.3	75.4	100

Notes:
1. There are wide variations within each group, so the table is largely indicative only.
*   In this group electricity is included, which is non-tradeable.
** Industrial wage rates have been calculated from UNIDO (1987), which has culled them from the industrial census data of individual countries; data is approximate as not all the countries in the group reported.

Source: Kravis *et al.* (1982) Tables 6.8; 6.12; Appendix Table 6.3.

prices. These groups include not only all 'exporters of manufactures' but also about 90–95% of all developing countries. Only a few developing countries, depending on high primary commodities prices, are in Group III. In the UN sample they consisted of only four market economies – Mexico, Iran, Uruguay and Ireland. Of these, after the collapse of commodity prices in the 1980s, the real wage rate of Mexico, Iran and Uruguay came down to Group II level [see UNIDO, 1987 for the 1983 wage rate]．We see that though the nominal wage rate in Group I developing countries was 8.4% of the US wage rate and in Group II countries 11%; when we adjust those figures for the price of consumption goods, they become 21% and 22% respectively. Thus in almost all the developing countries (i.e., Groups I and II) the real wage rate is about one-fifth of that of USA which might just be sufficient to meet the 'necessities' of life. This may be conceived of as a 'subsistence wage' for industrial labour.

All these developing countries are part of an international economic system where they must export to get the basic wherewithal for survival and growth. The nominal wage rate is determined by the price their export commodities fetch in the international market and the nominal prices of 'necessities' are determined by the nominal wage rate. However, in Group I countries the nominal price of foodgrains is so low that it will hardly be feasible for them to use imported inputs like fertilisers and fuel in the production of these 'necessities'.

TWO GROUPS OF DEVELOPING COUNTRIES

This clearly demarcates developing countries into two groups – one whose price structure cannot support modern agriculture and the other whose price structure can just support it. In the Group I agricultural production depends on the traditional techniques of production; with such techniques, there is an upper limit to agricultural output per unit of land as well as per unit of labour. As these countries cannot import non-subsidised foodgrains from outside, their total employment can hardly be increased. For the land-constrained economies among them any transfer of land for growing commercial export crops will only reduce the area under food crops and thus tend to reduce the availability of foodgrains and thus lead to the creation of additional unemployment and/or famine conditions.

For labour-constrained economies, any diversion of labour from producing food crops to working in export agriculture or industry will, similarly, tend to reduce the production of foodgrains, etc. This will again show itself in famine conditions. The recurring famines in Africa in the 1970s and 1980s may have something to do with their efforts at export promotion and development in these decades. Similarly, the endemic famines of the late nineteenth and early twentieth centuries in the Indian sub-continent were primarily related to getting export crops out of a limited land supply.

These countries cannot change their price structure by a relative increase of foodgrain prices so as to make their production non-loss-making after paying for inputs like fertilisers and after investing capital for modernisation of agriculture, because that will increase the wage rate in the country. This in its turn will raise the cost of producing export commodities. As the price of the export commodity is determined in the international market, either the country will be priced out of the world market or it will have to devalue its currency. This will bring it back to the starting point, with some extra internal inflation as the consequence of its endeavour. The new price of foodgrains will still not be able to support the modernisation of its production process, as the primary inputs of the improved techniques of production (chemicals, fertilisers, etc.) have to be imported. And with the given interrelationships between different sectors, the local price of foodgrains in international units just cannot be increased.

The price structure of Group II developing countries is such that it can support the modernisation of foodgrain production. However, for that they require imported inputs. So production becomes constrained by the availability of foreign exchange. The greater the amount of their foreign exchange earnings, the greater amount of wage goods they can produce, so they can have higher employment. But to be able to increase their exports they may have to reduce the price of their export goods. This will have repercussions on the wage rates they can offer, and therefore on the price of wage-goods.

The standard of living of the average wage worker in the two groups of developing countries thus is almost the same after all. The ability of Group II countries to be able to use modern techniques of agricultural production has not helped its labour force to attain a higher standard of living. Temporary increases in the price of export commodities create a temporary advancement, only to have it painfully reversed as the international price regains its normal level. In some of these countries the wage rates in the 1970s increased significantly, only to fall back in the 1980s. Some of these countries are represented in Group III countries in Table 1.1.

MACROECONOMICS OF DEVELOPING COUNTRIES

Lewis's Macro Model of Development

Following Lewis (1954) and Myint (1958), we can use the notion of two *Sub-economies* to tell the development story. A developing country consists of two sectors, one modern and the other traditional. They have been referred to in the literature as 'capitalist' and 'subsistence' economies. We shall retain this nomenclature as it does not have any institutional implications. The 'traditional' sector does not imply that all people getting their income there are living at subsistence level only; it may consist of landlords, chiefs, etc. living lavishly compared to the poor people around them. Similarly, the 'modern' sector may give bare subsistence wages to its workforce.

The 'modern' sector also does not consist only of modern industry, but will have plantations, mines and agricultural cultivation using modern production techniques with fertilisers, etc. Similarly, the 'traditional' sector will consist of traditional peasant agriculture, cottage industries and traditional services. In their purest form the two economies can be conceived as closed and working in complete isolation of each other. The traditional economy has been self-sufficient for many years, and the modern economy may be conceived of as an implantation of a self-sufficient economy from already developed countries. Like the developed countries, this modern sector may grow from its own savings and provide capital goods, etc. from its own produce; it should not require help from any other sector for its growth.

Lewis conceived the traditional economy as having surplus labour, which implies having limited land; there is thus open or disguised unemployment. On the other hand Myint looks at an economy where land is abundant while labour is fully employed in the traditional sector itself. The wage rate in the traditional sector is conventional, determined partly by subsistence and partly by custom. In purely family enterprise, with no hired workers, the 'wage' is the average product, it equals average consumption. The traditional sector hardly ever saves.

In such a setting, the modern sector can develop with a low fixed real wage. This wage may be slightly higher than that in the traditional sector and may be considered as subsistence wage in a new setting. With low wages, the profit rate will be high and, as most of profits would be saved, this will imply a high saving rate in the modern sector. This should be higher than if the modern sector had been paying the wages it was paying in its country of origin. This will lead to a high rate of growth which will be sustained by the capital produced within the modern sector itself and by absorbing labour from the traditional sector. In consequence the traditional sector will shrink, but whatever is remaining will remain self-sufficient. This process over time should lead to the whole of labour eventually working in the modern sector. Then, in the absence of any reservoir of the cheap labour power, any further capital accumulation would lead to an increase in the real wage rate in the modern sector. This process will continue until the country has become a developed one. It will have acquired modern technology and also acquired a real wage rate equal to that of a developed country.

Lewis's Development Model: A Diagrammatic Representation

Two periods of the functioning of the economy according to the Lewis schema are depicted in Figure 1.1. The upper panel depicts the period subsequent to that depicted in the lower panel; the left-hand panel represents the traditional and the right-hand panel the modern technology. Total labour in the economy is $n+N$ and land $l+L$. In the first period n labour together with l land produce an output in the traditional sector. All this output consist of consumption goods appropriated by labour which consumes a units of goods per labourer.

In the modern sector, N labourers, together with L land and K capital produce AN amount of output with the help of modern technology. Out of this $a'N$ amount consists of consumption goods which is distributed to the labour working in that sector. Per unit consumption of labour a' is slightly greater in this sector than in that of traditional sector (a), but much less than A – the productivity of labour with modern technology. The remaining output of this sector $(A-a')N$, is produced in the form of investment goods. Let the output–capital ratio be B. Then the output of the modern sector is equal to BK. Therefore, the amount of investment can be written as $(A-a')BK / A$. This gives us the rate of growth of capital in the modern sector as $B(A-a') / A$ per period.

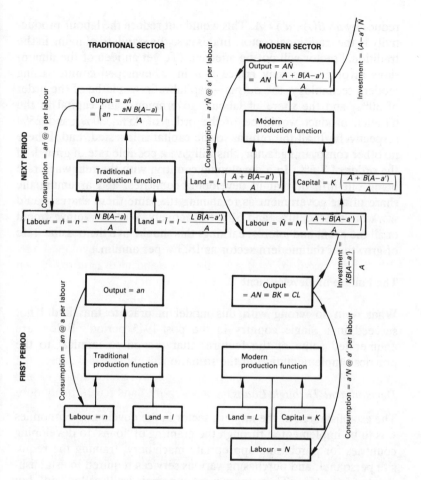

Figure 1.1   Lewis's development model: diagrammatic representation

As this sector is able to take land and labour from the traditional sector according to its requirements, they will also increase in the same proportion. Labour and land in the modern sector in the next period will thus be $N \{ 1 + B(A-a') A \}$ and $L \{1 + B(A-a') / A \}$ respectively. Then labour, and land in the remaining traditional sector would become $n - NB(A-a') / A$ and $1 - LB(A-a')/A$ respectively. The decrease in its output would depend on whether labour or land was the bottleneck for production in that sector. If labour was the bottleneck, the output of the traditional sector would reduce by $aNB(A-a') / A$. This would not reduce the labour productivity in the traditional sector. In this case the standard of living in the traditional sector will not be affected. (To get an idea of the dimensions involved, we may notice that in a developed country using modern technology, the output – capital ratio would be of the order of 30%, and the share of labour, government, and capital in the national product would be of the order of 45%, 30%, and 25% respectively. If all the returns to the capital is invested, and if there no other constraining factor, this will give a possible rate of growth of the order of 7.5%. In a developing country, with the real wage rate being one-fifth of that in developing countries, and assuming the share of the government as remaining the same these shares would work out as 9%, 30%, and 61% respectively. With the reinvestment of all the profit and interest earnings this should give the possible rate of growth of the modern sector as 18.3% per annum.)

The Failure of Development

What went so wrong with this model in practice that it did not succeed in a single country in the post-1945 period? Below are enumerated some of the features that proved so inimical to the practical implementation of the scenario.

Development Through Loans

The establishment of the modern sector in the developing economies was to be implemented through the granting of 'loans' to developing countries for purchasing appropriate machinery, training the requisite personnel, and purchasing various services required in establishment of industries. These loans were euphemistically called 'aid', but the grant component in them was not very significant.

This implied that a significant amount of surplus from the modern sector of the economy would have to be transferred to the industrialised world that provided the loans and expertise. The 'higher' profits were thus not available for local savings and investment purposes. Further, due to transport and trading costs, the capital equipment was more costly in the developing country than in the country of origin and similarly the commodity whose international sale provided the wherewithal for servicing the loan had to be priced sufficiently below its price in the developed countries to meet the transport and trading cost of reaching its market from the country of production.

To get a feel of the dimension of the problem, let us assume that in the modern industrialised country, $1,000 worth of capital is producing gross output worth $300; of which $200 goes to labour as wages, and $100 towards capital servicing. The cost of the same amount of physical capital becomes (say) $1,300 as transport and trading costs are added to it. If the output is to be exported to the industrialised country, its value in the country of origin would be say $230. The capital servicing cost at the rate of 10% per annum would be $130, leaving $100 worth of goods for payment to the local factors of production. Assuming the wage rate to be one-fifth of that in the developed countries, wages will absorb $40, leaving only $60 for profits and/or investment. This will hardly suffice even for the replacement of the capital goods. The question of net investment is therefore somewhat academic.

However, the low wage rate will also mean that the consumption goods can be produced cheaply within the modern sector of the country. Assuming that the consumption goods thus produced are at about half the price in international currency, the real wages worth $40 in the developed country would cost only $20 in the developing country. That would leave $80 for profit and gross investment. The progress of the modern sector may thus roll on, though at a much reduced pace than that implied in Lewis's celebrated model.

Importing Intermediate Goods

In many cases the technical transfer is only partial. Some intermediate good or part of the product is even then required to be imported. The cost of that has to bear the transport and trading cost, which has to come out from the local earnings; this will further reduce the local income in the developing country. Suppose in the above example, a part valued $100 in the developed country is imported, and assume that the capital and labour requirements of the remaining production are correspondingly less, then the capital exported to the developing country will be worth only $667, whereas its price to the receiving country will be $867, assuming the cost of transport, etc. as 30% of the cost. This will reduce the loan servicing charges to $87 only. However, in the current cost of production there will be an imported element of $130 ($100 the cost in the exporting country and 30% cost of transport, trade, etc.). Thus out of the $230 price of the product, only $13 will remain as local income. This would not even suffice to pay the wages at the rate of one-fifth of those in the developed countries, as that itself would absorb about $27. However, with consumption goods at about half the price in nominal terms it may just suffice to pay the wages.

The above hypothetical example seems to approximate the price structure observed in Group II developing countries, as shown in Table 1.1. Prices of non-imported tradeables were about two-thirds of those in the USA, of imported goods nearly one-third higher and of services about one-third. Thus consumption goods prices were about half of the US level, the nominal wage rate about 10% while the real wage rate was one-fifth. We cannot thus expect the modern sector of those countries to expand under its own steam as it will hardly produce sufficient for its own renewal. However, it may produce sufficient to be able to pay the interest on its foreign loans, and its continued existence may depend crucially on getting new loans equivalent to the gross repayments. An increase in the size of the modern sector depends thus not only on the net investment from outside, but also from the current earning of the foreign exchange. For its current working it requires sufficient foreign market to be able not only to service its foreign loans but also to import the intermediate goods and parts required for its current production.

This has two implications. The size of the modern sector would depend on export performance. And changes in the international price of the export commodity will directly lead to the fluctuations in the size of the modern sector. Hence, decreasing commodity price will lead to decreasing employment, and there is hardly any chance that this strategy of development will bring about increases in the real wage rate, even in the long run.

High Cost and Low Productivity of Technology Transfer

The development loans given under 'aid' programmes are often 'tied' in one way or other; that substantially increases the real servicing charges for the loans provided as aid. 'If over-charges resulting from the restrictive terms of the aid are subtracted from the total amount, the average net flow, according to calculations of the Inter-American Economic and Social Council, is approximately 54 per cent of the gross flow' (Santos, 1970). This may significantly increase the servicing charges even if an account is taken of the easy terms on which loans are provided under aid programmes.

At any time there are various 'layers' of techniques of production in the industrialised countries. The productivity of the best technological layer may be as much as twice that of the worst layer still producing (Popkin and Mathur, 1989). Frequently the technique that is transferred to the developing country is one that is on its way out in its country of origin. Its productivity would thus be about half that of the best firm or of the order of two-thirds the average productivity in the same industry in the developed country at the time of transfer. But within a few years as the old techniques become increasingly obsolete, productivity may be reduced to the order of half the average of that in the developed country. This implies that to be economically viable the developing country must provide substantial savings in the wage costs.

Dependence of the Modern Sector on the Traditional One for Wage Goods

In countries having a sizeable traditional sector, there is another way to nurture the modern sector and simultaneously keep international competitiveness. That is to confine the modern sector to non-wage goods industries only. Wage goods for the labour in the modern sector would then be provided by the traditional sector. This will allow the nominal wages in the modern sector to be depressed sufficiently to ensure international competitiveness without in turn depressing real wages. This solution to the dilemma depends on the fact that the traditional sector does not require any imported input in its production process; this makes the cost of the production in this sector independent of the exchange rate. As the local real wage rate depends on the nominal wage rate in the local currency and also the prices of the wage goods in the same local currency, it can be made as low as necessary in the international currency as the requirements of international competitiveness through exchange rate manipulation dictate. The prices of wage goods can be suitably depressed to keep the real wage rate at the subsistence level.

This strategy violates Lewis's condition that both the modern and the traditional sectors of the economy should be closed and self-contained within themselves. Really it makes the modern sector a parasite on the traditional sector. Productivity in the traditional sector cannot be increased without modern inputs, the total output of wage goods it can produce being limited by the availability of either land or labour. A voluntary transfer of wage goods from traditional to modern sector can be only on a limited scale, conducted primarily by the landlord class in the traditional economy who have the wherewithal to live a life of luxury. Any extra transfers will have to be accomplished by means of extra taxation of the traditional sector.

After a time it may become necessary to have an autocratic and repressive state apparatus to accomplish this task; no wonder quite a few developing countries end up having dictatorial political regimes. Even then, there is limit beyond which such attempts at modernisation cannot go. At that stage, bigger developing countries may be able to modernise a part of the wage goods sector by subsidising it so as to keep the prices of the foodgrains and other wage goods at the same level as that prevalent before the modernisation programme. This will enable them to increase the total output of the wage goods and thus of the modern sector itself. However, the subsidy will have to be given from the savings of the modern sector itself; this will drastically reduce the potentiality of growth of the modern sector. This strategy of growth will also quickly reach a limit due to the heavy cost of subsidies, leading to too slow growth of the modern sector. With this strategy, there will be hardly any possibility of an increase in the real wage rate.

Commodity Export-based Development and the Fallacy of Composition

Implication of Low Nominal Wage   Most of the developing countries are basically exporters of primary commodities. In the international competitive market the countries having low nominal wage rates are at a competitive advantage in selling their export commodities. This hardly allows them to have a wage rate higher than the subsistence level of living. Usually, this truncated modern sector subsists on the wage goods provided by the subsistence sector of the economy. When the production of the export commodity, entails the use of a scarce factor of production the total production of the traditional sector is proportionately reduced. Thus if in a land-scarce developing country, an export commodity like cotton takes up (say) one-third of the cultivable land, the production of the subsistence crops will be reduced to two-thirds of their previous production. Their productivity cannot be increased by traditional means not requiring the inputs of the products of modern sectors. This implies that the total labour that can be employed even at a subsistence level is reduced to about two-thirds, and we get a situation of chronic unemployment. The creation of the modern export sector thus leads to a decrease in the total employment in the economy instead of the creation of new employment. Similar results will follow if labour instead of land is the bottleneck in the traditional economy. As the labour transferred for working in the export industry will not be available for working in the traditional sector, this will reduce its total output, which will lead to a reduction of the total available wage goods, resulting in a decrease in total employment.

The way out of this is the modernisation of foodgrain production. But that requires inputs of fertilisers, etc. and the use of modern machinery and plant. This not only requires foreign exchange for investment, but also for the purchase of intermediate inputs. That will not allow the nominal wage rates to be as low as necessary in terms of international currency; thus it will tend to reduce the competitiveness of the export commodity in the international market, which virtually rules out this mode of escape.

Almost every developing country tries to increase its export earnings, as foreign exchange is not only the key for development but also for defence and for the luxurious living of the ruling class. Once they have contracted international loans for development purposes, the foreign exchange for servicing the loans becomes an international obligation; this induces the country in turn to try further to increase its foreign exchange earnings.

The Fallacy of Composition and Barriers to the Increase of the Long-run Real Wage Rates   In order to increase foreign exchange availability, every developing country will try to increase its exports. They will tend to project the benefit of their efforts by assuming constant export prices (even World Bank experts advising individual countries on how to restructure their economies use a constant price assumption in calculating the cost/benefit ratios of their recommended policies). However, as all the developing countries are in a similar situation, this will lead to the world supply increasing faster than demand especially if most of these countries are getting financial assistance for this increase in capacity from international agencies. This will lead to a fall in the world price of the commodity in question, nullifying part of the effort. Thus an action which is good for one, if others do not act similarly, becomes dubious in its results if others also act in the same way. This 'fallacy' of composition is largely ignored by both policy-makers and their international adviser.

Ordinarily, real wage rates of formally employed labour cannot be reduced beyond a certain level, although this level can be further reduced to some degree in a totalitarian regime. As most of the developing countries try to increase their export earnings as much as they can, in the long run they tend to increase exports until their wage levels are reduced to this level; in the pursuit of this aim many such countries then find themselves saddled with totalitarian regimes and a bare subsistence level of wage rates.

With these dynamics, it is highly improbable that these labour- or land-constrained developing countries will be able to raise their wage-rates high enough to transform the price structure in such a way that modern techniques of producing foodgrains become economically feasible.

Similar considerations apply for the import-constrained developing economies having all their production from modern fossil fuel-using techniques; the fallacy of composition also prevents them from increasing their 'real' wage rate on a long-term basis. Whenever there is a world commodity price rise, they may be able to increase their 'real' wage rate for a short time. But the increase in commodity prices generates a scramble for creating new capacity, until prices settle back to approximate the cost of production based on 'subsistence' level wage rates only.

NOMINAL WAGE RATES IN DEVELOPING COUNTRIES

To get an idea of how the above factors have affected various developing countries, Table 1.2 shows the average manufacturing wage rates for 1985 as culled from the individual country's Census of Manufacture by UNIDO (1987). Twelve developing countries were designated as exporters of manufactures by the World Development Report 1987 (World Bank, 1987: xi). Table 1.2 gives their average wage rate for 1985. We have also given information on seven other countries whose manufacturing exports were more than 30% of their total exports, though they do not meet the World Bank criterion, which was that 30% of exports should consist of non-agricultural processing industries (textiles are included in agricultural processing industries).

Apart from the exporters of manufactured goods, we have also included the countries whose nominal wage rates were less than 10% of that of the USA. These wage rates imply that to have a subsistence level for labourers the foodgrains and other wage goods should be so cheap that it would be difficult to produce them with modern higher productivity technology of production. Therefore in these countries the modern sector is either parasitic on the traditional sector, or agricultural production is heavily subsidised. (It is worth remembering that 82 countries did not report the results of their Census of

Table 1.2   Average industrial wage in developing countries (1985)

Country	Average wage (US$)	% of US av. wage
1. USA	22,694	100.0
Developing countries classified as exporters of manufactures		
2. BRAZIL	2,050	9.0
3. CHINA	n.a.	
4. HONG KONG	4,643	20.5
5. HUNGARY	1,381	6.1
6. INDIA	1,013	4.5
7. ISRAEL	6,922	30.5
8. POLAND	1,611	7.1
9. PORTUGAL	3,405	15.0
10. REPUBLIC OF KOREA	3,282	14.5
11. ROMANIA	n.a.	
12. SINGAPORE	6,777	29.9
13. YUGOSLAVIA	1,903	8.4
Other developing countries having > 30% manufacturing exports		
14. Bangladesh	539	2.9
15. Greece	5,940	26.2
16. Pakistan	1,182	5.2
17. Philippines	1,357	6.0
18. Turkey	3,404	15.0
19. Tunisia	3,016	13.3
20. Morocco	2,883	12.7
21. Uruguay	2,201	9.7
Other developing countries having < 10% of US wage rate		
22. Dominican Republic	1,239	5.5
23. Egypt	1,474*	9.0*
24. Ethiopia	1,381	6.1
25. Ghana	561	2.5
26. Indonesia	874	3.9
27. Kenya	1,708	7.5
28. Madagascar	1,449	6.4
29. Mauritius	1,396**	6.8*
30. Sri Lanka	486*	3.0*
31. Thailand	1,981	8.7
32. Tanzania	1,146	5.1

Notes:
n.a. = not available.
*   The figures are for 1980; the percentage is also taken from the 1980 US wage.
** The figures are for 1983.

Manufacture, if any, to UNIDO, and so we do not have information about their wage rates; as they are mostly small countries with an undeveloped statistical system, it is expected that most of them would be part of this class.)

Apart from these there are developing countries whose prosperity is based on the export of some high value minerals. They have a comparatively higher wage rate in their mostly rudimentary manufacturing industry. We have not included them in Table 1.2 as a modern sector in them is hardly a harbinger of development: they are more like mining enclaves for the developed world.

Of the developing countries which are exporters of manufactures, four (namely, Greece, Israel, Hongkong, and Singapore) had wage rates between 20 and 30% of that of the USA. These countries can be supposed to have been transferred the best techniques of production. Many of the new establishments are run by multinationals for the purpose of producing or assembling goods for export to other countries and sometimes for import in developed countries themselves after taking advantage of the cheap labour conditions. In quite a few places the production facility is more like that of an off-shore assembly unit (World Bank, 1987: 45). Small wonder that these multinationals put up plants embodying latest technology for the purpose. The Republic of Korea may be considered as a genuine intermediate case; it also has quite a few plants of the 'Off-shore assembly unit' type, which account for a large part of its exports. Four manufacture-exporting developing countries that have wage rates around 15% of that of the USA are situated around the EC, having preferential arrangements with it; their transport costs, etc. are also low.

The remaining nine developing countries which are exporters of manufactures do have wage rates less than 10 percent of that of the USA. The technological transfer to them has been largely by the multinationals to exploit their protected markets or by the purchase of the technology by local entrepreneurs, private or public. In such cases, more likely than not, a technology on the verge of obsolescence in the developed country will have been transferred. This gives a new market for the capital goods producing capacity as well as a new lease to the intermediate goods industry associated with it; a developing country has to have a really low wage rate to use such a capacity for export promotion.

Table 1.2 also gives the nominal manufacturing wage rates of eleven more countries that are less than 10% of that of the USA. These are mainly exporters of primary commodities and can export at international prices due to their low wage rates. The 82 countries, noted above, for which UNIDO could not collect manufacturing wage rate information, mostly belong to this category.

THE INTERNATIONAL ECONOMIC ORDER AS AN IMPEDIMENT TO DEVELOPMENT

We have seen above how low wages in developing countries sustain their labour force, through the lower prices of essential consumer goods in low-wage countries. Groups I and II in Table 1.1 included not only all 'exporters of manufactures' but also about 90–95% of all developing countries. Only a few developing countries depending on high primary commodities prices were in Group III. These results have far-reaching implications. They signify that developing countries that adopt the strategy of industrialisation via technological transfer and which involves a continuous earning of foreign exchange by export of their produce cannot increase their wage rate beyond a certain proportion of the wage rate in the developed countries. In other words, they will always remain under-developed countries until the time these conditions cease to prevail.

We also saw two types of technology transfers – one where the transferring country transfers a part of the most efficient techniques to some small countries, which enable them to become processor of some labour-intensive part of production for multinationals. That allows such countries to go ahead of other developing countries in the development race, though they seem to be stuck at the new position attained. The second type of technological transfer has been that of sending near-obsolete techniques to the developing countries. They have had to pay for the privilege in the shape of compulsory exports at any cost. To make this feasible, wage rates had to be significantly depressed. This in turn forced the price of wage goods to such a low level that it made it difficult to modernise the sector. Alternatively, the economy becomes so dependent on foreign exchange for its running that it is unable to extend the modernisation process for the employment of its total labour force, nor to increase the real wage rate of the labour already employed: the process of modernisation thus remains stunted. So the technique of development through technical transfers is not likely to lead to the graduation of the developing countries into the 'developed' world, if this implies a compulsion to export.

In primary commodities exporting countries, the manufacturing sector is mostly rudimentary. Due to international competition, the price of primary commodities is so reduced that in many cases the sector becomes parasitic on the traditional sector of the economy. In such cases, the growth of the modern sector brings only deprivation on the common man as the traditional sector which is primarily a wage goods producing one shrinks due to paucity of land or labour. Further the attempt to transfer wage goods from the traditional to the modern sector sometimes requires autocratic government. The path of transformation of an economy to a developed one through this route is therefore in practice blocked.

However, some primary mining commodities can sometimes provide the wherewithal for sustained growth for small countries, if the income is invested in creating a Lewis-type closed modern sector. Such attempts have, however, been conspicuous by their absence in the development scene since 1945.

Part II
Development Theory and Experience

2 Metaeconomics

ECONOMIC ENVIRONMENT AND FACTORS OF PRODUCTION

Every economy works in its own physical, human and technological environment. The physical environment relates to the geographical position, availability, fertility and other special characteristics of the land, and the types of minerals, etc. found in the area, as well as the difficulties associated with exploiting them. The human environment is dependent on the socio-political conditions, property relationships, and distribution of decision centres for different types of decisions; individuals with various skills, educational attainments, tastes, etc. form an important element of the human environment. The technological environment is the sum total of not only technical but also practical knowledge of how to do or accomplish the production of commodities with precision and efficiency. This is termed 'know-how', and its availability to the economy for production of different commodities, as well as the possibility of getting such know-how from external sources, constitutes the total technological environment in which the production processes in the economy have to work. In the case of external sources, the terms on which such know-how can be obtained become of vital importance; it also depends on the extent and the types of various assets the economy has accumulated.

The world economic environment is becoming more and more important as the world is becoming more and more integrated; on this depends not only the possibility of trade and its favourable conditions, but the geographical, human and technological environments of other countries, as well as the power relations between the various countries of the world: all become important determinants of the economic well-being of each individual country.

These environments give us the constraints under which an economy must work. Technological knowledge, called 'the state of the art' by classical writers, shows us the alternative ways in which various goods and services can be produced by the economy. The make-up of the decision centres, together with their respective degree of command over various economic decisions, gives us the objectives which are sought to be achieved in the economy. The political and social environments and the existing property relations tell us the degree of command that various decision centres enjoy; on this depends the interactions and coordination of their various activities.

Economics has been defined as 'A study of human behaviour as a relationship between ends and scarce means which have alternative uses' (Robbins, 1935: 15). Human wants are more or less insatiable; they cannot be fully satisfied with the scarce resources available. Since the resources have alternative uses, they can be utilised to satisfy different sets of wants of the individual commanding them. The possibility of this choice determines the behaviour of the individual decision-maker. The repercussions of this choice throughout the system, and the ways of reconciling the choices of various decision units, is the subject matter of economics.

Choice is exercised by selecting various commodities that can be produced from existing resources in such a way that no other combination of commodities that is also feasible is preferred to the one chosen. The resources that are necessary for production, and determine its extent, are called 'factors of production'. Traditionally, they are classified in three groups – Labour, Land and Capital. Each of these groups may contain non-substitutable entities – for instance, there may be land suitable for cultivation of rice on which wheat cannot be produced, and vice versa. These two areas of land are then de facto two different factors of production and the availability of one is no help in the production of the other. Similarly, an unskilled labourer is no substitute for a skilled one. This 'specificity' of fixed capital goods is well recognised: for the production of an individual commodity specific factors of production are required. However, it is convenient to group these factors of production in the three categories noted above.

Not only are factors of production required for production, but also intermediate goods. 'Intermediate goods' are the goods that are required as inputs in the production of a commodity. For instance, one requires wheat in the production of bread; fuel is also required, and so on. A thin line divides intermediate goods from capital goods. Capital goods – machinery or buildings, for example – are means of production in the same way as intermediate goods. But once produced they help in the production process over several production periods. To distinguish them, they are sometimes therefore called 'fixed capital'. Intermediate goods, if storeable at all, are more often than not stored for less than one period of production; they are called 'working capital'. (There may be some intermediate goods, like electricity, that are hardly storeable). But the time period of storage is not the only distinguishing feature of these two types of capital. Working capital remains stored in the same form as it was acquired until the time it is used in production. If it is found to be surplus to requirements for the immediate purpose, it can be disposed of in the same form in which it was acquired; fixed capital, by contrast, gets more or less fixed before it can be even slightly used. If its services are not required further, it can be disposed of only as a second-hand good. In the case of a building, for example, if it is found to be bigger than necessary for carrying out production, the spare capacity may have to lie unutilised unless it is demolished or the production facility is transferred to some other location.

FORMALISATION OF THE PRODUCTION PROCESS

For an individual decision maker-the parameters of his economic choice determine his production decisions. First let us look at an independent self-sufficient producer-cum-consumer who hardly needs to acquire anything from any outside body. We can think of him as a medieval feudal lord, who produces all his requirements from his manorial land with the labour of his serfs. Almost all the intermediate goods required for the production process he adopts are produced there, as well as the fixed capital products, like buildings, hand tools, etc.

Let the utility function of the lord of the manor – the decision-maker – be indicated by the function

$$U(Y_1, Y_2, Y_3, \ldots Y_i, \ldots Y_m) \tag{2.1}$$

where Y_i denotes the amount of the ith commodity available.

These commodities are the final products made available to the decision-maker by the production processes in that period, and the total number of commodities available for use by him are m. These are produced under two types of constraints: those of the availability of intermediate goods and of the factors of production.

Intermediate Goods Constraints

To keep the algebra simple, we shall assume constant returns to scale and no joint products in production. Then the production process of commodity i can be represented by the list of commodities that are required in its production as intermediate products per unit of its output, together with another list detailing the quantity of various factors of production necessary for its unit production. Let the first series be represented by a list

$$(a_{1i}, a_{2i}, \ldots a_{ji}, \ldots a_{ni}) \tag{2.2}$$

where a_{ji} indicates the amount of jth commodity thus required.

The number of commodities in (2.2) are n, of which only m are required by the decision-maker for his use. The remainder may be necessary for use only as intermediate goods in the production process. Some part of the output of the commodities required for use by the decision-maker may also be used as intermediate products. The production of each commodity should thus not only be equal to the amount to be used by the decision-maker, that is the amount given in function (2.1), but should also meet the needs of intermediate goods required in the production of all those commodities.

This is not all. The decision-maker will also have to produce the goods required by the dependent workers working on his estate. What those goods will be depends on his relationship with them. In the case of the medieval feudal lord they would amount to the goods required for the minimum subsistence of the serfs. Those were the days of surplus labour, and lots of destitutes were roaming the countryside. The feudal lord could pick up as many serfs as he required. But the serf had to be maintained at the standard that was considered as minimum subsistence by the society. No serf could be got at a starvation level of emoluments. The physical amount of commodities required for this subsistence wage should also come from the production output. Once the amount of goods to be given to these labourers is fixed, their production become as necessary as that of intermediate goods. So these may be treated in a similar way in defining a production process.

Factor of Production Constraints

The second type of constraints facing the decision-maker relates to the availability of the various factors of production. The paucity of suitable land is an obvious example. The richness of the feudal lord depended on the amount of the land he could command. In many situations, the only means of acquiring more land was to win it in war or through marriage alliances.

In certain situations the paucity of labour may itself become an effective constraint. In the ancient Graeco–Roman world wealth depended upon the number of slaves owned. Arable land seemed to be plentiful, the scarce factor was the number of workers that could be commandeered to work on the land.

Similarly, the ready availability of the means of production, or fixed assets, may become an effective constraint. For each type of production, different types of assets are normally required. If that production is to be carried out the availability of the specific assets in the requisite quantities are an effective constraint on the quantity of the commodity that can be produced.

It is not only land or labour in general that can cause bottlenecks in production, however, but their specific type. Specificity of land, both as regards the items that can be produced from it as well as its fertility are well known. The same is true of the skills of labour. When, (say), in Roman times agricultural implement-makers were in short supply, they were plying their services in the cities, and charging for their expertise. When the expertise became common, every feudal lord could keep his own implement-maker, who got no more emoluments than the ordinary labourer. There were hardly any monetary returns for the training for his skill; only that he could get a job in preference to an unskilled labourer.

These constraints on the availability of various factors of production, property relations, ownership of assets and politico-legal conditions for their use, as well as the political, legal, and social rights of the individuals forming the society, determine the macro conditions prevailing in the economy. For production to be viable all these conditions should be satisfied. The availability of various factors of production determine the physical constraints under which the whole of the economy works, while the other conditions determine the way the whole economy is organised, the extent of the decision-making power of various decision-makers, the economic relations between them, etc.

If the whole economy were like the private estate of one decision-maker, the economic problem would be simple. The economic problem would become merely that of maximising the decision-maker's utility function (2.1) subject to the inequalities given by these overall conditions. In an economy where there are many decision-makers with various degrees of interdependence, these macro conditions, together with the production functions, give only the alternative production possibilities (production possibility curves) for the economy as a whole. Whether an economy can realise any of those possibilities in practice depends on the total economic organisation.

Central planning exercises are bold attempts to view the whole economy as one big economic estate and then attempt to realise one of the available possibilities. Out of them, the planning authority would select the best by maximising the community utility function. However, no such utility function is apparent since, unlike an individual, the community as a whole cannot express its preferences. The planning authority, however, assumes that it knows whatever is the best for the rest of the community; and it is this perception of the good of the community which can be formalised as a community utility function, or a social welfare function.

MICRO MANAGEMENT AND MICROECONOMIC PROBLEMS

This formalisation of the decision process of production and consumption as an entity which can take its own decisions and is in command of certain quantities of the various factors of production required for production with a known technology can be considered as a problem of *micro management*. Within its confines, it is a command economy; the management decision is taken by the person in control of the whole process, and it has rules which help in taking the decision under the prevailing conditions.

However, the economy may be so organised that it has many decision-makers. There may be different persons deciding about different aspects of the economy; different entities may be making decisions about production; there may be different owners owning some quantity of the different assets that are necessary for production and deciding how they are to be used and whom to allow to use them. And all these decision-makers will choose to optimise their individual utilities by means of their production, hiring and exchange activity.

Coordination of the activities of these different operators has been attempted through various means. These can be classified in three broad ways. One is where some central authority allocates different functions to different individuals, arranges for the exchange on the terms it considers fit, and decides the consumption or living pattern of each, as well as how much of the production should be used for consumption and how much for investment, military and other uses and in what form. This type of economic arrangement has been termed by Sir John Hicks (1969: 14–15) as a 'command economy'. This can be conceived in the same formal way as in the case of the self-sufficient decision-maker that we considered above. The constraints in this case will be national rather than individual; the total land of different specifications available in the country will determine the production of various agricultural goods, the total amount of various assets in the country will form the upper limit of the fixed capital capacity, and it will be the total labour force of various skills that will be constraints on the scale of the economy. The objective function to be optimised will be that determined by the central authority. There have been attempts to approximate to this format in various centrally planned economies. It is almost impossible to achieve this in its pure form, due to the difficulty of getting the information necessary to make a comprehensive model and carry out the extensive calculations required. Delay in these operations may make the information base of the plan obsolete, even before the plan is formed in requisite details; it is also almost impossible administratively to organise and supervise a command system in that much detail.

We therefore do not find the command economy in a pure form. It has been combined with a market economic system with various degrees of success, and conceptually, the formal schemata developed for it is easy to use. Even those who detest the command economy as a system, use the schemata outlined above for policy derivations, changing the utility function of the central authority to some more nebulous concept of a 'social welfare function'.

The other extreme form of this coordination *of production* and *resources* is the concept of a free competitive market. The theory of microeconomics deals with this category of economic relationships. Coordination by this route depends on the development of a price system which will equalise the demand and supply of each commodity and of each factor of production in the economy. The formal theory also gives the restrictive conditions under which this form of coordination can be achieved without any interference from the central authority, or other operators.

Some basic assumptions are made – that the economy is in long-run equilibrium, that there is perfect foresight, that future prices, demand and its pattern, etc. are known. All production functions operate along a smooth curve – i.e., production processes are available that can use any combination of factors of production, so no bottlenecks and no unemployment, and no unpredicted technical change. Also no increasing returns, no non-market interdependencies, no externalities, no indivisibilities, or uncertainties, etc.

The formal theory also shows that in the Pareto sense pure competitive equilibrium can be considered optimal. That is, after a competitive equilibrium is achieved, no person can be made better off without somebody being made worse off. This considers given property relations as sacrosanct, and skewness in the living standards of different people is not considered at all undesirable even if the people at the bottom are completely destitute; the theory is also based on all the simplifying assumptions of competitive equilibrium. After examining its place in the economic conceptualisation, Nath (1969: 28) concluded that 'For long time this theorem was given great importance by economists: and significant corollaries were derived from it for practical policy purposes. But the theorem in fact is hedged by so many restrictive (and therefore unrealistic) conditions that it is trivial'.

Much popular economic understanding is based on this special case of pure competition, and that it is in some sense optimal. Of course, the necessary conditions determining its existence and optimality are beyond the popular understanding, and hardly any attempt is made to popularise them. As Galbraith (1958) pointed out, we have seen the spectacle of half-baked economists lecturing the developing countries on the theory's advantages without having any understanding of the theoretical limitations of the analysis or whether the assumptions underlying it are satisfied by the economies of the developing countries. They seem to be ignorant of the ever-present guidance of the economy by the state, its active seeking of various kinds of investment, etc. against the canons of pure competition in the developed countries themselves. They are also ignorant of how the presently developed countries organised their economies when they were themselves developing. Despite this basic ignorance, they go on wilfully extolling the virtues of pure competition to the developing countries.

Standing between the above two extreme forms is the theory of management, which implies that various decision-makers can formally or informally bargain and/or make coalitions in such a way as to coordinate their decisions to their mutual advantage. A formal schemata for this scheme was presented by Edgeworth (1881) at the end of the last century in his theory of 'the core', although its practical development into a corpus of management science is a more recent development. Edgeworth's theory deals with the coordination problems of complicated modern economies with multiple centres of economic power where monopolies or monopolistic competition is the main market form. We can consider this as macro management in contrast to the micro management discussed above.

In practice, we find none of these pure forms anywhere. The prevailing world economic systems are combinations of all the above systems, one system determining one aspect of the economic working of the nation, while another determines another part. Countries differ profoundly in the importance and role attached to the different systems in their economies.

THE MACROECONOMIC PROBLEM

When formalising the production process, we found that two types of constraints faced the decision-maker. One related to the availability of intermediate goods, the other to that of the factors of production. We have seen that if the factors of production are available in sufficient quantity, the requisite intermediate goods can be produced within the production unit itself. If we look to the economy as a whole the basic constraints that limit its production possibility are again those of the factors of production. Individual production units within the country can increase their production and income by acquiring more of that factor of production which has proved to be an effective constraint to their production by purchase, transfer or conquest. For instance in a slave economy, where labour is in short supply, slaves can be purchased in the market. In a feudal economy with land shortage, new land can be acquired by the grace of the monarch, through marriage, and in some cases by direct purchase. In a modern market economy the services of all the factors of production are subject to sale and purchase in the market.

However, there is an overall physical limit to such services in the economy, and the implications of overall constraints is the subject matter of macroeconomics. The physical quantity of the land in a country cannot be substantially increased; that may provide an upper limit to the quantity of food that can be produced. As food is an essential part of the subsistence wage of a labourer this provides an effective limit to the number of labourers that can be employed in an economy. From this is derived the wage fund theory of classical macroeconomics. Only when the colonisation of America effectively made the land constraint redundant did economists give up the wage fund theory, and the neoclassical system of economics come into existence.

In a command economy this coordination is supposed to be achieved by the central authority. In the market or macro-managed economy there are hardly any short-term signals that will induce all the operators to remain together within the limits of effective constraints. As one operator does not know the actions of other operators in response to the same price and other market signals, it is very unlikely that the sum total of their activities will use the scarce resource so as to remain within the overall limit without leaving any of it unutilised. If, in the long run, the total quantity of the resources does not change, various economic agents may ultimately hit on consistent decisions through progressive approximations.

Coordination failure can work both ways. When more of a factor of production is demanded than is available, the economy is subjected to specific cost-push inflationary pressures. Until the time some operators reduce their demand so as to make the total demand of the scarce factor of production equal to its supply, inflation will not only continue but will show itself more and more vigorously.

In the case of demand falling short of the availability of some factor of production, recessionary pressures may build up. The price fetched by the factor is likely to fall until it reaches a floor below which it may not be able to fall due to physical, or socio-economic, or organisational reasons Keynes envisaged that interest rates could not fall below a certain level because of the 'liquidity preference' of the operators; the minimum level of wages in the organised sector is the well known 'subsistence wage rate'. The returns to a factor of production will tend to fall towards the floor level whenever the macro constraint relating to it is redundant – that is, whenever demand does not reach overall available quantity. It does not matter whether any other macro constraint is effective or not. In the Middle Ages, when the land constraint was effective, the labour constraint was not. And in that situation labour could command only a subsistence wage, and labourers had to be grateful if somebody employed them even at that miserable rate as it saved them from destitution. However, in classical times or in early colonial America, where the labour constraint was effective, a system of slavery became necessary to force labour to live on a subsistence wage.

INTERNATIONAL CONSTRAINTS OR WORLDWIDE MACRO LIMITATIONS

Before the development of mercantile trade after the colonisation of America, the constraints on production were basically national. International trade in those days was confined largely to luxury items, which hardly figured as a bottleneck to any further production. But as colonial trade began to provide the wherewithal of the production economy and of essential consumption, and as the exports of goods and services to the colonies and empire from the mother country became a crucial sector of their economies, the international constraints started to provide a framework under which national economies could work. There is no international government that can do the necessary work of coordinating various activities in this regard. During the period of empires, this type of dependence was primarily confined to the various sections of the empire; the so-called 'mother' country used to perform the coordinating function – primarily, of course, for its own benefit. With the dissolution of the formal empires, a sort of hegemony or spheres of influence developed through which these activities were coordinated, with various degrees of success.

The situation has become more and more complex in the modern world with its many centres of power. Various international institutions have appeared to regulate and coordinate affairs at a worldwide level. For the mutual coordination of their economic activities, the developed countries have devised the Organisation for Economic Cooperation and Development (OECD). For regulating trade there is the General Agreement on Tariffs and Trade (GATT), for currencies and exchange rates there is the International Monetary Fund (IMF), and for general credit regulation there is the World Bank, and so on. The coordination of activities is done through operators and policy-makers taking guidance from the governments of the developed countries. As we shall see, their biases are transparent.

International constraints on individual countries are primarily commodity constraints, unlike the national constraints which are primarily factor constraints. However, the total availability of foreign exchange should be considered as a factor constraint. This total availability effectively limits the amount of commodities that can be imported, and therefore it becomes one of the constraints that limit the possibility of total production.

For internationally traded commodities, the whole trading world is like one big country: somehow its demand has to be contained within total factor availability. When a constraint on its supply becomes effective, this will be achieved by a similar mechanism as that experienced within an individual country – that is, its relative price increases will create inflationary pressures. However, unlike the case of intra-country scarcity, these inflationary pressures do not mean a redistribution of income within a country, but involve the necessity of increased exports by the user country. If, due to conditions in the world market, it is not able to increase exports by the requisite amount, its output will suffer.

When this constraint is not effective, the international price of a commodity will come down to its marginal supply price. However, there is no mechanism that will equalise such prices in different countries, so the competition between different producers will not only bring down the price to the minimum possible cost of production, but the attempt to sell more and more of it in the international market (by reducing its international price) may also bring down the value of the currency of the exporting country as against other currencies in terms of purchasing power parity. When the internal price cannot be reduced beyond a limit due to an effective lower limit to some factor payments like subsistence wages, the only way to compete further is through currency devaluation. In the case of a foreign exchange deficit, this course is widely recommended for the countries concerned by international agencies like the IMF. The reduction in the price of export-commodities will of course lead to a foreign exchange deficit. The motive for taking international competition to the bitter end will be enhanced if the requirement of foreign exchange is a high priority with the country. For a developing country there may be a need to import investment goods so that it can accelerate its economic growth. It may have an urge to purchase weapons for self-defence or for aggrandisement over neighbours, or it may be simply in order to repay international debt and/or the interest thereon contracted in the past. For some countries, necessary inputs in its production process (fertilisers, etc.) may have to be imported, and it may have to succumb to this price-cutting exercise just to keep its production going.

RECAPITULATION

We have given above a sketch of the general system within which modern economic activities function. National economies work under international constraints in the same way as the economies of a firm work under their national macro constraints. The usual country-centred economic analysis is not illuminating, and can lead only to the economic dogmatism which results from attempts to theorise without taking into account an essential extra dimension: it reminds one of Plato's famous allegory of people confined in a Cave trying to decipher the happenings in the world outside only by the movements of the shadows of the wall. All macroeconomic analysis should be done within the parameters provided by international constraints; this is true irrespective of the type of internal institutional regime a country is following to achieve economic coordination.

3 A Synoptic View of Economic Historic States in Theoretical Perspective: Before the Industrial Revolution

AN IDEALISED HISTORY OF ECONOMIC PROGRESS

Our economic founding fathers like Adam Smith and Karl Marx organised their analysis in terms of stages of growth as phenomena in historical time, demonstrating how changing physical and technical environments led to different types of institutions. This particular methodology has been followed in our own time by quite a few scholars, most notably W.W. Rostow. The economic historians have criticised this approach as neither good history nor good economics; when one goes into details one tends to agree with this assessment. However, we may recall that all the attempts at economic theory building have been castigated in almost the same terms by the historical school. After all, economic theory is hardly able adequately to explain historical experience. This does not mean that the theory has to be discarded, but it does indicate that it has to be extended and modified with the creation of new paradigms so that the theory is able to account more accurately for actual economic happenings. Similarly, the stages of economic growth should not be viewed as a necessary sequence of economic systems and institutions explaining every facet of economic phenomena. The historical states that are depicted in such an exposition may not describe the situation completely, but they should help us to bring out the salient features of the situation. Their function is to give an 'overall' picture of the dynamic situation in individual cases to see whether we can explain it through our theoretical understanding of economic progress. A theory that has passed the test of explaining historical experience of the stages of growth may be able to guide us better. We shall now examine the characteristics of some of the historical economic states experienced in the past. A few of these can be discerned in the situation of some present-day developing countries, so this may help us to understand their problems better.

TRIBAL SELF-SUFFICIENT ECONOMY: NO SURPLUS

In most of the tribal economies the techniques of production are so rudimentary that the task of keeping a human being alive and reproducing itself is a full-time job. There is hardly any leisure from the pursuit of earning a living and keeping predators, both animal and human, at bay. The economy repeats itself year after year. Mostly there is economic specialisation on a sexual basis, but there is hardly any other specialisation in performing economic activities. Most transactions are customary. There is hardly any problem of pricing, distribution, cost assessment, etc. though notionally all these concepts can be used to aid our understanding. Though the scale of the economy is determined by the number of the people in the labour force, there is no use in enslaving them as they can hardly produce anything more than is required for their bare living. In some parts of the world, where marginal land can hardly produce more than is necessary for one person to eke out a bare living with traditional cultivation techniques, we can even today find people whom nobody needs to disturb for any economic gains.

LABOUR AS THE SCARCE FACTOR: SLAVE ECONOMY

As soon as man made sufficient technological progress to be able to produce essential goods for his own needs in less time than a complete working year, the possibility of leisure and leisure pursuits appeared. It was possible for every person to enjoy that leisure for himself, but in hindsight we know that that was not to be. It was soon found out that if some persons could be employed full-time in producing the necessities of life, another section of the population could be free to enjoy that leisure and to pursue other interests in life. This led directly to the institutions of slavery, or some variant of it, in classical times.

In this case the main constraining factor for economic activity is labour. There is sufficient land to be cultivated; capital requirements are simple. In such a situation, a free labourer could have easily established his independent farm and enjoyed a better standard of living than slave labourers working for other farmers. An independent farmer could become rich only if he could command the labour services of others who could be employed full-time. Then the extra production over and above that needed for maintaining such a worker(s) could be appropriated by himself. So there was an economic necessity to force a labourer to stay on one's estate, otherwise he would just move away to another free plot to make a better living for himself over there. This implies an institution of slavery, or bonded labour. Historically, it may be that those tribes who could not defend themselves against marauding tribes had to submit to slavery, which made their owners comparatively rich. As the marauding tribe automatically become the ruling one, the laws against escaping slaves could be enacted and enforced. So the state ceased to be the only protector from outside attacks but also became the guarantor of the rights of the slave owners. Mostly these slaves were distinguished from their owners by the way they spoke or the colour of their skin.

Slavery was not only prevalent in the classical times, but also in the nineteenth-century USA. The situation then was comparable in the sense of scarcity of labour but not of land. Even after the abolition of slavery similar economic conditions produced similar institutional arrangements. In Mauritius, Fiji, Jamaica, Guyana, etc. similar conditions prevailed with plenty of land that could produce sugarcane and other commercial crops but hardly any suitable labour. The British invented the system of indentured or bonded labour to meet the situation; under this system unemployed people from India 'voluntarily' offered themselves to go abroad and found themselves bound in law and unable to return if they wanted to, or even change their job while they were there. In an indentured situation, the person accepted bondage 'voluntarily', though mostly in the ignorance of the conditions involved, while in slavery labour was forced. This difference can also be attributed to the conditions in the country of origin. If in the country of the origin there was no dearth of land, the person would have to be physically forced to be a slave; if there was such a dearth of land as to inflict large-scale and long-lasting unemployment with consequent ever-present hunger, people would voluntarily sell themselves in perpetual bondage.

This leaves the question of why the local tribal labour in these countries could not be enslaved, which would have avoided the need to bring bonded labour from outside. My study at Guyana (Mathur, 1978) revealed that the local labour force could not be policed. They knew too well the byways of the forest and hills in the country; whenever any attempt was made to use them, they would in a few days escape into the jungle and could not be brought back. They themselves could make their living in the traditional way in the forests without any economic necessity of coming in contact with foreigners. That type of life was not possible for the indentured labourers or slaves, who were kept out of the forests by the local tribes who would not hesitate in murdering such intruders. This strengthens the general point that with an abundance of land a landlord can only have labour working for him in primitive conditions only by force – legal, physical, and or environmental.

LAND AS THE SCARCE FACTOR: FEUDAL ECONOMY

The character of the economy changes as soon as land instead of labour becomes the scarce factor of production. As soon as a person has a control over land, he need not control labour; labour, to earn its living, will have to come to him to work at a 'subsistence' wage. This gives the landlord a further advantage; he need not sustain his labour force through health and sickness, or support them in rearing children as his future labour force. Once one has the control of land and there is a surfeit of labour, one can dispense with a labourer's services as soon as he is no longer useful.

In such a system the economy can be explained in terms of the 'physiocratic theory', where the net product was produced only by the land. Wages of labourers were an input into the land, like seeds, and only land was the productive factor. Landlords were not interested in what we now call GDP, as the part that was going as wages to the farm labourers was not available for alternative uses of the landlord or the king. The surplus of land, however, could be used for providing luxury goods for the feudal class, or spiritual, temporal, or educational services to the community as a whole, or could be used for the upkeep of the army for the safety of the realm.

INTERNATIONAL TRADE AS A FACTOR: MERCANTILISM

It is mercantilism that brought the almost independent national economic systems of the world into mutually interdependent organisations. After the discovery of the sea routes to America and Asia at the end of the fifteenth century, a triangular system of exchange between these regions, Europe and Africa developed, and remained in place for about 250 years. The main driving force behind this was of course the European merchants, conquerors and colonisers.

The first stage was that of the Spanish and Portuguese conquerors collecting gold and silver from Latin America and using it to purchase oriental spices and manufactured goods (primarily textiles) brought in mainly by British, French, and Dutch merchants. There were no European manufactures worth the name that could be sold in the Orient, and there were hardly any purchasers in the American continent. Adam Smith (1776) wrote about this phase as follows:

> The discovery of America, and that of the passage to the East Indies by the Cape of Good Hope, are the two greatest events recorded in the history of mankind (590) . . . In the cargoes of the greater part of the European ships which sail to India, silver has generally been one of the most valuable articles. It is most valuable article in the Acapulco ships which sail to Manila. The silver of the new continent seems in this manner to be one of the principal commodities by which the commerce between the two extremities of the old one is carried on (207).

This phase was based on exploiting the tribute or loot of the Americas by Spain and Portugal, and then a straightforward trade with the Orient by Dutch, French, and English merchants to supply oriental spices and textiles to Europe. However, an effort was made, even in those early days, to see that these mercantile interest did not disturb the industrial interests of the trading countries. Though England had been reexporting Indian cotton textiles – the famous calicos – for quite sometime, these were prohibited in England itself until 1774, to protect the woollen goods industry and the owners of sheep farms that were springing up in the countryside, displacing crop production in their turn. Though initially the conquest of America brought riches to the Iberian Peninsula, this mercantile trade also brought prosperity to other West European countries. The new riches thus created were concentrated in the hands of enterprising seafaring merchants who were ready to grasp economic opportunities as they presented themselves on the worldwide stage. As the opportunities of expanding this simple trade on the same basis dwindled, the accumulated capital found its way into the development of colonial economies in the newly discovered territories, opening up the mines and establishing agricultural plantations. Soon simple mercantilism was supplemented by a much more trading-cum-production relationship that characterised the mercantile-cum-colonial economies.

COLONIAL ECONOMY

The first mines opened were the silver and gold mines of Mexico and Peru, worked with the forced labour of the defeated local people. This was in a way a continuation of the tribute gathering of the early mercantile period, when the accumulated precious metals of American Indians were near exhaustion. In the other areas of the vacant continent European colonial immigrants were slowly establishing themselves as small cultivators, and the colonising companies were perfecting the new system of large-scale commercial agriculture where the capital provided by European merchants could be matched with the vastness of natural resources of the continent. However for these large-scale operations a considerable and permanent labour force was required that would not leave at the time of crucial agricultural operations. Free immigrants could not be relied upon, in view of the cheap or free good land which would tempt them to become independent small farmers. The institution of indentured labour and slavery filled the bill, and so grew up a class of professional agricultural managers called planters, and the development of the first large-scale factory-type organisation. The marketing specialisation of the company as well as the professional specialisation of the agricultural managers dictated that it should be a monoculture; the early plantations to develop were devoted to sugar production. About them Adam Smith had this to say,

> The profits of a sugar plantation in any of our West Indian colonies are generally much greater than those of any other cultivation that is known either in Europe or America (Smith, 1776: 366).

These plantations in the Caribbean, Latin America and the Southern USA were soon producing such staple crops as sugar, molasses, indigo, tobacco and cotton, the processing of which in due course created new industries in England, while the maintenance of the labour force and their owners on the plantations provided another market for British industry.

The Northern USA and Canada did not participate in this large-scale commercial agriculture as their land was not suitable for tropical crops, and large-scale production of wheat, for which their land was suitable, could not take off as the Corn Laws in Britain prohibited its import until 1846, to protect the income of the British landowners. But these areas were singularly well placed to meet the demand of plantation workers and owners for consumption and other simple goods, due to their short distance from them and cheaper agricultural production. They found those countries with plantations a good market for their corn, oats, peas, rice, dried fish, onions, timber, pigs, horses, poultry, etc. from which to pay for their imports of the British goods. The British were of course paid by the plantation crops themselves.

North America could also develop its shipping industry at a fast pace due to the ready and cheap availability of timber, and the enforcement of the seventeenth century British Navigation Act which stipulated that trade can be done only in the vessels of the trading country, cut the Dutch and other European powers out of this lucrative trade. This gave sufficient protection to the infant shipping industry of North America and simultaneously made its merchants middlemen for much of the trade with the interior of the continent.

As the plantation crops and other colonial production became established in the Americas, the mercantile trade absorbed the new requirements and became more complicated. In the words of Eric Williams (1966: 51–2), the simple mercantile trade, 'was supplemented, but never supplanted, by direct trade between the home country and the West Indies (or other colonised regions), exchanging home (and Oriental) manufactures directly for colonial produce. The triangular trade thereby gave triple stimulus to British industry. The Negroes were purchased with British (and Oriental) manufactures; transported to the plantations, they produced sugar, cotton, indigo, molasses, and other tropical products, the processing of which created new industries in England; while the maintenance of the Negroes and their owners on the plantations provided another market for British industry, New England agriculture and Newfoundland fisheries. The profits obtained provided one of the main streams of that accumulation of capital in England which financed the Industrial Revolution'.

The development of a mining and plantation economy in America was a virtual extension of the productive territory of Europe, not only an extension of the quantity of land but also the availability of qualitatively different land for cultivation and of mineral deposits that were not otherwise available in Europe. However, the land was far off and the transport cost of the produce and payment in terms of manufactured goods and slaves was not inconsiderable. Marketing in Europe required not only a significant capital base but also a considerable organisation, a large-scale operation that could be supported only on a base of large-scale agriculture. Availability of almost free land, which would allow a free wage labour to desert a plantation at will, meant that it was not economic for the company to incur the expenditure of bringing such labour from the Old World; only indentured labour or slaves met the situation. Once the labour was bound, there was no necessity to give it more than the minimum for survival. The monetary value of this wage of course depended on the price of wage goods that were being produced by the independent free farmers rather than by the virtually forced labour of the subservient natives. We shall see below how this in turn affected the structure of the price system, and through it the development of the economy as a whole.

SUBJECT ECONOMY AND ECONOMIC DRAIN

By the beginning of the eighteenth century, the erstwhile colonial powers were starting to develop political rule over the thickly settled countries of Asia. They developed a new system of collecting tribute; they were not interested, as the Romans had been, in collecting foodgrains from the empire to feed the home population with free gifts of grain nor, as the Spaniards had been, in simply amassing silver and gold from their empire and spending it on manufactures, mainly from the Orient, brought by British, Dutch, and French merchants. The colonist of Asia collected tribute in terms of manufactured goods like textiles that they had already been purchasing for many years in exchange for bullion. Even before they were in any position to collect any tribute, these merchant companies had several foreign trading stations in these countries, from which they were importing manufactures. When their trade increased, they could not purchase enough in the open market, so they employed the traditional local craftsmen to manufacture in their trading stations, known as factories since the merchant-employees of the company managing the trading station were called 'factors'. The factory organisation of purchasing, producing and marketing was born before the advent of the industrial revolution in Europe.

When these countries became subject countries a tribute became payable, though more often than not it was disguised under the name of various charges for services performed. In the first form of the 'drain', the tribute was taken out of the country in the form of manufactured goods; out of the total produced manufactured goods a large proportion was so exported. However the tribute was not primarily levied to the manufacturing sector itself: it was mainly collected as land revenue, and so reduced the demand of manufactures from the local landed classes and farmers.

With the increase in manufactures, the employed labour in that sector correspondingly increased. The labour in agriculture remained the same, as the area was not reduced; however, its consumption was reduced by the amount of the tribute. The manufacturing and other cottage industry labour satisfying that need became unemployed. The increase in manufacturing was thus not equal to the amount of manufacturing exports from the country, only to that corresponding to the reduction of the consumption of wage goods by the agricultural sector. So not only was agriculture greatly reduced but significant unemployment also showed itself in the manufacturing sector.

After the advent of the industrial revolution, when the manufacturing factories of the subject country could be transferred to the ruling country and its workers trained in the requisite arts, the pattern of tribute-gathering changed. Now, it was not manufactured goods that were required as tribute but the raw material themselves. The economy of the subject country changed for the worse, since while the reduction of agricultural income remained the same, as did the reduction in the local demand for manufactures, the extra income and employment created in the manufacturing sector by export demand disappeared. This lead to a further significant increase in unemployment in the manufacturing sector.

When the Europeans developed their own industries, Asian tribute was taken in terms of raw materials and tropical products similar to the ones that were pouring in Europe from the plantations of the New World. This conversion of monetary tribute into commodities was achieved through the mechanism of the market system, and implied significant distortion of both price and production structures in the subject country.

In these Asian subject countries, unlike the New World, land was not abundant, and (as in contemporary Europe) was the effective constraint on the economy. The amount of the labour that could be employed depended upon the availability of wage goods, which in turn depended primarily on the land under food crops. The tribute, or 'drain' as the Indian economists headed by Dada Bhai Naoroji termed it (Naoroji, 1901), required the use of certain amount of land. For tropical crops the land requirements were direct; manufactures such as textiles and rubber, were also land-intensive as their raw materials, such as cotton, preempted significant amounts of the scarce resource. All this land was taken out of cultivation for crops providing wage goods; this led to the decrease in total wage goods available for labour in the dependent country: a portion of labour was working only to produce things that were required to pay the tribute. That led not only to the pauperisation of the populace but also to the undermining of profitability of other local industries as the purchasing power of the local consumers of these goods declined. In other words, the macro decline of employment indicated by the declining availability of the wage goods showed itself primarily in the failure of local industries.

IMPERIALISM AND STRUCTURAL CHANGE

Imperialism in Land-constrained Countries

We have seen above that in a subject country the effect of tributes in terms of agricultural commodities, reduces the size of the economy in terms not only of the production of agricultural consumption goods, but of the production of industrial goods as well. With the maturity of industrial revolution in the United Kingdom, it began to develop the techniques of mass production of manufactured commodities, especially textiles, by harnessing the motive power of fossil fuels. It became profitable to become the workshop or 'factory town' of the world, supplementing its production of manufactures for its usual markets with markets in the subject countries from which the raw materials were themselves imported. If the ownership of the enterprise had been foreign, it would have been called 'offshore' production, but in this case all the profits of the enterprise, accrued to the residents of the ruling country.

We can discern three distinct stages in the development of the manufacturing activity of the ruling country. First, importing manufactures from the old Asian civilisations and selling them in the rest of the world – Old as well as New – in the process, transforming the collection depots in the Asian countries into factory organisations where these manufactures could be produced. Secondly, bringing those factories to the metropolitan country itself after training the local workers in the appropriate arts. This changed the imports of the manufactures from the Asian countries into the imports of the raw materials. But the second part of the link – the selling of the manufactures to the rest of the world – remained undisturbed. The third stage involved reexporting the manufactures to the country which originally produced them. This third stage, as is well known, was achieved not only by technological improvements, but also required coercive measures to ward off competition from the well-established older industry, as well as the development of an extensive railway network to give access to markets in remote areas, and to facilitate collection of raw materials at reasonable cost.

As a result the subject country turns into a predominantly agricultural country, in spite of the paucity of suitable land in relation to the labour force. Alternatively, it is termed as an over-populated country, where according to some development economists it should cut down the reproduction rate of the population by family planning techniques.

Imperialism in Labour-constrained Old Countries

When the imperial powers established their sway in the old countries of Africa, these countries were not producing any manufactures worth exporting. As noted earlier, the opening of West Africa was primarily motivated by the possibility of getting slaves for the American colonies in exchange for guns, rum, and oriental manufactures. Slowly the continent was opened up for mining and plantation crops grown on the most suitable area cleared of the natives and based on the cheap labour of the native population. The richer among the natives were slowly induced to consume the imported manufactured goods other than the rum and guns.

Though the best land was occupied by the colonisers, there was no dearth of land suitable for cultivation; the extent of the economy was limited by the availability of labour. Labour came out to work on mines or plantations through the inducement of the new types of the consumer goods, but also to earn some cash to pay the taxes or tribute which was levied by the ruling powers and which had to be paid in their currency. Only by the use of cheap local labour could these mines and plantations compete with similar products of the New World based on slave labour. The cheapness of the labour was due to the fact that no essential consumption good required by the labour was imported or made from an imported commodity, making the cost of living independent of the exchange rate. So until wage goods were locally produced from indigenous materials, the international value of wages was a matter of indifference.

As labour was the real bottleneck to the economy, the production of wage goods depended on the number of labourers engaged in their production. Total production would of course decrease in almost the same proportion as the proportion of the labourers withdrawn from production to produce export goods in the mines or plantations. So the effect of this type of imperialism was the deterioration of the native's standard of living. At the macro level, this availability of wage goods put an effective upper limit on the extent of the exaction of tribute, as well as on export possibilities.

Imperialism in Foreign Exchange-constrained Economies

In the new countries, which were either empty lands or cleared of natives by the early settlers, modern techniques of production were used – there was hardly any traditional technique that could have borne the burden of providing wage goods for labour. Modern techniques of production and their competitiveness depended on the use of slave labour and the abundance of land; as these areas were producers of raw material commodities whose international price was prone to stay at the supply price determined by subsistence or slave labour emoluments, there was hardly any possibility of any significant development. With development there being based on loans and or foreign capital, most non-wage income was transferred to the industrialised countries, leaving hardly any resources for the growth of other modern sectors than raw material producing ones and those appurtenant to theirs.

This implied that all production required direct or indirect inputs of imported goods from the industrialised countries. Total production and employment thus depended on the foreign exchange that could be earned and this in turn depended crucially on international 'commodity' prices. These countries also provided a ready-made market for manufactures and the industrial intermediate goods for the industrialised countries.

SOCIAL THEORIES OF ECONOMIC GROWTH

It is interesting to consider economic development and growth as a part of bigger field that embraces the theory of the growth of civilisation as a whole, even the growth of species and the ascent of man. The earliest theories of evolution denied the process of growth itself; the Creator was supposed to have created all the species as they are now from the very beginning. There is a reflection of this in the genetic theory of civilisations: until recent times it was maintained that some races were biologically superior to others and that they were intrinsically prone to develop a civilisation. The myth of Aryan race dies hard, and we can still find protagonists of crude or thinly-disguised racial theory of economic development. This attributes basic human characteristics in the population of different countries as the cause of differing experiences of economic growth. The Younger Pitt was neither the first nor the last to say that 'the English were active, sober, and industrious; the Irish were the contrary'; a wealth of theories exist to show how the climate of the tropics leads to lethargy and saps the will to develop. Even a slight acquaintance with history should have convinced these thinkers that almost every race and almost every geographical part of the world has as some time sustained a well-developed civilisation which contained the richest, most wise and cultured people of the contemporary world, and had comparatively the highest standard of living.

Only slightly more elevated in sophistication are the theories attributing economic differences to psychological attitudes and other social characteristics. The essence of this argument is that the economic and social characteristics of 'backward' areas places them in a far worse situation as regards potential development than were the modern developed nations in the late seventeenth and eighteenth centuries when they themselves were 'developing'. They enjoyed important advantages, they were part of Western culture combining an empirical and scientific frame of mind with an ideology that accepted innovation and change and encouraged both hard work for material ends and voluntary postponement of present consumption in favour of capital accumulation. It is postulated that the social institutions and ethos of the modern under-developed countries is different and is not conducive to the activities that lead to economic development.

There is a grain of truth discernible in this argument; given the instability of existing political and social conditions it is difficult to see how economic growth can occur. But the difficulty with this type of reasoning is that static conditions in a society are misconstrued as dynamic ones; a researcher is overwhelmed by existing social and political conditions and ethos. At present, we do not have a widely accepted theory of social change, we are not still technically competent enough to understand its complex dynamics. The feudal political organisation and guild organisation of industry in old England, the nation that pioneered economic development in modern times were, after all, hardly conducive to economic growth. However, a historian can now find several subtle processes working at that time, which with hindsight look as if they were conducive to the economic development that later occurred, although an observer at that time could not have perceived their importance.

The experience of economic growth so far has been confined to so few countries that we still have no general understanding of all the processes that can lead to these changes. A tendency to assert that the way it happened in England is the only way it could happen is clearly not being borne out by the experiences of countries like Japan and the USSR. The importance of any specific ideology in this regard is much more doubtful. We are told on the one hand that people must be prepared to work hard for the material benefits, they must not be satisfied with their lot as it is at the moment, they must strive for a better standard of living. On the other hand, we are told of the role that a Puritan ethic played in the economic development of Great Britain and we are warned against the tendency towards conspicuous consumption in the under-developed countries which may make the whole development programme stillborn. All such pressures of sociological development seem at the moment to be more indebted to the fertile imagination of the analyst, which allows him to be able to assert at least something about a baffling reality.

INNOVATION AND THE PROCESS OF GROWTH

Human growth is the result of innovation. Innovation is a response to some challenge; however, innovation is not biological, it is technological and social and also, as a consequence, psychological. So when a challenge occurs that threatens a particular society with extinction, and if that society successfully innovates as a response to it, it does not mean that biologically the society has become different from the rest. The innate biological tendencies of all human societies are the same; over the whole span of human existence there has not been a single biological improvement in the human being. This is not to deny the importance of the heredity factor in the make up of an individual or the effects of heterosis in the development of civilisations; but here the heterosis that lead to growth is cultural rather than biological. Human beings, biologically, are a single species all over the world, and each group of them is capable of the highest achievement. When we encounter primitive societies eking out their sheltered existence at what we call now a very low standard of living, we should remember that this lack of growth on the part of those societies is simply due to the absence of any challenge to their style of living in the very long historical period of their existence. Their admittedly low standard has never been challenged, either by nature or the fellow human beings, so they go on living as they were. Any society that faces a challenge either makes a response by suitable innovation or is swept away, just as thousands of animal species have been swept away and are now extinct.

For human beings, innovations are not biologically transmitted, they are transmitted through communications. However the process of adoption of an innovation is not a simple thing; it becomes more and more complicated the higher we are in the scale of socio-economic development. A suitable institutional framework becomes necessary, so that the cost of adoption may be borne by someone. The laws of social dynamics are such that every human society can form a suitable framework for the purpose. But 'can' does not mean that it will: the main purpose of this socio-politico-institutional framework is to be able to force a group – indigenous or foreign – to bear the privations which the process of the adoption of an innovation entails.

These privations, in the case of economic growth, have so far been borne by 'Internal and external proletariats', in the sense given to them by Toynbee: 'Any social element or group which in some way "is" and not "of" any given society at any given stage of society's history' (Toynbee, 1934: 41). It will be seen that this is a much wider definition than that given by Marx. He included all the workers in the modern industrial proletariat, and owners of the means of production in the bourgeoisie. For Marx, conflict between them determined the course of progress, while for Toynbee, this was part of the internal proletariat. Another part of it was the unemployed, displaced by innovational activity within the country. On the other hand, the external proletariat was foreign people affected by the successful innovating activities of the creative minority within the country. Such a group may be affected by direct conquest or indirect political-cum-economic control, unequal trade relations, or control of some resources used by them etc, etc. This wider definition is much more useful in understanding the total repercussions of the innovations resulting in modern economic growth triggered off by an 'absent minded creative as well as dominant minority'. In these 'proletariats' will be included not only workers in the machine industry during the industrial revolution but also those displaced by it within the country and outside, not only directly but also indirectly, not only through the economic reverberations 'heard around the world', but also through the repercussions of the socio-politico-institutional superstructure which played a part of 'catalyst' for the emergence of modern industrialism. These different proletariats will have different economic interests. While workers in jobs will wish to improve their own standard of living; they will hardly be concerned with the plight of those whose jobs have been destroyed in the building up of their own industry. Though the internal proletariat may wish to partake in the profits being made by their firms, they will hardly be interested in recompensing the external proletariat for sacrifices extracted from them in the cause of the country's industrialisation, as this may involve sacrificing some the standard of living of the internal proletariat themselves. The slogan of the unity of the proletariat of the world may be excellent on a moral and idealistic plane, but it is not based on any commonality of economic interests and thus lacks any motive force.

A theory of development should tackle these problems for future growth. What are the conditions for the transference of knowledge or 'know-how'? Have the techniques developed in other places been, or can they easily be, adopted to the conditions prevailing in the less fortunate parts? What are the suitable institutional conditions that can be developed in the places that are trying to adopt the innovations, and how can we get them in? How are the costs of growth to be borne? How much by nationals and how much by wider international community?

4 A Synoptic View of the Industrial Revolution in Theoretical Perspective

THE BASIC CHARACTER OF THE INDUSTRIAL REVOLUTION

In an international environment of mercantile capitalism, colonialism and imperialism, the present industrialised countries in general and the United Kingdom in particular embarked on an 'Industrial Revolution'. This industrial revolution was basically characterised by the use of fossil energy (coal, oil, etc.) instead of biological energy (humans, horses, oxen, etc.) for the large-scale production of goods for human use. The supplanting of human and animal power by coal, oil and electrical energy greatly extended human capability: it was a quantum leap forward in the evolution of human society in its everyday business, which should be ranked with such milestones in human progress as development of agriculture and domestication of cattle in about the tenth millennium BC or of irrigation technology in the valleys of the Nile, Tigris–Euphrates and Indus in the fourth millennium BC which led to the growth of the first civilisations.

Technical change to the application of non-biological energy did not alone result in the industrial revolution. Even in the Middle Ages there had been important developments in the application of water and wind power, for instance in the grinding of corn and working of forge hammers. Technical change in the sixteenth and seventeenth century led to coal-burning processes in the manufacture of glass, bricks, the smelting of copper and iron and the development of forging, etc. For the launch of the industrial revolution, it was necessary that this technical change be on a sufficiently large scale to make the entrepreneurs and leaders of these industries important and independent centres of power in the economy as well as in the body politic of the country, rather than a mere appendage to the ruling oligarchy, as had been the case during previous technical improvements. Only with these changes would the prestige of the new

62

creativę minority be sufficient to attract new enterprising young men to carry on the revolution to its mature phase; otherwise there was a danger of such promising efforts petering out.

For large-scale production it was necessary that the product should command a large enough market, and that the entrepreneur should have sufficient funds to embark on a large enough production operation; this could happen only after the emancipation of the producer-entrepreneur from the tutelage of overlords. And to command a large enough market, especially overseas, the price of raw materials should be so low that the final product could compete successfully even after bearing the trade and transport cost of a long-distance transfer. The price of imported raw materials would need to be much lower in their own countries as their price in the manufacturing country would have also to include their cost of transportation, etc. from the producing countries. All this presupposed a relatively developed transport system, both internal and international.

In the industrial revolution, apart from the basic technology, a major role was thus played by the availability of risk capital, cheap raw materials, and a buoyant market. Only these permitted the successful implantation of the basic technology. We cannot know whether the industrial revolution would have been possible in the absence of the support these availabilities gave to its establishment.

AVAILABILITY OF RISK CAPITAL

Innovation is a risky activity. We hear only about the successful innovations and innovators, but with every successful innovator there are dozens of unsuccessful ones. If you look at the patent register of the last two centuries in the UK or the USA you will be amazed at the hundreds of patents which have left no trace on industrial history. Many of them must have been tried, and many of them must have ended with the bankruptcy of their inventors and their backers. As Professor Leontief says, if we want to commemorate the pioneers of the industrial revolution, we shall have to raise the largest number of plaques to these unknown heroes who ruined themselves in the cause without leaving a single trace of themselves or their deeds behind.

This gives a rough idea of how much risk capital must have been invested in the process; only the tip of that iceberg is now visible in the shape of the history of the successful enterprises. The origin of that huge risk capital is intimately entangled with the origin of the industrial revolution. This capital at the beginning of the industrial revolution was the profits – some would say loot – of the trade with the Indies. Eric Williams (1944) maintained that a large part of the capital accumulation which financed the industrial revolution came from the profits of the slave trade. We need not completely agree with him, since his evidence is largely anecdotal, to realise that those profits also played their part in the capital accumulation process. We have seen above how tribute was extracted from subject countries and how huge profits were made through the 'unequal' mercantile trade with the colonies and dependencies. As is natural most of these profits were squandered in conspicuous consumption, but even then sufficient was left to form the risk capital for a large number of entrepreneurs, a few of whom were successful in laying the foundation of industrial revolution.

Another type of invested capital was in overheads like canal construction, improvement of roads, etc. for easier and cheaper transport. This primarily came from the landed gentry who expected to gain from easier access to the market centres conducting international and internal trade in the produce of their estates. They were already making fortunes from the success of the foreign trade in woollens, and were actively pursuing a large-scale enclosure policy by the substitution of their arable agricultural land by sheep farming.

M.M. Poston (1935), after reviewing the relevant evidence, pointed out that in eighteenth century Britain there was no shortage of capital on a nationwide basis:

> There were enough rich people in the country to finance an economic effort far in excess of the modest activities of the leaders of the industrial revolution. [On the other hand, the imperfections of the capital market were such that] new enterprises in the search of capital were not much assisted by the fact that England happened to be at the time the richest land in Christendom.
>
> The most important – indeed perhaps the only important – supply of such capital came from commerce, especially from merchants who invested large sums in industries producing goods they sold (Crouzet, 1972: 123).

W.A. Lewis (1955) defines the industrial revolution as a 'sudden acceleration of the rate of capital accumulation'. He writes that, 'We cannot explain any industrial revolution until we can explain why saving increased relatively to national income' (1955: 208ff).

The idea that capital formation proportions doubled from 5 – 6% to about 12% during the industrial revolution, first put forward by Lewis, was made the central mechanism of industrial revolution by W.W. Rostow in his famous book *Stages of Economic Growth* (1960); Rostow terms the period of history when this change occurred the 'take-off'. While these are of course approximate figures, any estimate of capital formation will fail to include the savings or investment that was 'wasted' in the experimentation which was so essential for an industrial revolution to 'take-off'. These extra savings were not the result of a sudden change in the saving habits of the population at large but were rather the result of a sudden increase in the income of savers from their usual or permanent income, largely due to colonial trade and enterprise.

The continuing profits of the colonial trade soon spilled over into export of capital from Britain. The capital requirements of the US industrial revolution, as well as that of Germany and France, were in no small measure indebted to exports of British capital. This explains the fact that banking institutions played a much bigger role in their development than in that of Great Britain, while in the construction of their social overhead capital the state played a significant part; these institutions could tap the international capital market much more effectively.

The servicing of these debts did not pose a great problem as their returns were mostly reinvested in the same country. This also increased the capacity of borrowers in new countries to produce and transport the primary products for which there were growing markets in Europe. In the case of the USA, it was further facilitated by the fact that many individuals from Europe themselves migrated there with their savings: the USA remained a net capital importer until near the end of the nineteenth century. In the early days of the industrial revolution most of the non-wage gross returns were reinvested. Patel (1961) refers to 'the immense power of the compound growth at higher rates'; Rostow (1960: 36) typifies a country's 'take-off' as a critical phase when 'compound interest gets built into society's structure'. As saving rates from these non-wage gross incomes were very high it tends to justify (even after the first phase was over) Arthur Lewis's characterisation of the industrial revolution as a period when the rate of investment increased from less than 5% to more than 12% (Lewis, 1955: 225).

However, financing industrialisation with the help of borrowed capital seems to work only when the gross returns on capital are not repatriated until the country has become fully industrialised. Once the country is fully industrialised net capital investment seems to have a more subordinate role; the use of accumulated depreciation funds for the replacement of the invested capital gives sufficient chance for the incorporation of new technical improvements. Solow (1957) has shown that between 1909 and 1949 only one-eighth of technical improvement in the USA was due to increased capital per man.

The industrialisation of India and Russia during the last decades of the nineteenth century was aborted primarily due to the repatriations of profits by the legal owners of the financial capital. These countries acquired their considerable railway network, modern textile, metallurgical, and other modern industries at almost the same time as the USA, France or Germany. Most of it was financed from the 'import' of capital, but due to the need to service the loans in exports, the compound rate of growth could not be built up: 'take-off' lended with a thud. The later industrialisation of the USSR was based on extracting savings from economically depressed populace in a way that only a tightly controlled political regime could have achieved.

CHEAP RAW MATERIALS

The consumer goods produced with the help of new innovations have to compete with products satisfying similar needs produced with traditional techniques. When the raw materials for the new product are imported they have to meet the trade and transport costs from the exporting country. So the cheaper the raw material price in the producing country, the easier it is for it successfully to compete with the established line. This becomes even more crucial if the industrialising country is producing for export, because then the cost of exporting and establishing in the new country must also be borne: in many cases the price of the raw material becomes critical for the success of the innovatory activity.

In a subject economy where the 'tributes' or 'service charges' to the imperial power have to be paid in foreign exchange, this poses no economic problem: the international trade is not an exchange of commodities on the basis of 'comparative cost' but a unilateral transfer of commodities in exchange for some imposed 'services' rendered. The local price or cost of production does not matter, as the exchange rate will be so determined that the users in the imperial country will get the materials at the price they can afford provided they can at least meet the trade and transport costs incurred in the currency of the imperial country. The position is only slightly different for economies that cannot produce the goods that they import, such as military hardware and/or industrial machinery. The countries that have to service capital imports with traditional exports not produced with the help of imported capital goods are in a similar boat: the export industries are parasitical on the local economy, which provides cheap raw materials. The particular institutional framework of international dependencies and economic relations at the time of the industrial revolution thus helped to make raw material imports sufficiently cheap for the industrialising countries.

Two strategies were available for getting cheap raw materials; one was to force the supplier country to send 'unrequited exports' in the shape of imperial charges or returns for the forced services rendered or repatriation of profits, etc. which would force the country to produce export goods at subsistence wages. This has been used extensively in imperial possessions, and was called the 'drain' by Indian economists. The other was the production of these raw materials with slave labour. When slavery was abolished, a substitute had to be provided, and it was found in the import of indentured labourers, mainly from India. Though their conditions of work were hardly better than slavery, at least they were not captured and tortured when brought to their new homes. They were pushed into this status by their abject poverty and pulled by the dream of the good life so deceptively painted by the people enlisting them. Britain could thus provide labour at subsistence level to its colonies, particularly in the West Indies.

However, British ships were also combing the oceans as self-appointed policemen chasing slavers of other nations. 'They recaptured and released some 150,000 slaves between 1810 and 1864' (Parry, 1971: 444). The number their activity prevented must, of course, be much larger. 'Here, from the British point of view, principle and self-interest coincided . . . It has even been argued that Pitt's support for anti-slavery was merely pursuing national economic advantage under a cloak of humanitarianism. Of course this is to push cynicism to the point of naivete' (Parry, 1971: 430–1). This did, however, contribute to the industrial revolutions of Spain and Portugal being stillborn, as they had hardly any source of indentured labour, and the British navy was patrolling the oceans to catch ships carrying slaves.

THE SIZE OF THE MARKET

The importance of the size of the market was emphasised by Adam Smith (1776) at the very beginning of the systematic study of economics. He maintained that the seminal innovation was the division of labour in the production of a single good: it is the division of labour that increases productivity. The extent of the division of labour depends on the extent of the market, so the extent of the market determines the scale of the operations; the bigger the scale of operations the larger number of cost-saving devices that can be introduced, giving a decreasing cost of production with an increasing market size.

Another role of the market has also to be appreciated in this context: giving a *chance to the innovating activity to be firmly established before the 'profits' on it become zero.* Here the word 'profit' is used in the Schumpeterian sense that excludes the normal returns to capital from the definition, and includes only abnormal returns due to the innovating activity of the entrepreneur. Such profits tend to become zero as more and more capacity to produce the good is created. Once they are zero, the investment will yield only normal returns that should be equivalent to the interest rate. (Schumpeter, 1934)

So the higher the potential market, the higher will be the 'profit' in this sense; and the higher the potential 'profit' the greater will be both the incentive for innovation and the chance to establish a successful innovation. Not the size of the 'profit' alone, but also the length of time that the 'profit' is available will determine the success or failure of permanently establishing the innovation. In most cases, the savings accumulated through the accumulation of the 'profits' will contribute to the creation of new capital for the propagation of that sectoral activity. During the early years of the industrial revolution, there was sufficient risk capital available as a result of mercantile profits, but it was available in separate 'pools' as there was hardly any national mechanism to bring the saver and investor together. Once an innovator had successfully established his industry, the pool from which he drew his resources was soon found to be inadequate, so he had to base his expansion primarily on the accumulated 'profits'.

The time of positive 'profits' for new enterprise should be sufficiently long not only to reward the original innovator adequately, but also allow sufficient followers to establish themselves in the industry; this will allow a healthy competitive modern industry to be established. This implies that even after the start of the innovating activity if market size can be further increased it will help in establishing the activity even though in the beginning 'profits' were not high enough. If this condition is not fulfilled there is a chance that the whole experiment will wither away.

This way of looking at the process of industrialisation also explains Rostow's (1960) phenomenon of the 'leading sector' of industrialisation. If the sector in which the potential 'profit' is highest is the first one to be developed, then it is likely to take more time before its 'profits' are reduced to zero. Given a longer period of profitability, there is higher chance of establishing the industrialising process, that sector becomes the leading sector, and this inaugurates Rostow's period of 'take-off'.

By the time 'profits' tend to zero, the changing price, market and know how situation should have created another sector showing a high potential for 'profits' by using fossil fuel in its production process. If this new innovation does not come in time, the country is likely to relapse. If it comes as soon as the old 'leading sector' is reaching a zero profit stage, the country will move into Rostow's 'drive into maturity' period. The success of the industrial revolution is signalled by the use of non-biological fuel-based technology in the industries employing most of the labour force of the country. The longer the time available for establishing an innovation, the greater are the chances that the industrial climate will be able to produce a new innovation that will take the economy into a 'drive into maturity: this available time depends on the *size of the market.*

The example of Spain is instructive. In 1795 there were over 3,000 small factories in Catalonia, employing about 100,000 people, mostly women, . . . importing its raw cotton and dyestuffs from the Caribbean and Mexico, shipping its product, the gay prints known as indianas, from Barcelona to all parts of Spanish America. The industry was protected by a decree of 1771, which prohibited the imports of cotton prints into Spain

and admitted colonial raw cotton duty free . . . Under protection
the industry throve, but opening of the Indies ports to the
neutrals in 1797 dealt it a heavy blow. Thereafter, the French
War, British competition, and the loss of control of Indies,
combined to kill it – not stone dead, for it had a home market;
but for a hundred years it limped along with little further
development. Europe as a whole suffered a similar setback as a
result of continental blockade. It was turned back upon its
internal markets and its own raw materials. Britain, conversely,
was driven outwards, obliged to seek compensation for its European losses by extending its markets overseas, especially in its
own and other people's colonies (Parry, 1971: 380–1).

No wonder that with savings from new and immense mercantile
wealth and with domination of cheap raw materials sources as well as
of the markets Britain became the first industrialised country. These
are the circumstances of unequal trade, internecine warfare in Europe and domination of overseas countries that enabled the industrial
revolution to take root at all. What circumstances would enable the
industrial revolution successfully to embrace the whole of humanity?

THE 'BACKWASH' MECHANISM IN DEVELOPING COUNTRIES

The great human achievement of the industrial revolution could thus
be successful in the modern industrialised countries primarily because there were several developing countries to endure the 'backwash' effect of this industrialisation. If it had not been so the world
would have missed this great revolution; however, the task of incorporating those countries into this great revolution is still incomplete.

The economy of these countries is not like the pre-industrial
economy of the currently industrialised nations. Any expectation that
the stages of economic growth as observed in these countries can be
repeated in the present under-developed countries is a puerile conclusion of the non-analytical historical determinist who has studied
his economic history in deceptive national formats, rather than in
international perspective.

These economies have been completely metamorphosed from the
ones that were independent and self-contained at the pre-industrial
level of technology into ones which are linked to the current indus-

trialised world as subordinate economies supplying raw materials to their industrial machines; their economies are now more or less completely integrated with the world economy. The world economic order – that is, the institutional framework and the market rules governing these relationships – are similar to the ones that governed relationships with dependent economies in the days of economic imperialism. The major difference is that while then each such country was attached to one or more industrialised countries in an unequal trading relationship, now each of them is related to the industrialised world as a whole. Previously, the imperial power was the guardian of the prevalent economic order; now that job is performed by world institutions like IMF and World Bank on behalf of the industrialised countries as a whole. Another most important difference is that while previously this arrangement proved to be a necessary sacrifice for the progress of the mankind to a new revolutionary stage in its development, now it is serving only as an impediment to the fulfilment of that very revolution by not allowing its spread into the rest of the world. Our job is to examine the working of this system in detail to discern, if possible, the steps that should now be taken to spread the industrial revolution to every corner of the world.

INSTITUTIONS FOR INDUSTRIALISATION

It is generally believed that for economic development the same type of institutional and social environments are necessary, like those prevalent at the time of the start of the industrial revolution in England or the USA. It is believed that all economic activities should be taken up by private individuals and that the state should interfere as little as possible. This is justified on the basis of an idealised economic history of the already developed nations. However, as Galbraith points out, 'Those economic advisors who advise smaller nations about pure private enterprise in the United States of America are ignorant of their own economic history.'

The nearest approximation to this idealised economic history is Great Britain. Here, two special circumstances must be remembered. One is that in the case of Great Britain the industrial revolution was an autonomous creative activity, it was not a copy of some already developed prototype. Such a case of original creativity can be done only by private individuals. Nobody could have foreseen the course of future growth, or could have planned for it: there was no model; it was a creative activity of some individuals who successfully innovated and started the path of industrial growth. In the process of the flowering of this creative activity, quite a few creative individuals did not make it, they were economically ruined and left no trace behind. Those who succeeded by trial and error were left as the leaders on the new path.

For success in such a situation, one of the primary conditions was non-interference by people who could not know what was going to come and non-interference by vested interests who would have been rightly or wrongly apprehensive of these new developments without understanding them fully. The best way to achieve that was to have as little government interference with the process as possible. However, government interference of previous centuries in the economic activities of the country were themselves responsible for creating these very preconditions for growth. It was a fortunate chance, but that chance had played a crucial role; it was government interference that had developed Great Britain into a really successful trading nation and one of the key instruments was the granting of a monopoly of trade of particular goods or regions to individual companies. This restrictive practice was responsible, to a large degree, for the growth of Great Britain as an international trading nation. This commercial capitalism was not only responsible for the accumulation of wealth, a part of which could be converted easily into risk capital, but also brought the technique of the cotton textile production to the UK from the Indies. This, in turn, was the harbinger of the industrial revolution. It also provided the large market for its manufactured products which was the sine qua non for the success of this unique enterprise. All these were the necessary preconditions of the triggering of the industrial revolution, and these conditions were created in no small measures by the actions of the government in restricting individuals' economic activities.

Another important point to note is that at that time each innovation in itself was small, so small that it could have been furthered by even small entrepreneurs. A new firm incorporating these new techniques of production need not have to be much bigger in size than already existing production units, and they did not require much more capital investment: they were well within the reach of an innovating individual and his immediate family and acquaintances. And as the market for the goods produced was fairly well developed, there was a ready excess for the merchants selling the commodity at home and abroad. In other words, the gap between the existing conditions and the conditions that would result after the innovation was not very big, and it could easily be filled by the existing entrepreneurs.

In countries that developed later, this gap was larger. This meant not only a larger technical difference, but also a larger requirement of risk-bearing capital, managerial skills required to manage an enterprise on a larger scale, etc. It required also knowledge of the whereabouts and the quality, price etc. of ancillary industries which became more and more necessary with the advance in the sophistication of industrialisation. With the increased sophistication of the industrial products, markets also became more and more specialised and had to be studiously cultivated. With international trade advantage existing to a much lesser degree market intelligence became much more crucial. Existing establishments and entrepreneurs were in a much less favourable position to surmount these hurdles to industrialisation, unassisted as they were in the first industrialising country. It was almost inevitable that some sort of help would have to be given by organisations which had greater recourse to risk capital and had the facility of gathering economic intelligence on a much wider scale. These organisations were able to look forward to economic developments for beyond the horizons of one firm or industry and to the forward and backward linkages that the industry might induce – to the developments of its supplier industries as well as to its markets. They should also be able to take an informed view about the future of the whole economy of which that industry was to be a part. Thus we find the industrialisation process being guided by the banking industry in France and in Germany during its formative period. While in Great Britain banks were advancing only working capital and were keeping aloof from supplying the risk capital which was primarily embodied in fixed capital, in France and Germany banks provided risk capital. They could not only spread their risk over many industries but also encouraged complementary industries to develop; they had much better market intelligence and so could reduce the inherent risk to themselves far more than was possible for an independent entrepreneur.

However, it may be worth remembering that at the time Germany and France were developing, interconnections between industries were rather simple and for large part linear. The production process went from the primary products to final output through intermediate products. There were hardly any indirect inputs except universal intermediaries like fuel and energy. Markets were also well defined, and it was within the capacity of the banking system to organise their intelligence so as to be able to reasonably guide individual industries through its implications. As the industrialisation process became more and more sophisticated, interconnections between industries became more and more complicated and remote, and the suitable size for a new firm became bigger and bigger; the whole economic process involved in industrialisation became more and more difficult for the banking system to comprehend. The pace and direction of growth started to be more and more dependent on few decisions about big and basic industries or few big commercial deals which were beyond the power of the banks to influence. Forecasting became almost out of the question – probability calculus can help only with large numbers of decision-makers and is useless when the establishment or otherwise of a few large industries makes so much difference to the performance and the direction of an economy. Clearly countries embarking on industrialisation at this stage required guidance at a higher level than banks – a level that not only could forecast the future movements of the economy but also had the capacity to guide the economy in the way that it had forecast, when forecasts were becoming themselves more and more dependent on a few unforecastable decisions of a small number of decision-makers.

This stage is best illustrated by the experience of Japan and the USSR. Japan chose to develop its major industries as public-sector industries. All the major activities that were conducive to economic growth were either undertaken by the state or were under its direct guidance. The directions required for industrialisation were by this time well known; there was hardly any necessity for technological risk-taking. The knowledge base at the state level, together with the attempts to develop related industries as a unit considerably reduced the risks associated with the disruption of the backward and forward linkages. As soon as these industries were sufficiently established, the state privatised them in the interests of efficiency as well as to prevent interference by political adventurers. However, this divestment was not done haphazardly; it was so managed that the whole industrial structure was divided into a few conglomerates, called 'Zaibatsu'. Each Zaibatsu was almost fully integrated vertically; this implies that for all the intermediate goods industries both backward and forward linkages were controlled by the same Zaibatsu. This of course considerably reduced the risk involved. Capital goods required for industries in a particular Zaibatsu were also supplied by the industries in the same conglomerate, and so could be produced in a planned manner. Even mobility of labour was socially and legally controlled and was quite small. Each conglomerate could thus function almost as a closed economy. There was competition in both the durable and the non-durable consumption goods sector; that kept the individual Zaibatsu on their toes, since inefficiency anywhere down the line would inflate the production cost of the final consumption goods: a Zaibatsu had to see that none of the vertically integrated sectors became flabby.

However, for the purposes of the international trade these conglomerates had cosy arrangements among themselves; these were masterminded by state or semi-state agencies. Thus in the international trade field, where there are many more uncertainties and thus risks, Japanese industry could operate as one big integrated institution collecting market information, and organising concentrated marketing operations. It became the counterpart of the trading monopolies granted by the British crown during the initial decades of the commercial revolution which was the precursor of the industrial revolution.

The industrial revolution in the USSR can now be considered. It occurred under conditions of strict state planning; almost every aspect of the economy was centrally controlled. This reduced the risk factor considerably in what was the transformation of the economy to the highly complicated and integrated industrial economy of the mid-twentieth century. Not only the whole production structure is planned, but also the price structure; a complicated system of open or hidden subsidies and taxes operates, and there are multiple exchange rates. However, there now seems to be evidence that, at the current stage of the country's development, this complicated command economy with extensive bureaucratic apparatus is becoming slowly counter-productive. After the completion of the industrial transformation through the accumulation of the technically right sort of capital which had proved itself in other places, a time of technological and other experimentation is dawning. This requires an individual initiative in an unknown direction and risk-taking with expectations of corresponding reward. As soon as mass consumption rises above subsistence level, the producer firms require signals from the market about the goods demanded, and some indication of their detailed specifications for this demand. A central authority is not capable of indicating this consumer preference in requisite detail. Then, of course, there is a perpetual problem of inefficiency dogging all sorts of monopoly production. No wonder that the USSR is slowly jettisoning the system of command economy, which stood it so well in its process of industrialisation; this system is now becoming an encumbrance for future growth after serving its purpose well in very different circumstances.

We have seen that the instruments and the institutions that are necessary to ensure economic growth depend on what Gerschenkron (1962) calls the 'degree of backwardness' of the country at the moment it starts on the economic development path. There cannot be any general rules about this. The later a country starts its industrialisation programme the greater its 'degree of backwardness' in relation to the prevailing technology, and the more elaborate instruments it will have to adopt for success. As modern development is becoming more and more gigantic and technically more and more complicated, even in the old developed countries and even with the instrument of joint stock companies there are some projects that are found to be beyond the capacity of private enterprise or even individual countries. The most spectacular example of this has been the space programme to send communication and other satellites to be stationed in space. Only a joint consortium of several European countries is able to manage it. The supersonic aeroplane *Concorde* had to be developed by a consortium of the United Kingdom and France, and so on. Many big industries are continuously seeking specific help or government orders for growth, or sometimes even for survival. Even a casual look at the financial papers of the modern developed countries will be sufficient to convince one of the enormous extent of government interference that is responsible for the growth and survival of modern industry. The days of pure laissez-faire no longer seem suitable for modern industrial growth, though a continuous vigilance against falling into the trap of monopolistic inefficiency resulting from state 'feather bedding' is necessary.

5 Types of Developing Countries

INTRODUCTION

That the developing countries are different not only because of their geographical and socio-political conditions, but also because of their level of economic growth, has been recognised at least from the time of Adam Smith. Marx gave it a central place in his socio-economic schemata of human development; he thought that his stages of tribalism, slavery, feudalism, mercantile capitalism, and industrial capitalism followed each other with something like historical necessity. In modern economic literature, it was Walter Rostow who has again brought this concept of stages of economic growth into economic thinking. His paradigm of 'take-off' has become a current coin of economic discussion; his characterisation of economic growth as the five successive stages of traditional society, pre-take-off stage, take-off stage, drive to maturity, and high consumption stage had a ring almost of historical inevitability.

These theories of the stages of economic growth, when applied to developing countries, all assume that the developing countries are at the beginning of the growth period. They are either like an undisturbed traditional society and/or are working under feudalism. And the path that they have to follow for development is the path followed by the current developed countries in the past. However, most of the current under-developed countries have been affected by the activities of the presently industrialised countries in the last few centuries; their participation in international trade has changed their economic structure, which can hardly be compared with that of the pre-industrial stage of developed countries.

Different countries face different types of economic constraint, and the economic situation will be effectively conditioned by the type of constraint a country is facing at any given time. International economic relations and the condition of the international economy at the time are also crucial to the economics of any country in our present highly integrated world. We have indicated previously the types of economic and commercial relations that were prevalent when the currently developed countries themselves developed. It should be

77

obvious that those conditions are not replicable for any country in the future. Both Marx's and Rostow's theories look at the economic growth of the developed nations as if they were a self-sufficient world in themselves; they do not adequately explain even the development achieved in so far as they neglect the crucial help such nations received from the international economic relations existing at the time, especially that from the underdeveloped countries of today. However, there is one important lesson that we can learn from their studies; that is that unique levels of achieved development and its structure require unique policies if the growth of a country is to be furthered. Therefore in analysing the development prospects and policies of different countries it is necessary to deal with countries at different levels separately.

There is also a qualitative difference between the economic structures of different developing countries. The under-development of various countries and their dependence on the developed world is of different kinds. Galbraith seems to recognise this when he opines that capital is the problem in South Asia, human resources in Africa, and social and political systems in Latin America (reported by Papanek, 1977). We have seen that these different characteristics are partly the result of different historical experiences and qualitatively different relationships with the international economic community. We therefore require both a distinct development theory and a distinct development policy for each type of developing country.

This seems so obvious as to be a banal statement; some development workers exaggerate it, claiming that one requires a different development theory for each case, you just cannot generalise, in fact there is no general development theory; and so on. This is not the case. According to the constraints faced, and in accordance with the historical development of their under-development, we can classify the developing countries into clear types, and then distinguish the policies that will only aggravate their under-developed conditions from the ones that look more promising in bringing them out of the historically-inflicted morass and putting them on the royal road to development. The short-term indicators of development so often used are mostly misleading, and do not tell us the capacity of such developing economies to withstand the pressures of adversity occasioned by changes in international circumstances. New indicators to assess progress to the goal will have to be developed, and these indicators will of course be different for different types of developing countries.

Surprisingly most of the current development theories do not make such a distinction among developing countries, and give a similar prescription for all. This is not only true of casual economic pundits but also of such operating agencies as the World Bank and the IMF, who seem to prescribe similar a medicine to all the developing countries which happen to approach them for financing purposes irrespective of whether they come from Latin America (with modernised agriculture and industry as well as efficient markets integrated with the rest of the world), or from Sub-Saharan Africa (dominated by traditional peasant agriculture, with fragmented markets and a rudimentary transport and communication network).

CLASSIFICATION OF DEVELOPING COUNTRIES

For our purposes, we shall divide the developing countries into five types, in accordance with the economic character relevant to their development performance:

**Labour-constrained Dual Economies: Traditional
Ones Almost Self-sufficient**

These show a dualism between a traditional self-sufficient society and commercialised enclaves. The export orientation of the enclaves was initially controlled by entrepreneurs from abroad, though now it has mostly been transferred into local ownership and sometimes nationalised. However, its basic character has hardly changed; technically, it hardly interacts with its stagnant rural backyard. The income levels in this traditional sector provide a yardstick for the real wage levels in the enclave. Though the traditional sector was originally self-sufficient, its better-off members now purchase modern commodities from the enclave economy either produced there or imported in exchange of the foreign exchange earned through the export of its products. These purchases and the state taxes make the traditional worker part with the products required to provide the wage goods in the enclaves. As the economy is labour-constrained, the output of the traditional sector is almost proportional to the labour force remaining there. This implies that with the development of the rest of the economy, the real wage rate of agricultural workers will decrease.

An ILO study (Ghai and Radwan, 1983) found that the real wages for agricultural workers had declined in three of the relatively better growth performers; Kenya, Ivory Coast and Malawi. According to the World Bank's World Development Report (1987: 205; 265), agricultural production in Sub-Saharan Africa increased at an annual rate of 1.9% during the period of 1965 to 1980; though the rate of growth of the total labour force was 2.5% per annum, the percentage of labour in agriculture decreased from 79 to 75, giving a growth of agricultural labour as only 2.1.%. In view of the fact that extra land is likely to have lesser productivity than that already under cultivation, this data fits remarkably well with our hypothesis. According to FAO estimates (FAO, 1979, Table 4.5) Africa's potential arable land is estimated at about 1.7 hectares for each African person while only about 0.55 hectares per person is being utilised at present.

This implies that in Sub-Saharan Africa the agricultural production is constrained by the agricultural labour force, and the bulk of the agricultural production is being produced by means of the traditional techniques. All development programmes as well as the export-creating plantations, mining, and other industries, that take away labour from agriculture serve only to reduce agricultural production. The way to increase agricultural production, conducive to development activity, is to use modern labour-saving devices for agricultural production. With the present price structure that is not feasible, as the returns from the agricultural activity will show huge losses; and if the prices of agricultural goods can be increased to make the labour-saving devices in agriculture profitable, it will increase the minimum wage rate and that will increase the prices of the export commodities.

A development theory dealing with these types of developing countries will have to deal with ways of solving this dilemma, where to provide sufficient foodgrains to the people, the price of foodgrains has to be increased, but that increase itself leads to a rise in the supply price of export goods, reducing their sale in international market. The dilemma becomes doubly acute due to the fact that for increasing foodgrain output fertilisers, etc. have to be imported which demands the availability of more foreign exchange.

**Land-constrained Dual Economies: Traditional
Ones Almost Self-sufficient**

In these types of developing economies it is the land rather than labour that is the bottleneck. This implies that with current techniques of production agricultural output is not sufficient to employ the whole labour force. There is a quite substantial unemployed or under-employed labour force, which cannot be employed in the formal sector as the economy cannot produce sufficient amount of wage goods to satisfy the extra demand that would be generated.

Any agricultural production for export again reduces the amount of production of agricultural wage goods in the country. However, this is due to the reduction of the area of land available for that production and not to the paucity of the labour force. This will lead to increasing unemployment in the economy due to scarcity of the wage goods as well as a reduction in consumption levels of food producers. Here the phenomenon of under-employment becomes important, because quite a few people work part-time or on a casual basis in the family business or agriculture surviving on less than the minimum necessary diet, and spending much less energy on work than they are capable of; this is a way of distributing deprivation. It is clear that this under-employment cannot be mobilised for productive purposes without the supply of additional wage goods to the economy.

But, unlike the case of labour constraint, an increase in non-agricultural activity in the economy does not decrease the production of agriculture; it can be sustained only if the necessary agricultural wage goods are transferred from the agricultural sector itself. These can be done by some sort of taxation of agricultural incomes or by selling extra non-agricultural goods to the better off among the agriculturists.

The exports of these economies depend on the low wage rate of labour in terms of the international currency. This is made possible because the basic wage goods do not require any imported input, and therefore the wage rate in international currency can move with the international price of the basic export commodity. All the extra export promotion effort is based on this low wage production capability; with the current development paradigm, this becomes essential for acquiring investment goods and other developmental assistance from developed countries, and also for acquiring luxury goods for the better off and military hardware for the protection of the country from external and internal enemies. It is also important for servicing any external debts that may have been contracted in the past on regular or on concessional terms. The later is termed as 'foreign aid'.

In such circumstances, the only way to move towards the betterment of the people is to increase land productivity; this seems to be the only way to increase the wage goods that may be able to feed the increasing labour force employed in productive activities. However, the techniques of increasing agricultural productivity require the application of fertilisers and other chemicals to the crops as well as the use of more advanced agricultural plant and machinery. For most countries, these have to be imported, and these inputs in the production of wage goods will make their supply price dependent on the exchange rate; as the wage rate is dependent on the price of wage goods, this may tend to price exports – developed on the basis of low labour cost – out of the market.

This dilemma of increasing wage goods supply requiring more imports, and its consequences on the price structure – making exports more costly and thus tending to reduce them – is a major hindrance to the development of this type of country. It is to this problem that the attention of the development economists should be directed. Some big developing countries in this category (like Egypt or India) have tried to tackle the dilemma by modernising some of their agriculture by using imported inputs but also directly or indirectly subsidising it to the extent that the price relatives in the economy are not much disturbed. This does not adversely effect an export market developed on the basis of cheap labour. However, the subsidies come directly or indirectly from other sectors of the economy and lead to a break in their growth potential. The comparatively low rate of growth of these countries can be partly attributed to the cost of this solution, and this route is not available for smaller countries or those which do not have any industrial sector that can take the strain. These countries, which could become exporters of the manufactures on the basis of this technique of judicious tariffs and subsidies, need to be studied as a separate sub-class for development insights: it has its own peculiar problems, strengths, and weaknesses that require deep individual analysis.

Foreign Exchange-constrained New Economies: International Trade-dependent Wage Goods Technology

The colonial economies of Latin America did not develop on the basis of cheap labour that was getting its sustenance from traditional agriculture; they depended mainly on the indentured or slave labour which was sustained from their own production or that of other independent farmers. With the progress of the industrial revolution those farmers kept abreast with the developments of modern technology and in many cases were themselves the inventors of farming techniques suitable for husbanding extensive land with limited labour, depending on fossil fuel for the requisite energy. By the very nature of the fact that foreign entrepreneurs were looking after these farming industries, which catered largely for foreign markets, there was no need to develop a self-sufficient economic base in the colony itself. Chemical inputs, metal products, machinery, etc. could easily be brought on the returning ships from the countries where the colonial products were sold with hardly any real transport cost. Thus there was hardly any need to develop supporting intermediate and capital goods industries, and to develop them for the small market of the individual colonies would have hardly been an economic proposition anyway. Further, the entrepreneurs familiar with those industries were not generally among the migrants attracted by the riches of these new lands.

The result of this historical accident is that we now have several developing countries whose production, both industrial as well as agricultural, is crucially dependent on intermediate imports. Any lack of foreign exchange will be reflected in the paucity of the intermediate goods; this in its turn will force the industrial establishments to run below capacity and the agricultural sector to leave the land either uncultivated or starved of the necessary inputs, thus reducing its output. This decline in economic activity will of course create a corresponding amount of unemployment.

Almost the contrary should happen in times of abundant foreign exchange. However, in such happy times a lot of the foreign exchange will be used for the luxury imports of the better off sections of the community, as well as in the purchase of defence equipment. Encouraged by a development conscious government, there will be entrepreneurial tendency to invest in new capacity creation and other development activities, little realising that in times of foreign exchange difficulties such newly created capacity will lie unutilised due to the paucity of the intermediate goods. In times of abundant foreign exchange the selected technique will be import intensive rather than import saving ones, thus making the days of foreign exchange deficiency even harder.

With the wide fluctuations of the prices of internationally traded commodities over years, the foreign exchange availability of these old colonial outposts will also change fast from relative abundance to relative scarcity, because these countries depend for their foreign exchange on the international sale of a few commodities in which they have historically specialised.

In times of scarce foreign exchange, unemployment will be generated; this will tend to drive real wages down to the minimum sustainable levels. However in times of relatively abundant foreign exchange, the labour of various skills will start to become the hindrance to growth; this should lift wage rates above subsistence levels, so we can expect to find some of these types of the developing countries having a much higher level of real wage rates than others. But all will be susceptible to the gyrations of the price levels of the internationally traded commodities, and real wage rates as well as employment levels will fluctuate in step.

Sovereign Entities Working as Service Centres and Locations for Offshore Assembly Plants

Apart from these three major categories, there are some minor but important ones that exist as simple appendages to major industrialised countries. They, like Hongkong, Singapore, etc. serve mainly as an offshore location for the manufacturing activities of the major international manufacturers. Their prime advantage for these international manufacturers is that they provide cheaper labour for the labour intensive chores of the production processes; they also provide a good distribution point for the metropolitan manufacturers for the region. To them can be shipped the parts of the major durable products which can be assembled there with cheap labour and shipped to a regional destination, providing economies in both assembling labour costs and in shipping due to bulk transport arrangements.

As they have no hinterland of traditional wage goods producers, their wage goods are also to be largely imported, so the advantage in such a country consists primarily in the lower real wage rates. These rates should be so much lower than in the original country that the transport, trade and extra administrative costs of such arrangements can be met from the savings. The wage rates in such countries cannot hope to approach those of the advanced countries even in the long run, and they have little hope of being able to develop any base through which they could independently operate their economies. This route is thus closed as a way to lead the economy into a developed position which would be resilient to the changing world economic environment as well as making it possible eventually to lift the real income level of its nationals to that of the advanced economies. However, this is a good arrangement for a short-term increase in the per capita income of a small sovereign entity to a much higher level than would be possible with any other development strategy.

As investments in these countries are made to serve other markets in the region, the multinationals and associates put techniques, machinery and plant incorporating the latest technology into the industry; this is in contrast to technological transfer in a country where the entrepreneur's intention is to get access to a large protected market. Here, a technique on the verge of obsolescence can be passed on. As the productivity of the first type may be as much as double than of the second, this gives a further boost to the economy of these offshore processing units. As will be shown later, wage rates here can easily be more than double than those in other manufacturing exporting developing countries.

Oil Exporters

Another special category of developing countries is the oil producers. They can be divided into two groups. One is the countries with the normal hinterland of the under-developed economy, with a respectable amount of arable land and population. These countries have the potential to become developed countries on an equal footing with the currently developed world in terms both of their economic resilience and of their per capita incomes. These countries – like Indonesia, Nigeria, Mexico, etc. – will have similar problems of development to the three major types discussed above. They may be colonial foreign exchange-cum-labour-constrained economies like Mexico; or old civilisations having a land constraint to growth like Indonesia; or like Nigeria a labour-constrained economy, having a considerable traditional sector. However, oil export does not necessarily limit the wage rate in the country; provided they do not depend on the export of other commodities, they have the potential to organise their economy on the Lewis model discussed in Chapter 1.

The other group consists of those sovereign entities that have hardly any economic hinterland to speak of. Their small populations have a high standard of living based on the sale of their important asset to the rest of the world in general and the advanced countries in particular. Economically, they are simply offshore oil fields with complicated political and trading relations with the rest of the world. Their real income level is of the same, if not a higher, order than that of the advanced countries. However, they are completely dependent on the current or future world political economic order. Their resilience to a changing international situation is minimal; it is difficult to conceive of them as strong economic units in themselves unless and until they become a part of some bigger economic entity. Their development problem is to find out a way to achieve this without diluting their high incomes in the quest to become a part of an independently viable economic grouping where most of their potential partners have substantially lower real incomes.

Technically, similar conditions are possible in other mineral exporting countries. But such conditions of the oil exporters are rarely found. Usually, unlike oil, the marginal cost of production of these minerals is not much higher than the prices they can fetch; so they do not present the opportunities the oil producers enjoy.

CONCLUDING REMARKS

We have seen above that the study of development problems can be made only in terms of international environments. The market and the fluctuations in the prices of the export commodities of the developing countries are the crucial elements of that environment; changes in the environment affect different types of developing countries differently, and the development problems faced by different types of developing countries are also unlike. In interacting with the international economic environments these different types not only throw up different types of production structures, with differing technology mixes; differing price structures also result. These all have profound effects on the chances of the success for various development strategies, and can be ignored only at the peril of analysis becoming irrelevant.

The classification proposed above is illustrative; we may find it useful in analysing the recent experience of various countries. But it must be emphasised that all countries cannot be classified exclusively into one class or another: many countries will have characteristics of more than one type, and show a preponderance of one characteristic at one period and another at a different period. But the classification is useful in helping to understand the way various decisions, and international economic events, are likely to affect individual types of developing country. For a particular country, the composite effects can be discerned only through detailed analytical judgement.

Part III
An International
Framework
for National Economies

Part III

6 Determination of International Commodity Prices

INTRODUCTION

In modern times a national economy has to work within the framework of the international environment. It does not matter whether the economy is a developed one or is in a developing phase. Though an insular national economy is exceptional nowadays, it is surprising to find how much economic analysis is conducted as if a national economy were governed solely by national conditions and policies. It is natural for politicians to attribute their failures to international environments if possible, and the economic betterment of their country to the successes of their policies, irrespective of the role actually played by international factors. The parochial analytical stance taken in much academic writing is less justifiable; it becomes downright misleading when it is taken in journalistic economic writing, which in its turn is responsible for the public perception of economic conditions. The public economic debate during the period of high inflation as well as high unemployment in the 1970s and of lower inflation as well as lower unemployment in the 1980s in the developed countries mainly attributed these to the economic policies of the state itself rather than to the changing international environment to which states were reacting in their own way. A moment's reflection should be sufficient to realise that the international economy's role in constraining the national economy is similar to the role of national macroeconomic conditions in constraining the microeconomic situations of individual economic agents.

This is obvious for the developing countries; for them most of the items that help to start and sustain the development process have to be purchased from outside, and the terms and the cost at which these can be acquired depend on international economic conditions. Not only modern technology, the associated machinery and expertise have to be imported but also many intermediate goods necessary for modern production. Most of these countries require imports of the fuel, minerals, and metals necessary for industrial production;

increasing agricultural production by the use of modern agricultural technology requires the inputs of imported fertilisers, pesticides, as well as the necessary farm machinery. All these have to be paid for by exports; however, payment is deferred if the country is able to get some international loans – commercial or concessional. Export earnings will depend on the price its export goods receive in the international market; these goods are mainly agricultural or mining commodities, and so its development is circumscribed by the international economic situation which determines what, how much, and at what price it can export. Most of the development efforts of the developing country can bear fruit only within the parameters thus imposed.

Not only are the developing countries so circumscribed, the economic health of the industrialised world is also crucially dependent on such constraints. The spectacular rise of fuel and other commodity prices in the 1970s not only fuelled unprecedented peace-time inflation in those countries, but also reduced their growth rates and created large-scale unemployment in their economies. The experience clearly demonstrated that any national model of the economy can rapidly be made irrelevant by happenings in the international market in countries that depend on the international market for fuels, minerals and metals, etc.

If we are to understand the framework in which any national economy can develop, we have to understand the determinants of the international economy. Like those in the national economy, these can be classified into two types – the market-determined and the institutional. The commodity prices of the primary commodities, except foodgrains, dairy products etc., are mainly market-determined. Long-term successful cartels of their producers hardly exist; though occasionally some have achieved short-term successes (like the cartel of the oil producers in the 1970s). However, for the movements of foodgrains, etc. most of these countries have not only erected barriers to protect their agriculture from the harsh winds of the international markets, but also practise a regulatory regime replete with various types of subsidies and incentives within their borders. On the other hand, there are a number of non-market restrictions in the international trade of the industrial commodities such as textiles, etc.. To understand their price and quantity movements requires a detailed consideration of the constraints imposed by formal or informal regulatory mechanisms. We shall now examine the international market mechanism for the market-oriented commodities on which the foreign exchange earnings of the developing countries primarily depend.

COMMODITY PRICE DETERMINATION IN INTERNATIONAL MARKETS

There are two ways in which the differences in demand and supply at current prices are adjusted in the economy – through stock adjustments or through price adjustments. In most modern manufacturing industry it is the stock adjustment that makes supply equivalent to demand, while changes in prices are basically determined by changes in the cost of production. This results not only in fluctuations in the stocks held by the industry and trade, but also, at one step removed, in the output produced. This in its turn leads to fluctuations in employment; changes in demand are thus accommodated by changes in stocks in the short run. However, if they persist, they lead to the changes in production and employment.

For primary commodities short-term quantity adjustments are quite difficult; production is planned in anticipation of demand several months to several years ahead. Some agricultural plantations have to be planted almost a decade ahead and once they start producing, there is hardly any way to reduce or increase production. The annual agricultural crops depend on the availability of alternative crop patterns and their profitability; for annual agricultural export crop substitution by food crops is not an economic feasibility. With the price structure prevailing in these countries, the returns to staple food production are comparatively quite low and as will be shown later, staple food prices move with the prices of the export crop. Further, the country will probably need foreign exchange badly, a need that food crops cannot fulfil. So far as the prices of agricultural commodities in the international market move in unison, there is hardly any advantage in substituting one export crop by another at the time of declining prices in world market. Moreover many developing countries are exporters of a single commodity; in their case, there is no possibility of substitution with international price decline.

Mines also take several years from planning to the production stage; a mine once commissioned generally has to be kept open unless it is decided to abandon it completely, as restarting a 'mothballed' mine is a costly and time-consuming process. However, within limits its production can be varied with changing demand. If the demand is significantly deficient, its production can be reduced, although the average cost of production would most likely increase, as the smaller the production the higher the proportion of the fixed cost in the unit cost of production. On the other hand, with increasing demand the production can be some-what stretched in the short run, but at significantly increasing marginal costs.

We can thus conceive of the price of these commodities as consisting of two components – a long-term and a short-term one. The demand and supply factors determining the long-term component are the long-term growth of the world's economic activity and the net investment made in extra capacity creation over the relevant period. As the gestation period of the investment is usually rather long, the key to the stability of this component consists in the accuracy of the long-term forecasting of demand by investors. Usually, there is a large number of investors creating capacity for the production of each such commodity in different parts of the world; naturally, their investment decisions are not coordinated, and it is very unlikely that the total capacity thus created will approximate the increase in its world demand: this implies alternate periods of scarcity and abundance of the commodity. The second component is the short-term one. In the short term the supply curve remains more or less fixed while demand fluctuates with the short-term fluctuations in world production. In the short run, changing demand thus leads to movement on the fixed supply curve, while in the long term both supply and demand curves shift.

SHORT-TERM PRICE DETERMINATION

The short-term supply curve will for the most part depict a slowly rising price with increasing quantity. Its gradient will go on increasing with increasing quantity, tending to be vertical as the quantity demanded approximates to capacity output. The demand curve, of course, will shift 'north-east' with the increase in economic activity and 'south-west' with its decrease. In the medium to long term the supply curve as a whole will shift to the right with the creation of extra capacity for commodity production and the demand curve will shift in a 'north-east' direction with the growth of the world's economic activity. If the two movements are in consonance with each other, the supply curve will have the same gradient at the point of intersection with the demand curve. Short-term fluctuations in de-

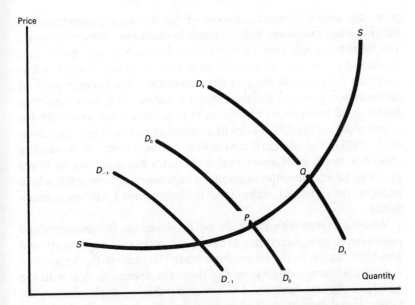

Figure 6.1 Short-term commodity supply–demand curve

mand are thus likely to bring about similar fluctuations in price. However, if the rate of capacity creation is less than that of the increase in economic activity, the intersection point will move upwards, where the gradient of the supply curve is larger. This will imply that short-term fluctuations of demand will generate much greater fluctuations in price.

This is illustrated in Figure 6.1. The line SS represents the short-term supply curve. Close to the capacity, its curvature increases fast with the increasing quantity, as it moves north-eastwards. $D_0 D_0$ represents the demand curve during the period in which the extra capacity coming on keeps pace with the growth in demand. When the growth of demand outpaces the growth in capacity, the demand curve shifts to $D_1 D_1$. It will be seen that in this situation the elasticity of price with respect to economic activity reflecting the quantity demanded will increase at an increasing rate.

DUTIES ON COMMODITY IMPORTS AND EXPORTS

The marginal cost of commodity production crucially depends on labour cost in the country of production. If the country suffers from persistent unemployment, as most of the developing countries do, the real wage rate there will gravitate towards the subsistence level. The nominal wage rate in international currency may be further depressed if the price of necessities in the producing country is less than that prevalent in the industrial countries. The average price of consumption goods in the developing countries in general has been found to be between 40 to 60% of that in the industrialised market economies (see the UN studies of purchasing power parities in Kravis *et al.*, 1982). The marginal cost is thus not only lower in developing countries because of lower real wage rates but also due to lower prices of basic consumption goods in international currencies, which reduces the nominal wage rate in international currency much further.

When a commodity can also be produced in the industrialised countries it can sometimes create problems; the huge tariff and non-tariff barriers erected by these countries against the imports of agricultural commodities is one of the ways devised to deal with the problem. At one time the USA was purchasing sugar, etc. in the international market at a higher price than the international price; of course, it gave a quota of such purchases mainly to the countries where the production of these commodities was organised by the US multinationals themselves.

If a producing country has a partial monopoly of the production of a commodity, it can use an export tax to recoup some of the loss due to this purchasing power anomaly. India, for instance extensively used the device of an export tax by putting export duties on jute and tea.

LONG-TERM SUPPLY CURVE

Long-term supply depends on capacity creation. For many commodities, the act of capacity creation has a long gestation period. For a stable relationship between demand and supply leading to stable prices, demand should thus be adequately forecast in advance by investors. If the forecast deviates too much from realised demand, we may find the demand curves meeting the short-term supply curves at points higher or lower than normal, like the curves $D_1 D_1$ and $D_{-1} D_{-1}$ in Figure 6.1. This implies a large increase in commodity price in one case and the existence of unutilised capacity in the other. The increased profitability in the first case will lead to feverish activity on the investment front, while in the other it may even lead to postpone-

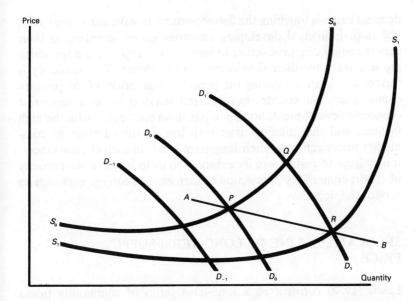

Figure 6.2   Short-term commodity supply–demand curve: movement over time

ment of some ongoing investment projects by multinational companies. However, with declining commodity prices, those developing countries which depend for their foreign exchange on their commodity exports will tend to increase their investment further in an effort to recoup their foreign earnings.

Figure 6.2 depicts the shifting of the short-term supply curve as a result of investment. The curve S_0S_0 depicts the short-term supply curve before investment activity. It shifts to S_1S_1 after investment. If economic activity has not correspondingly increased, the curve D_1D_1 will meet the new supply curve at R, which is in the flatter portion of the curve. As we shall see below, we may conceive the situation in the 1960s as demand curve D_0D_0 meeting supply curve S_0S_0 at P, which is in the flatter portion of the supply curve, while that in the 1970s demand curve D_1D_1 met the same supply curve at Q, which is in the steeper portion; in the 1980s demand curve D_1D_1 met the new supply curve S_1S_1 at R which is again in the flatter portion. It seems that these flatter portions depict the long-run supply curve for most of the time; as soon as the demand curve touches the steeper portion, a flurry of investment activity moves the curve to the right, and so the demand curve again touches the flatter portion. However, when the demand curve is touching the flatter portion, investment activity does not stop; individual developing countries go on investing in their export commodity production to increase the export earnings which are necessary for their development and defence. This tendency is further aggravated if during the period of high prices of the primary commodities, the country has incurred heavy debts to achieve fast economic development, hoping to pay them back easily with the high income, and then finding itself with low export earnings as commodity prices return to their long-term level. In such circumstances, it may have to restructure its economy so as to increase the capacity of export commodity production to earn enough foreign exchange to service the debt.

SECULAR DECLINE OF LONG-TERM SUPPLY PRICE

Lewis (1952) constructed a long-term series of commodity prices from 1870 to 1950. He found that the relative prices of raw materials with respect to manufactures had been declining over the years. As shown by Spraos (1980), and Sapsford (1987), this trend has continued into the 1980s.

Prebish (1950) and Singer (1950) both propounded an hypothesis that the deteriorating trend in the net barter terms of trade between primary commodities and manufactures was not just an observed fact but was inevitable with rising world income, as the income elasticity of demand of the primary commodities was much less than that of manufactures and technical progress results in more and more proportionate savings of industrial raw materials.

However, international trade is not conducted on barter basis, and the textbook model of international trade consisting of only two commodities and two countries is too much of a simplification of the reality to be of any practical use. Most of the developing countries exporting primary commodities are not advanced enough to be able to produce the manufactured goods they import; thus there is no 'comparative advantage' as envisaged in international trade models. The price determination of primary commodities as well as that of manufactures is made in different markets with hardly any reference to each other. As Kaldor (1983) has pointed out, 'primary product prices were determined in highly competitive markets, whereas industrial products were marketed under monopolistic conditions with producers setting their prices mainly by reference to their costs. In the latter case, the response of supply to demand took place not through the agency of price changes, but as a result of stock management. Manufacturers expanded or contracted their rate of production according to whether the flow of new orders exceeded or fell short of what was required to keep stocks in a normal relation to turnover. The highly competitive markets in basic commodities on the other hand rely on the variations in prices for keeping demand and supply aligned to one another, both in the short run and long run! Hicks (1974) has termed these two types of markets as 'Flex' and 'Fix' price ones.

In the flex-price market of primary commodities, long-run prices tend to gravitate towards the floor level given by the marginal cost of production based on a subsistence level of wage rates. Temporary increases in world prices are mainly absorbed by the middlemen's profits. Even when they are transferred to the workers they tend to be reversed at the next downturn of prices. This transference of profits is a slow process, as the entrepreneur waits to see the normal trend of the markets, while the reversal is a swift one to save the existence of the business itself. One further result of this distinction in market behaviour has been that most of the productivity gains in primary commodity's production have been transferred to the users through the flexibility of the price mechanism.

In the fix-price markets, the downturn of demand leads to unemployment, rather than a cut in the real wage rate. We thus find that even in such recessionary periods as the 1930s the real wage rate in industrialised countries did not come down. However, the industrialised countries found that their agriculture was subject to the same vagaries as the primary commodity markets in the developing countries; to protect their farmers' standard of living they had to adopt a complicated scheme of farm support prices and/or farm subsidies, etc.

Grilli and Yang (1988) have constructed a new index of commodity prices and related it to modified indexes of prices of manufactured goods. This shows (from 1900 to 1986) a cumulative fall of about 36% in the market prices of all primary commodities relative to those of manufactured products. Relative metal prices fell at the rate of 0.82% per year, non-food agricultural product prices at 0.84% a year, non-beverage food prices at 0.54% a year, and cereals (wheat, maize, and rice) prices at 0.68% a year. The relative prices of tropical beverages – which include coffee, tea and cocoa – on the other hand show a strong positive trend, rising at the rate of 0.63% a year.

If we view these long-term trends in terms of the basic component of a subsistence wage, we see that metal production as well as non-food agricultural production shows some gains in productivity that are being passed to the user of these products, while beverages are showing the classical signs of decreasing returns in face of limited land suitable for their production.

AN ILLUSTRATION OF THE SHORT-TERM SUPPLY CURVE

As pointed out above, international trade is not conducted on a barter basis; it is conducted in terms of money prices. We should therefore expect a relation between the money prices of commodities and world industrial production, which should give us the short-term supply curve. To derive a long-term supply curve we should expect some relationship with capacity creation activity. Using time as an independent variable assumes only that the relationship between the trend of increase in the demand and the trend of capacity creation is uniform over time; it should be possible to get more precise relationship with the new capacity creation itself.

We should expect this relationship to be stable only during the period when the price of cereals is not fluctuating wildly; in other words when the long-run trend of the primary product prices gravitates towards the marginal cost of production based on the subsistence level of wages, the basic unit in which the short-term supply response can be studied is that given by prices in terms of the prices of cereals. Mahdi (1988) selected the years 1958–1971 as a period in which cereal prices did not change very much. He estimated the following equation as showing the relationship between the price of raw materials and the world demand:

$$P = 84.4 + 0.258 \, M - 0.001 \, L \qquad (6.1)$$
$$(18.76) \quad (5.51) \quad (-1.06)$$

$R^2 = 87\%$; D.W. = 1.58

(figures in brackets are t values with 11 degrees of freedom).

P is the index of non-oil raw material prices and M is that of world industrial output with 1963 as base. L are the total financial flows to the developing countries in millions of dollars in 1963 prices, lagged 4 years. Really, the total investment in primary commodities should have been taken instead; but as that was not available total financial flows were taken, as it is expected that they would have been highly correlated with total investment. The coefficient of M is of the expected sign and highly significant while that of L is of the expected sign but statistically not significant.[1]

Mahdi (1988) has done a similar study for the years 1972–83, with the following results.

$$P = -246 + 4.12 M - 2.00 L \qquad (6.2)$$
$$(-3.40) \quad (6.94) \quad (-3.97)$$

$R^2 = 0.92$; D.W. = 1.64

(For this the year 1975 was taken as base year and the degrees of freedom were 9, and the lag in L was three years only.)

In this all the coefficients were found to be of the right signs and highly significant statistically.

Comparing equations (6.1) and (6.2), we can see that the portion of the supply curve met by the demand curve in the 1970s was about 16 times steeper than the portion it was crossing in the 1960s. The new capacity creation in the 1960s was keeping pace with the increase in demand, and therefore had hardly any effect on the slope of the supply curve in the neighbourhood of its point of intersection with the demand curve. In the 1970s, the extra capacity creation was helping to bring the intersection point to the flatter portion of the supply curve. There is a slight presumption that the investment activity was done at a less leisurely pace, reducing the average effective lag between investment and its effect on prices from four to three years.

It may be noted that in the above formulation both the independent variables are quantity variables and no adjustment is made for world inflation in estimating commodity prices. This implies that the rise or fall of primary commodity prices during that period was almost completely determined by demand and supply conditions rather than by cost-push forces; the inflationary forces in the industrialised world hardly affected the process of the price formation for the primary commodities. However, these two periods need to be distinguished as the former was one where new capacity creation was keeping pace with increasing demand and hence represented the long-run condition, while before the second period capacity creation seems to have lagged sufficiently behind the growth of demand creating conditions of shortage.

IDEALISED STORY OF COMMODITY SUPPLY CURVES AFTER 1945

In the post-1945 period, the high prices of primary products attracted investment. The capacity for 'commodity' production grew faster than demand for about two decades. This creation of more than adequate capacity was hardly the result of conscious farsightedness; it was just as much the result of comparatively lavish 'humanitarian foreign aid' disbursed to keep the developing world on the side of the free world. This 'aid' was largely used for developing the capacity for the production of primary commodities, often with the help of the multinationals. As shown by Prebish (1950), the consequent improvement of the terms of trade of the industrialised world was partly responsible for the two decades of unprecedented growth and prosperity in the 1950s and 1960s.

In the 1960s, the developing countries started clamouring for 'aid' to develop manufacturing sectors. Some of them started nationalising the exploitation of their natural resources. The 'donor' countries, taken in by their own propaganda of 'philanthropy', found that they were not so ' philanthropic' after all; aid was considered as a part of the conduct of foreign policy. Donor countries thus slowly tended to replace a part of their developmental 'aid' by military aid, thinking that it would give them a bigger say in the affairs of the debtor countries and thus they that would have more chance of saving them for the free world. So that while the official development assistance of OECD (industrialised market economies) increased by about 27% from 1960 to 1965, it decreased by about 11% from 1965 to 1970 in real terms (World Bank 1981a, p. 164.)

As a consequence, the growth of the supply of primary commodities slowed down in comparison to the increases in demand. These were the decades of the highest growth of the world economic activity; the industrial countries grew at just over 5% a year in the 1960s. By the early 1970s the imbalance in the supply of primary commodities and their demand reached crisis proportions, bringing in its train a sudden correction of the relative prices of the primary commodities. The World Development Report (World Bank, 1981) describes the situation concerning the oil price rise of the early 1970s as follows:

> Until 1970 the post-war period was characterized by rates of discovery of oil in the Middle East and elsewhere that were far in excess of demand. As a result the real price of petroleum fell steadily. . . . Cheap energy made an important contribution to the unprecedentedly rapid growth of world output. This pattern could not be sustained indefinitely. As the rate of growth of oil consumption began to exceed the growth of additions to reserves, prices would have risen regardless of the way the world oil market was managed. The fourfold rise in the nominal oil prices that took place in 1973–74 was triggered by short term political and economic factors, and somewhat overshot the real level sustainable by market forces (World Bank, 1981: 35).

This situation was not peculiar to oil alone. It was true for almost all primary commodities, though political factors and the cartel arrangement among the major oil producers made the price change in the oil industry spectacular. World prices of the non-fuel primary commodities almost doubled between 1972 and 1974. The rise was evenly distributed over the commodities; the price index for food commodities was 113% higher over the same period. Those for beverages, agricultural raw materials and metals were respectively 54%, 66% and 86% higher in that two-year period (IMF, 1986). All commodity markets were faced with the similar situation as the market for oil, though the effects were felt with lesser intensity due to institutional differences.

This sudden increase in commodity prices had two predictable consequences. The rate of growth of the real GDP of industrial market economies plummeted from 4.7% per annum during 1965–73 to 2.8% per annum during 1973–80 (World Bank, 1988: 189). This was a necessary adjustment to the reduced relative supply of the primary commodities. But as it was achieved through commodity price increases, it involved a real resource transfer per unit of output to the producers of these commodities. The economic struggle within the industrialised countries as to which factor of production should bear the brunt of this adjustment led to unprecedented inflation, labour troubles, erosion of real profitability, high interest rates, and high unemployment rates in those countries in the 1970s.

These high prices triggered an increase in investment in capacity creation for commodity production. The real net official development assistance of the OECD countries to the developing world rose from US $18.68 billion in constant 1980 prices in 1970 to 22.68 in 1975 to 27.68 in 1980 – an increase of 50%. Total financial flows (in constant 1980 dollars) to developing countries jumped from 44.1 billion in 1970 to 61.9 in 1973, 83.9 in 1975 to 104.2 in 1978, easing to 96.1 in 1980. Apart from this there was an accelerated investment in developed countries themselves in commodity producing activities.

The combined result of these two activities restored the relation of demand and supply of primary commodities by the beginning of 1980s. That led to a precipitate fall in the relative prices of primary commodities; the terms of trade of the developing countries, which increased at an average annual rate of 1.6% during 1973–80 decreased at an annual rate of 0.9% per year during 1980–4.

In 1985 its rate of decrease was 2.3% and in 1986 it fell at the high rate of 7.3% (World Bank, 1988: 192). The terms of trade of oil exporters fell precipitately by 38.7% in 1985, in the same way as they had risen spectacularly in 1973–4.

RECAPITULATION

We have seen above that the short-term commodity supply curve is of the standard shape, rising slowly with quantity until it reaches the vicinity of its capacity production; then it quickly rises steeply. Its height during its flatter portion depends on real wage rates in the producing countries and the purchasing power parity of the currency for necessities. In countries having chronic unemployment, this real wage rate is at the 'subsistence' level. Short-period fluctuation in commodity price can be explained as the movement of the intersection, with the demand curve oscillating with the fluctuation of world economic activity. The elasticity of the commodity price with respect to the economic activity will depend on the gradient of the supply curve at the point of the intersection.

In the medium period, with the creation of the new capacity, this curve keeps on shifting to the right. Empirically it has been inferred that the rate of capacity creation is greater than that of the increase of demand, making the intersection of the demand curve more and more to the left and thus decreasing the relative price of the commodities over time. As this process proceeds the rate of capacity creation falters, and demand outstrips the capacity, in its turn moving the intersection point precipitately up on the steep portion of the supply curve. This completely changes the short-term econometric relationship between commodity price and world economic activity; it also gives a favourable jolt to investment activity in commodity production, shifting the supply curve to the right and restoring the long-term price relationships.

7 Commodity Price Shocks and World Economies

INTRODUCTION

It is well known that the unprecedented and uninterrupted world economic growth of two decades after the Second World War came to an abrupt end with the oil crisis of 1973. It is less well known that the prices of the internationally traded world non-fuel commodities of agricultural and mining origin also increased by 60% in 1973 and another 20% in 1974. It seems that by the 1970s the supply of these commodities could not keep pace with the fast growth of demand generated by the high and continuous growth of the world economy over two decades. These commodities are after all a crucial though small part of the raw materials for the production of industrial goods.

Most of the developing countries are exporters of these primary commodities. Their exports mainly consist of agricultural and mineral products. The manufacturing exports of most of them are products of agricultural processing, like sugar, textiles, etc. The World Bank (1987) classification of 'Exporters of Manufactures' did not include these. It included seven market economies; of these Hong Kong, Korea, and Singapore are primarily 'offshore processing facilities', giving the benefit of cheap labour, overall tax reduction, etc. Their inclusion as developing countries serves only to obscure the real problems of development. Israel and Portugal are effectively part of Europe, with qualitatively different problems. This leaves India and Brazil only, in the non-European world, as exporters of such manufactures that are almost wholly produced within these countries together with their intermediate inputs.

The wage rates, employment, income and productivities of the developing countries mainly exporting primary commodities are intimately related to the international commodity market. And so to some extent is that of the developed countries, though much less transparently. We have looked already at the main reasons for the fluctuations of these commodity prices in the short run, as well as to their discontinuous jumps in the medium term. We need now look at the repercussions on the world economy. We shall see then how so many developing countries have found their incomes and wages

104

collapsing with these fluctuations and try to look at the possible routes of getting out of this dilemma; foreign exchange-constrained developing countries will be differently affected by this than land-constrained and labour-constrained ones. But, first, we shall look at the repercussions of commodity price changes on the industrialised countries.

COMMODITY PRICES AND INDUSTRIAL PRODUCTION

As the surge in commodity prices has been due to the capacity of their production not keeping up with increases in demand, the primary effect of any increase should be on industrial production. In fact, industrial production declined as the immediate aftermath of the commodity price rise. With the abatement of the rise in the real commodity prices it recovered and continued its growth, but at a reduced rate. Table 7.1 gives the industrial production for some important developed countries for selected years to bring out the point.

Table 7.1   Industrial production in some developed countries (1973–85)

	1973	1974	1975	1976	1979	1980	1985
1. USA	100.0	98.5	89.9	98.2	117.3	115.1	131.9
2. Japan	100.0	96.0	85.5	95.0	112.9	118.2	140.9
3. Germany (FDR)	100.0	97.8	91.4	95.7	107.5	107.5	110.8
4. France	100.0	102.2	95.5	103.4	111.2	112.4	111.2
5. UK	100.0	98.0	92.7	95.7	107.6	100.4	108.3

Source: IMF (1986).

It is clear from Table 7.1 that with the dramatic rise of commodity prices in 1973–4, industrial production was adversely affected. By 1975, non-oil real commodity prices had swung back to their pre-1973 level, though the real price of oil had come down only slightly by 1979. The result is the resumption of the growth of industrial production of developed countries in that year. Another oil price hike in 1979 was responsible for another slight dip of production in 1980 in the USA and the UK.

COMMODITY PRICES AND INFLATION

High prices of primary commodity inputs in production imply that the real value added per unit of production declined; thus for the same commodity output less was left for distribution in wages, interest and profits. A portion of this in manufacturing is usually recouped by price increases of the final product; as Kaldor (1983: 23) puts it, 'Primary product prices . . . were determined in highly competitive markets, whereas industrial products were marketed under monopolistic conditions with producers setting their prices mainly with reference to costs. In the later case the response of supply to demand took place not through the agency of the price changes, but as a direct result of the so-called stock-adjustment principle. Manufacturers expanded or contracted their rate of production according to whether the flow of new orders exceeded or fell short of what was required to keep the stocks in a normal relation to the turnover'. Hicks (1974) terms the former 'flex-price' commodities and the latter as 'fix-price': 'In fix-price markets, prices have to be "made"; they are not just determined, from day to day, by demand and supply. This applies most of all, to markets for labour, where wages have to be negotiated; but it also applies to fix-price markets of many other kinds. The only markets to which it does not apply are speculative markets, such as the markets for the staple commodities and market for securities . . . Now wherever prices have to be made, there is a question how they shall be made . . . When prices in general are fairly stable, that is often rather easy . . . To be obliged to make them anew, as one is obliged to do in continuous inflation, involves loss – direct economic loss, and (very often) loss of temper as well', (1974: 78–9).

The rise in commodity prices thus not only produced the rise in industrial prices but also a chronic conflict between various factors of production about the equitable distribution of this real reduction in the value added per unit of output. This real reduction has been occasioned because the foreign exchange inputs in production have increased due to the increase in 'commodity' prices. Until the time the relative price of industrial output to that of 'commodities' comes back to the level prevalent before the commodity price rise, this real reduction has to be borne by one or other domestic factor of production. There are three relevant domestic factors of production – labour, industrial capital and financial capital. Each of these will try to pass on the burden to another's shoulder. To protect their standard of living, labour can use its muscle of collective bargaining and strikes. Industrial capital can use its power of price fixing to recoup its share but often at the cost of quantity of production. Financial capitalists mostly consist of small savers, and they have hardly any protection unless and until the monetary authorities protect the real rate of interest. As industrial capitalists use their power of price fixing in this distribution struggle, this automatically leads to inflationary consequences. The extent of the inflation depends on the intensity of this struggle, and how soon the losing factor of production gives up. As we have seen, with the present rules of the game, it is the foreign factor of production, whose power is represented by commodity prices, which ultimately loses this struggle. To take advantage of the situation various countries try to increase the capacity of commodity production within their own frontiers; this increases world capacity and brings 'commodity' prices back to their long-term level. However, during the transition period one or other domestic factor of the industrialised country has to bear the brunt.

Components of the Cost Price (Hicksian Fix Price)

For the Hicksian fix-price commodities, the price will be equal to the cost of production of the marginal producer. The marginal producer will of course be the least efficient producer of the product whose output is still required by the market to meet the overall demand. This cost of production can be divided into the following six components:

(1) Wages and salaries $\qquad = W^0$
(2) Cost of domestic intermediate goods $\qquad = M^0$
(3) Cost of imported intermediate goods $\qquad = Im^0$
(4) Interest on borrowed capital $\qquad = I^0$
(5) Return on investment $\qquad = R^0$
(6) Taxes *less* subsidies $\qquad = T^0$

Thus for the fixed price commodities the price can be written as

$$P = W^0 + M^0 + Im^0 + I^0 + R^0 + T^0 \qquad (7.1)$$

Similarly,

$$M^0 = W^1 + M^1 + Im^1 + I^1 + R^1 + T^1 \qquad (7.2)$$

where superscript 1 indicates that the items enter the cost of production one process before the final production process. We can go on reducing the value of intermediate goods backward two steps removed from the final production process, and so on and on.

Substituting the cost of domestic intermediate goods the price can be written in terms of other items of costs as follows:

$$P = [W^0 + W^1 + W^2 + \ldots] + [Im^0 + Im^1 + Im^2 + \ldots]$$
$$+ [I^0 + I^1 + I^2 + \ldots] + [R^0 + R^1 + R^2 + \ldots]$$
$$+ [T^0 + T^1 + T^2 + \ldots] \tag{7.3}$$

Let the sum of the series in the brackets be W, Im, I, R, and T respectively. Then,

$$P = W + Im + I + R + T \tag{7.4}$$

(It is obvious that each item of the cost in the production n steps removed will be smaller than the one $n-1$ steps removed. So each of the above series can be added up as convergent infinite series.)

W, Im, I, R, and T are called the direct and indirect wage cost, direct and indirect import cost, direct and indirect interest cost, direct and indirect returns to the capital and direct and indirect taxes respectively.

In equation (7.4) W is equal to wL, where w is the average wage rate and L is the direct and indirect labour used in the production of one unit of the product. I is equal to iB where i is the interest rate and B is the direct and indirect borrowing required during the production of that unit. Similarly, $R = rK$ where r is the rate of returns and K is the value of the directly and indirectly invested capital. Thus

$$P = wL + Im + iB + rK + T \tag{7.5}$$

When the prices of imported intermediate goods rise Im gets increased to (say) Im'. If the price of the product is not to increase, either w or i or r or T or a combination of them should decrease by such an amount that equation (7.5) above holds with unchanged P even when Im' has increased equal to Im'. Even if P increases just equal to increase in the import cost and all the other items of the cost remain the same, the real wage rate, real interest rate, etc. would have decreased due to the increase in the general price level. However, all these receivers of factor incomes will try to increase the nominal rate of their income in an effort to maintain their real income. If they are able to achieve their aim, the cost of each item making up the total cost of production of the product will have risen proportionately and the decrease in the domestic income due to the increase in the import price will have been completely compensated for it. During the transition period, the country will have faced a price inflation equivalent to the initial price rise of the imported intermediate inputs.

The above satisfactory outcome is possible only if (a) labour is so organised as not to allow its real wage rate to fall; (b) the monetary authorities are so enlightened as to allow the creation of extra money so that businessmen can discharge their increasing monetary obligations of paying higher wages, higher intermediate goods prices, higher value of the production and commercial stocks to be maintained, etc.; and (c) by the end of the cycle the world capacity for producing the internationally traded 'commodities' has increased sufficiently to meet the world demand at almost the old relative prices.

If labour is not vigilant enough, it may have to pay the higher cost of imports by reduction of its real wage rates, and hence its standard of living. If the monetary authorities do not allow the monetary expansion of the money supply, the economic system may collapse as various economic operators will not be able to meet their economic obligations. This will lead to large-scale bankruptcies; a similar situation led to the deep recession of the 1930s. Further, if sufficient new capacity for 'commodity' production is not created in the meantime, there will be a new jump in commodity prices as a consequence of domestic factors of production trying to get back their purchasing power and thus a revamping of the demand for the commodities. This will result in the perpetuation of inflation until some domestic factor of production is prepared to acquiesce in a reduction of its share of payment.

Movements in Factor Payments in the UK: An Illustration

This is illustrated below by the factor payments in the post-Second World War economy in the UK. Table 7.2 gives the primary input content of final demand in the UK for various years. This is the

Table 7.2   Primary factor contents in final demand in the UK

Primary inputs	Year 1954	1963	1968	1974	1979	1984
Income from employment (*W*)	48.0	50.2	48.7	48.1	46.4	43.6
Imports (*Im*)	17.0	16.4	17.6	24.8	22.0	22.5
Indirect taxes, etc. (*T*)	10.0	9.6	11.6	7.7	10.3	10.9
Gross profit, interest, etc. (*I* + *R*)	25.0	23.8	22.1	19.4	21.2	23.0
Total	100.0	100.0	100.0	100.0	100.0	100.0

Sources: CSO (various years); HMSO (various years).

distribution of the ultimate cost of producing the total final product of the UK economy into various components, as detailed in equation (7.4) above.

We thus see that in the 1960s when the world 'commodity' prices were slowly decreasing, the import content of UK final production slightly decreased. But it increased with a vengeance in the mid-1970s, and did not reach its usual value again until 1984. We may note that although non-oil commodity prices collapsed in the early 1980s, it was only in 1986 that the oil prices finally fell to the usual rate.

Table 7.2 gives an idea of the movements of the shares of various factors of production over the years. However, the changes in the shares of labour or profit do not tell us whether the wage rate, the interest rate or the rate of return on investment is affected, and if so how. These are given for the UK in the Table 7.3. Table 7.3 gives a manufacturing price index as well as a manufacturing output index; it also gives the real price index of both oil and non-oil commodities, real wage rates, and both nominal and real interest rates. For returns to capital it gives the nominal returns on the historical value of the capital, as well as returns on its replacement value (real). The former is the traditional accountant's view.

Rates of Factor Payments

It can be seen from Table 7.3 that the real wage rate in the economy hardly declined. Through its militancy and monopoly power to do

Table 7.3   Inflation, manufacturing production and factor returns
in the UK

Year	Manufacture Price index	output index	Real price commodity Non-oil	Oil	Real wage Rate	Rate of return Viewed	Real	Interest rate Nominal	Real
1960	59.9	67.9	77.8	80.0	73.8	19.3	14.2	4.88	3.70
1965	67.8	79.8	80.3	76.7	78.1	15.8	11.2	5.91	1.16
1970	81.2	90.7	78.5	68.3	90.0	14.4	8.6	7.01	−2.03
1973	100.0	100.0	100.0	100.0	100.0	19.8	9.1	9.34	−5.05
1974	123.4	98.0	100.4	270.4	101.5	18.7	5.2	11.37	−12.37
1975	151.9	92.7	74.2	252.6	103.4	18.5	5.3	10.18	−3.98
1976	176.5	95.7	80.2	265.7	102.5	20.1	5.4	11.12	−2.43
1977	208.6	100.7	81.5	267.2	97.5	19.4	6.2	7.68	−3.10
1978	229.2	103.7	71.5	232.8	103.3	19.0	6.2	8.51	−5.15
1979	254.0	107.6	76.5	299.1	104.9	18.5	4.3	12.98	−5.77
1980	289.7	100.4	73.6	443.3	105.7	16.6	3.3	15.11	3.11
1981	317.4	97.0	69.1	511.0	107.1	15.0	4.0	13.03	5.12
1982	341.9	98.8	63.3	500.8	109.8	14.5	5.0	11.47	6.25
1983	360.4	102.3	69.5	457.5	114.0	17.1	6.2	9.59	5.48
1984	382.6	103.6	73.1	461.7	114.8	18.3	6.9	9.30	2.63
1985	403.9	108.3	63.4	437.5	120.3	19.1	8.0	11.56	4.75

Notes and Sources:
1. Manufacture price index is calculated from that given in IMF (1986): 684–5.
2. Output index is that of industrial production (IMF, 1986).
3. Real commodity prices are from IMF (1987): 136.
4. Real wage rate is average monthly earnings of all industries divided by consumer prices. Taken from IMF (1986): 684–5.
5. Rates of return are from *Bank of England Quarterly Bulletin*, (June 1981) and subsequent issues. It is approximate as the exact value is frequently revised by the Bank of England. 'Viewed' rates are as viewed by accountants and are based on the historical cost of fixed capital, 'real' rates are based on replacement cost.
6. 'Nominal' interest rates are Treasury Bill rates and 'real' ones are the same adjusted for the increase in the GDP deflator in the next year. Data for both are taken from IMF (1986): 684–5.

damage, especially in the nationalised industries, labour was successful if anything in increasing its real wage during this crucial period. The brunt of adjustment had thus to be borne by real non-wage incomes. Industry, of course, tried to keep this reduction as little as possible, by trying to pass on the extra cost to the consumer by means of increasing prices. The continuous efforts of labour in not allowing a decrease in its real wage in spite of the high foreign exchange cost of commodities led to the roaring inflation of the 1970s. Industry, on the other hand, maintained the fiction that it was getting sufficient returns on the historical cost of investment; this of course becomes progressively smaller than the replacement cost of the equipment in an inflationary period, thus the owners or shareholders of the establishment not only suffer a huge capital loss on their investment as the value of investment does not keep pace with the inflation but they also get a 'reasonable' return on only that low value of the investment, rather than on the real value of the assets. A large chunk of the burden of adjustment is thus passed on to the industries' financial owners. Not only that, but with under the same fiction the depreciation is also accumulated on the historical cost of investment which at the time of replacement would amount to the cost only at which the equipment was originally purchased; this of course will be totally inadequate to replace worn out machinery.

STRATEGY OF MONETARY EXPANSION

These price increases were made possible by the monetary authorities' connivance in making available the necessary funds representing the higher working capital, though at a higher nominal rate of interest. This higher nominal cost of borrowing was also passed on to the final consumer; the total inflation rate thus became higher than the nominal rate of interest, forcing the real interest rate to be negative and putting a major burden of meeting the cost of increases in import prices on the shoulders of savers; this led to high growth of the money supply, but by this device, the returns on investment could be maintained in nominal terms, though in real terms they fell precipitously.

Higher prices, low real non-labour income, and higher mortgage rates impinging on current income would have naturally depressed demand and through the multiplier effect would have brought in a depression, as it did in the 1930s. But the general Keynesian economic education was at least ready to deal with that problem this time; the state resorted to deficit financing and thus saved the country from a huge fall in production and employment that would otherwise have resulted. However, the phenomenal growth of the 1950s and 1960s was now a thing of the past. The global availability of raw material commodities could not have supported any higher production levels.

The strategy followed by the industrialised world avoided large-scale bankcruptcies as well as large-scale unemployment, in contrast to the experience of the 1930s. At that time, the policies of the balanced budget and tight money had plunged the world's economies into the Great Depression; constrained by the Gold Standard the bankers behaved as private money lenders, foreclosing their loans at the first sign of declining profitability of the enterprise, and the state behaved as a private enterprise that had to balance its accounts.

The unprecedented inflation of the 1970s was precipitated by a concerted effort of local factors of production to ward off the transfer of real resources from themselves; it also induced a frantic activity for creation of new capacity for production of 'commodities'.

In this they were not only helped by international institutions like the World Bank, but also by the profits earned by the commodity producers in general, and the oil producers in particular. The latter mostly deposited their profits in the banks of the industrialised countries who recycled this money as loans to other developing countries primarily for investment.

TRANSITION TO LOW COMMODITY PRICES

By the time these capacities were coming on stream, the industrialised countries were getting tired of continuous inflationary pressures, and paltry gross non-wage incomes. As an antidote to this malady, they resorted to the old classical formulae of using restrictive deflationary monetary policies and a reduction of the governmental deficit. Though these policies reduced employment as expected, and led to quite a few bankruptcies, they were not applied with the rigour that a balanced budget or gold standard would have done. By this time, increased production of commodities had also started coming on the market. The combined effect of the changes in the policy of the industrialised countries and the increasing capacity of commodity production turned out to be the 'collapse' of 'commodity' prices in the early 1980s. With hindsight, we can now say that this 'changing gear' by the industrial market countries resulted only in the creation of extra unemployment; the real hindrance to the availability of primary commodities was already on the way to being eased. The resumption of the growth of the industrial economies would have been smoother without this effort.

This collapse of commodity prices is of the same order as that experienced in the Great Depression of the 1930s. For most of the developing countries the Great Depression has now arrived, and for them it is worse than the one in the 1930s, because then the plantation and mine owners were multinational companies of the industrial countries and therefore the capital loss was sustained by them. This time, however, the investment was made by the respective government or nationals through commercial or semi-commercial foreign loans called 'aid'. So even after the collapse of the commodity prices, the debt burden remained. In the 1930s the debt burden was on firms of the industrialised countries. These went bankrupt, in turn transferring their insolvencies to their banks and thus aggravating the Great Depression. In the 1980s the nominal owners of these plantations, mines, etc. were developing countries, though the lenders of the finance were the banking institutions of the developed world. A suitable counterpart of the bankruptcy law relating to the individual companies is not available at the country level; it is high time that international legal experts paid attention to this. One guiding principle might be that debt repayment in foreign exchange should be legally restricted to an amount that would not result in the decrease of employment in the country.

This collapse of the economies of the primary goods producing countries also affected the industrialised countries beneficially by reducing their cost of production. If all the industrialised countries had faithfully acted on their professed economic policies of a balanced budget and tight monetary policy, this would have carried the recession to them also. Fortunately, the USA had no intention of doing so; it ran a huge deficit during these years and thus it pulled with it the economies of all the industrialised countries into comparative prosperity; the Keynesian stimulus of deficit financing was being provided by the USA to the closely integrated economies of the OECD countries.

COMMODITY PRICES AND DEVELOPING COUNTRIES

Until the end of the 1970s growth in the developing countries remained generally strong. This was mainly attributable to high commodity prices; in 1985 primary commodities accounted for 72% and 51% of the total exports of low- and middle-income countries (excluding China and India) respectively. The proceeds from these exports are needed to pay for the imports of manufactures, which are vital for continuing industrialisation and technological progress, as well as for paying for the imported intermediate goods required in the production of recently established capacity. Shifts in the relative prices of commodities and manufactures can therefore change the purchasing power of the developing countries' exports dramatically, often with major repercussions for growth, and even for sustaining the current level of production.

Between 1980 and 1986 the real prices of primary commodities fell sharply. The purchasing power of Latin American exports fell by 26%; that of Sub-Saharan Africa was cut by more than half between 1980 and 1987: 'Rising debt service and cuts in lending led to a reversal of net resource transfers to developing countries. For highly indebted countries the net resource transfers of $61 billion in 1978–82 became a net loss of $93 billion in the next five years. This in turn meant that the trade balance had to move strongly in surplus. This could be achieved only through import compression, lower investment, and reduction in per capita consumption. In twenty-two debt-distressed Sub-Saharan African countries per capita consumption dropped by about 3.2 per cent a year and investment by 2.6 per cent a year between 1980 and 1986'. (World Bank, 1988: 3, 27, 30).

DETERMINATION OF EXCHANGE RATES IN DEVELOPING COUNTRIES

Commodity exporting developing countries have to sell the commodities they can export at the prevailing world prices; these prices should cover the indigenous cost of production of the export commodities, and this condition will then determine the rate of exchange for the local currency with the international currency. If the international price of the commodity that can be exported is (say) a dollars per unit, and its cost of production in the developing country is (say) b in the local currency, the exchange rate that is feasible for this local currency is its b units exchanged for a dollars. If the exchange rate of the local currency becomes higher, the country will not be able to export that commodity so effecting its capacity either to pay for the imports necessary for its growth and/or to service its debts incurred in the process.

However, if f dollars worth of imported inputs are necessary for the production of one unit of the export commodity, and the exchange rate is e, then the domestic portion of the cost (say) c, will be equal to $b - ef$. As b is equal to ea, we get,

$$c = e(a-f)$$

giving the exchange rate

$$e = b/a = c/(a-f) \qquad (7.6)$$

In the above formulation, we have not taken account of the transport and trade cost of imports and exports. Introducing them, let t_a be per unit transport and trade cost of export and t_f be the trade and transport cost of the imports required for producing one unit of the export commodity. Then the equation (7.6) becomes

$$e = b/[a(1-t_a)] = c/[a(1-t_a) - f(1+t_f)] \qquad (7.7)$$

If

$$a[1-t_a] > f[1+t_f] \text{ then,}$$

e will be positive. If the prices of export goods decrease without a corresponding decrease in the price of inputs, production of export commodities become less and less profitable. With domestic cost being constant, this will reflect in a depreciation of the currency. However that will increase the prices in the local currency, creating not only a spiral of depreciation but also a spiral of price rises.

It may be noted that f here does not represent the foreign exchange contents of direct inputs only, but also the imported inputs required in the production of those inputs. This also should be true for the inputs that go into the production of those inputs, and so on. In short, we can say that f represents all imported direct or indirect inputs in the production of the export commodities.

This condition applies not only to material inputs but also to the necessary consumption goods used by persons working on the production process, as they also form an essential component of the cost of production of the commodity. Thus if imported fertilisers are required for the production of the cereals in the country and those cereals form a necessary part of the consumption basket of the labour force, it should be counted as import content in the cost of production of the export commodity.

In many cases the capacity for the production of the export commodity was created because the cheap labour cost made the production of the commodity in that country quite profitable. The labour was partly cheap because of the comparatively low standard of living of the people in the developing country and partly because of the fact that there was no imported input in the consumption basket of the labourer. In such a case the mechanism for fixing the exchange rate could do the required trick. However, the increasing standard of living will slowly erode this advantage of the commodity exporter. The task before a development economist is to find out the extent to which the standard of living of the worker can increase without upsetting the vary applecart on which the whole development strategy may be based.

CHANGING WAGE LEVELS IN DEVELOPING COUNTRIES WITH CHANGING COMMODITY PRICES

In Table 7.4 we give the change in the nominal wage rates of a few developing countries relative to that of the USA for the years 1975, 1980 and 1985. They have been taken from the *Global Reports* of UNIDO for the years 1986 and 1987. UNIDO collected their data from the industrial census data of individual countries.

In 1980, six out of eleven highly indebted countries had a wage rate higher than that of 25% of the USA. All of them except two had lower than 25% of the US wage rate in 1975 as well as in 1985; the two exceptions are oil exporters. The oil price collapse came only in 1986, and except for the oil exporter Nigeria the relative wages of all these highly indebted developing countries declined in the 1980s with the decline in commodities prices. Surprisingly, except for Singapore, the relative wages in all the exporters of the manufactures also declined during this period. The comparatively high level of wage income seems to be based on the high level of 'commodity' prices which were products of agriculture and mining. The increasing commodity prices in the 1970s are reflected in the increases in wages; it seems that these countries could attract a high level of loans for development on this apparently solid foundation, but when this foundation gave way with the collapse of the 'commodity' prices, their creation of manufacturing capacity and infrastructure was unable to sustain them in economic adversity.

The way prices are formed in the developing countries, as described above, implies that the burden of adjustment of the fall of prices of the primary 'commodities' produced will be borne by the wage rates and the structure of prices within those countries. With

Table 7.4   Movement of relative wages in some countries (US$)*

Country/Year	Average wage (US $) 1975	1980	1985	% of US wage 1975	1980	1985
1. USA	11,096	16,406	22,695	100.00	100.00	100.00
2. UK	5,689	12,371	11,123	47.82	75.41	49.01

Developing countries: exporters of manufactures[1]

1. Brazil	1,949	2,714	2,050	17.56	16.54	9.03
2. Hong Kong	2,006	4,396	4,643	18.08	26.80	20.46
3. India	639	949	1,013	5.76	5.78	4.46
4. Republic of Korea	964	2,890	3,282	8.69	17.62	14.46
5. Singapore	2,582	4,125	6,777	23.27	25.14	29.86
6. Yugoslavia	2,050	3,546	1,903	18.48	21.61	8.39

Developing highly indebted countries[1]

1. Bolivia	1,660	2,629	n.a.	14.96	16.02	n.a.
2. Chile	1,532	5,782	4,468	13.81	35.24	19.65
3. Columbia	1,214	2,586	2,765	10.94	15.76	12.18
4. Ecuador	1,635	4,859	4,138	14.74	29.62	18.23
5. Mexico	4,168	6,249	5,560	37.56	38.09	24.45
6. Nigeria	1,656	4,264	7,438	14.92	26.00	32.78
7. Philippines	773	1,305	1,357	6.97	7.95	5.98
8. Uruguay	n.a.	4,462	2,201	n.a.	27.20	9.70
9. Venezuela	4,767	7,932	9,485	42.96	48.35	41.80
10. Brazil	1,949	2,714	2,050	17.56	16.54	9.03
11. Yugoslavia	2,050	3,546	1,903	18.48	21.61	8.39

Notes:
1. For classification, see World Bank, *World Development Report* (1987): xi.
* From UNIDO *Global Report* (1986) and (1987); they collected it from the industrial census data of individual countries. Due to exchange rate variability over the years, they should be taken as indicative of changes only.

the reduction of the price of 'export' commodities, the wage rates in the producing developing country get reduced in terms of the downward demand curve of foodgrains and other subsistence wage goods. As wages come down, the cost of producing these goods also comes down pari passu. If no foreign imported goods are required for their production, these prices can go down in terms of foreign currency (say dollars) as much as necessary to be able to provide subsistence to the labourer with reduced wages.

However, if some imports are required as intermediate goods in the production of these subsistence goods, they will provide a floor below which these prices cannot fall in terms of the relevant foreign

Table 7.5   Real wages and terms of trade in the Philippines (1965 = 100)

Year	Real wage	Terms of trade	Year	Real wage	Terms of trade
1955	115	111	1971	101	86
1958	107	112	1972	97	78
1960	105	113	1973	88	88
1963	103	101	1974	71	89
1965	100	100	1975	71	68
1966	102	99	1976	70	60
1967	100	98	1977	69	55
1968	109	96	1978	66	61
1969	112	94	1979	60	63
1970	109	92	1980	52	53

currency as those imports have to be purchased with foreign exchange. With the reduction of the available foreign exchange, the total output of the wage goods may get reduced, reducing the potential employment in the country in its turn.

These changes in the structure of price, though providing employed labour with a similar subsistence standard of living, makes imported and other manufactured goods made from imported components and capital, etc. comparatively costly. Obviously the people and classes consuming these goods feel the pinch and have to reduce or postpone their purchases. Even labourers postpone and thus reduce the consumption of semi-durable goods like clothing, footwear and other manufactured goods. This in its turn leads to unutilised capacity in manufacturing industries. Unutilised capacity in manufacturing will of course lead to postponement of investments reducing production in capital goods industries in its turn.

This process of adjustment of the real wage rate to the declining terms of trade is well illustrated by the Philippines, which is one of the poor countries having a wage rate only about 6% of that of the USA. With declining terms of trade, we expect almost proportional reduction in the wage rates. Table 7.5, giving terms of trade and wage rate in the Philippines from 1955 to 1980 has been calculated from the information provided by the 1986 *International Financial Statistics Yearbook* (IMF, 1986). The long-term relationship between the two is obvious.

We have also seen in Table 7.4 that with the collapse of the commodity prices in the 1980s, the manufacturing wage rate in developing countries fell. Even though, in many cases, this wage rate did not relate to activities connected with the production of commodities for export, if the export commodities have imported inputs, we will expect the wage rates to decrease more than the decrease in export prices, as prices of imported inputs do not decrease and their cost becomes the first charge on the revenue of the export good producer before any factor payments are made. These decreases are achieved through the mechanism of devaluation of the exchange rate without corresponding increases in the wage rates; as such, they are general rather than confined to export industries only. However, if in the previous periods the benefit of high prices of export goods was not proportionately passed on to labour, it may happen that a larger portion of the decline is absorbed by non-wage incomes. We may expect this to happen in some oil and other mineral exporting countries.

PRICE STRUCTURE WITH DIFFERING IMPORT REQUIREMENTS

The demand price of 'necessities' will be given by the nominal wage rate in the country. It should be such as to allow a marginal wage earner to purchase at least the goods needed for subsistence living. But the marginal wage rates depend on the international price of the commodity that the country exports, as the production of the export commodity should not normally be loss-making. On the other hand the supply price will be given by the marginal cost of production. If in this cost of production there is no direct or indirect input of any imported commodity, the supply price is independent of the exchange rate. In such a situation, it will be the function of exchange rate to equate the cost of production of the export commodity with its international price. Then the nominal wage rate and the prices of the intermediate goods will follow; the nominal wage rates and the subsistence requirements of the labourer will determine the prices of the basic subsistence goods.

Where the subsistence goods require the inputs of imported materials, the supply price of these goods will have a foreign exchange component. This will set a lower limit to which its price can fall in terms of international currency. Of course, this implies that these developing countries will not be able to compete on the same terms as the ones relying on completely indigenous inputs for subsistence goods. However, if they are situated physically near their markets, the savings in transport cost may compensate for some of the disadvantage. Further, due to the modern methods of cultivation available to them, they will not have the hindrance of an unavailability of subsistence goods until they can get sufficient foreign exchange to purchase the required inputs.

These nominal differences in wage rates and the prices of cereals, etc. between different countries thus depend upon the extent of imported inputs in the production of these 'necessities'. Thus if imported fertilisers, fuel, etc. are used as inputs in foodgrain production, the prices of cereals can be about 55% that of the USA as the local part of the cost of production is produced by labour that is paid only the minimum wage. Where no imported inputs are necessary for the production of necessities, the exchange rate can be further lowered in the quest for competitive bidding in the market for export goods. This need not affect the internal price and wage structure within the country, but it may lower the prices to a level of only 35% of international prices. Further, some countries, though using modern inputs in the production of a part of their necessities, directly or indirectly subsidise it to mimic the prices that would have existed if they had not been using them. We have discussed these in details elsewhere; a specimen of the price structure of these different types of countries is given in Table 1.1 (p. 14).

POVERTY AS A NECESSARY CONDITION OF EXPORT PROMOTION?

Even after three decades of continuous 'development', most developing countries have not been able to increase the standard of living of their labour force; the price of the export commodity of the country determines the maximum real wage rate that the country can afford to give. As a country which has taken any loan which is not already completely repaid must export to repay the interest, etc. it cannot opt out of the export market however much that market may be depressed. There is no alternative to depression of the wage rate. This implies that the long-term wage rate of the country cannot improve, unless and until some way is found to get a long-term improvement in the real price of the export commodity. Theoretically, it may be possible to get out of the commodity export, and start exporting manufactured products instead, but we have seen that this route has also not been conducive to the improvement of the standard of living of the labour force, except for some countries who are engaged in the offshore processing activities for the multinationals. This is due to the basic fact that the requirements of the wage savings in manufacturing exports, if they are to compete with the manufactures of the industrialised countries themselves in their own markets, is so great that not much scope for increasing real wages is left.

We have seen before that the deterioration in the terms of trade of 'commodity' exporting countries was not a fortuitous event but was a *necessary consequence* of the way the international commodity market is organised. This implies that the reversal of development in the 1980s in those countries was itself a natural consequence of the way the world economy works. Continuation of poverty seems to be the necessary condition of export promotion. And if during the temporary supply stringency in commodity markets there is a decrease in this poverty, it is reimposed with a vengeance as soon as normal conditions return.

This proposition is not true only for those countries which use imported inputs in the production of their necessary wage goods, but also for countries that produce their wage goods without recourse to imports for intermediate goods. The growth of these countries is limited by the land and/or labour productivity of the traditional techniques of production of the necessary wage goods; to be able to increase the standard of living above that level they will have to resort to more productive modern techniques of production. This will force them to import intermediate goods at least during the transition period, and they will be subject to the same constraints to growth as these latter countries.

We may also recall that in the development strategy dependent on 'aid' in the form of long-term loans, the development of commodity exports becomes a must for the developing country. This triggers the mechanism which keeps the commodity prices so low that poverty becomes a necessary condition of export promotion. Is there any way out from this well-intentioned but usurious international relationship?

8 Changing Export Income and the Developing Countries' Economy: A Diagrammatic Representation

INTRODUCTION

We have now distinguished three main types of developing countries that crucially depend for their current production and growth on their export earnings, and for whom changes in commodity prices affect the whole fabric of their economies. (1) those having their traditional production restricted by the availability of labour force; (2) those whose traditional production is restricted because of the availability of suitable land; and (3) those whose production requires some imported inputs directly or indirectly, and thus have the extent of their output restricted by the availability of foreign exchange.

We shall deal below with the effect on each type of developing economy of the changing value of their exports. However, a formal analysis of a land-constrained economy is similar to that of a labour-constrained one and if we substitute 'land' for 'labour' in the description of the latter we shall get a corresponding description. We shall therefore not repeat this chapter's arguments in that regard.

LABOUR-CONSTRAINED ECONOMIES WITH TRADITIONAL TECHNIQUES FOR PRODUCING WAGE GOODS

Let there be three sectors in the economy, one producing wage goods (foodgrains, etc.), another producing export commodities, and the third producing capital and other non-wage goods for investment and government and private consumption. We further assume that all the three sectors are completely vertically integrated but for the imported inputs required for production; thus there is no indirect

123

domestic cost. The total income of the economy will be the sum of the incomes from the individual sectors, therefore if, l_f, l_e, and l_c are labour employed in the three sectors, and Y denotes the total income, then

$$Y = wl_f (1 + r_f) + wl_e (1 + r_e) + wl_c (1 + r_c) \qquad (8.1)$$

where r_f, r_e, and r_c are non-wage/wage ratios for the three sectors.

Further assuming, as a first approximation, that wage earners do not save, then total production of wage goods should be equal to total wages. Therefore, $wl_f (1 + r_f)$ is greater than or equal to

$$w (l_f + l_e + l_c) \qquad (8.2)$$

If the value of export goods produced by a unit of labour is k dollars and it requires q dollars worth of imported inputs, then

$$w(1 + r_e) = k-q, \text{ or } w = (k-q)/(1+r_e) \qquad (8.3)$$

This gives wage rate in terms of international money. However, the real wage rate is independent of the international prices as the price of the wage goods produced by one labourer will be $w(1 + r_f)$ irrespective of the rate of exchange.

So the purchasing power of a labourer is unaffected by changing exchange rates. But increasing world commodity prices or foreign aid for development may increase developmental efforts as well as non-wage income to be spent on non-wage goods, increasing the labour engaged in the production of investment goods in turn. In a labour-constrained economy, this will be at the expense of labour engaged in producing wage goods. This will reduce the wage goods' availability. Further, getting the wage goods for the consumption of other labourers from the producers will imply increasing taxes on them, for they do not require or even cannot afford any non-wage goods produced by that sector in exchange. As this implies a high handed treatment of traditional farmers, it goes a long way towards understanding the phenomenon of non-democratic governments in most of developing countries. This will also lead the country towards famine-like conditions where a downturn of usual yearly fluctuation in yield may be sufficient to trigger off widespread deprivation.

The situation does not improve when the world prices of export commodities fall, as the falling prices do not lead to a reduction in production, as envisaged in the neoclassical supply curve, but behave perversely as the reduction in export earnings induces the country to increase production of export commodities by employing extra labour. This results in the reduction of labour engaged in the production of wage goods, with similar disastrous consequences.

A DIAGRAMMATIC REPRESENTATION OF MACRO RELATIONS

In Figure 8.1, labour is measured on the X axis; the positive Y axis measures the foreign exchange availability, while in the negative direction it measures the output of wage goods. OA represents labour employed in export production, AB that employed in modern activities and development, etc. and the remaining BC represents that left to produce wage goods through traditional techniques. CD represents the total output of the wage goods industry and therefore the tangent of the angle CBD represents labour productivity in the traditional wage goods industry.

AG represents the net foreign exchange from exports produced with the help of labour OA. That foreign exchange is used as inputs in the modern activities of development, capital creation, industrial production through modern techniques, etc. The extent of these activities, and thus the labour employed in them, depends on the availability of foreign exchange. The tangent of angle HAB represents the foreign exchange required for employing one person in these activities. As foreign exchange available is $GA = HB$, the total labour employed in these modern activities will be HB.

As CD, the total wage goods produced, should be sufficient for consumption of all the labourers, the tangent of angle COD represents the real wage rate in terms of consumption goods. AJ and JG represent the wage and non-wage income in export industries respectively. Then AJ is the total wage of OA labour in international currency. So the wage rate in international currency is tan AOJ, the real wage rate is COD. The equality of the two gives the purchasing power parity of wage goods in international currency.

EFFECTS OF EXPORT COMMODITY PRICE INCREASES

In Figure 8.2 we have superimposed on Figure 8.1 the macroeconomic situation after an increase in world commodity prices; the latter situation is depicted by dashed lines. The increase in world prices of

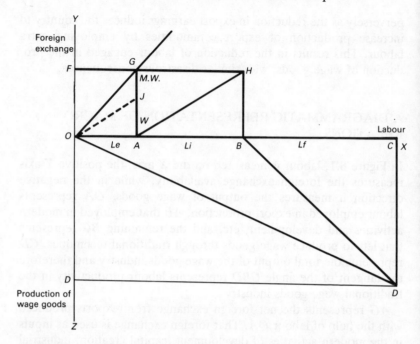

Figure 8.1   Macroeconomics of labour-constrained developing countries

export commodities is depicted by increasing the angle *AOG* to *AOG'*. Thus with this increase the net foreign exchange availability has increased from *AG* to *AG'*. Availability of this extra foreign exchange makes it possible to increase the modern development sector. The extent of this we find by extending line *AH* to meet the parallel line to *OC* from *G'* (F'G' extended to H'). This implies that the labour employed in this sector increases from *AB* to *AB'*, leaving only *B'C* labour for wage goods production.

This will reduce the output of wage goods from *CD* to *CD'* where *B'D'* is parallel to *BD*. This implies that the real wage will reduce from tan *COD* to tan *COD'*. This will tend to put workers more and more at subsistence level, which may turn into virtual famine in years of bad crops. The more annual fluctuation of weather moves the point *D'* up and down the line *CD* and lowers the angle *COD*, the more vulnerable are the labourers to this fluctuation.

Foreign loans or 'aid' will have similar effects. Though they will not increase foreign exchange earnings, the increase in the availability of foreign exchange will shift *B* to *B'*, with all the above-mentioned

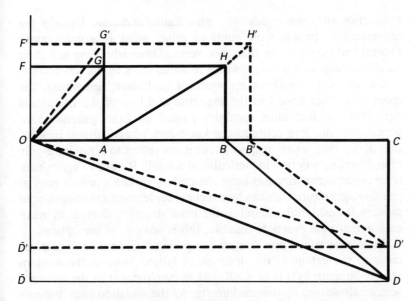

Figure 8.2 Macroeconomics of labour-constrained developing countries: with increasing commodity prices

consequences. However, if this is accompanied with food aid of the order *DD'*, the deterioration of the real wage rate can be suspended.

These are short-term effects. In the medium term, with high export commodity prices, there will be a tendency to increase the capacity and production of the export commodity, which will tend to move *A* and *B* to the right. This will aggravate an already bad situation.

EFFECTS OF DECREASES IN COMMODITY PRICES

The short-term effects of a decrease in commodity prices should be opposite to those just discussed. As pointed out above, a decrease in commodity prices only induces the developing countries to produce more of the export commodity to fill the gap in their foreign exchange earning; the employment in the export commodity production will not decrease. However, that in the modern sector will decrease. So *AB* will contract. This implies not only that development efforts will have to be scaled down, but also that quite a bit of fixed capital created by past efforts may have to be left unutilised.

However, it does not imply that the labour employed in the

production of wage goods will immediately increase. Usually the movement of people from rural to urban areas is a much more natural and easy process than vice versa. Those who have lost their rural moorings find it very difficult to adjust back to the low income and much more backbreaking work of traditional agriculture, the more so as they have lost the expertise and lore of the traditional agriculture of individual localities passed on from generation to generation; this lore contains the know-how of agricultural production of the area, a person ignorant of it can return to agriculture only after spending a period in 'agricultural school'. Return to agriculture from urban occupation has been attested only when a person goes to practise agriculture with modern techniques learned in colleges or in modern farms. Until and unless the price structure changes to make such agricultural practices feasible, this is not one of the options.

So decreases in export commodity price usually create unemployment to the extent of the decrease of labour force in the modern sector. Sometimes it is camouflaged as employment in the informal sector. However, in the medium term, the situation may become different. The reaction of countries to the decrease of world commodity prices is likely to increase the production of export commodities. The restructuring of the economy would imply a rightward shift of A and a contraction of AB; the end result may be that the position of B remains more or less the same. If it is the same, it implies a contraction of the modern development sector, leaving the wage rate unaffected. However, if the country is able to increase its foreign exchange earnings so as not to affect the modern sector much, we may expect B also to move to the right, further squeezing the wage goods sector. This is illustrated in Figure 8.3. The new situation is given by dotted lines and double dashed letters.

LAND-CONSTRAINED DEVELOPING COUNTRIES WITH TRADITIONAL TECHNIQUES OF FOODGRAIN PRODUCTION

A similar analysis can be developed for the developing countries having land instead of labour as the bottleneck. If we substitute land for labour in the *discussion above* we get the macroeconomics of the land-constrained economy. The total land resource can be conceived of as distributed into three uses: production of wage goods, of export commodities, and (directly or indirectly) for the production of mod-

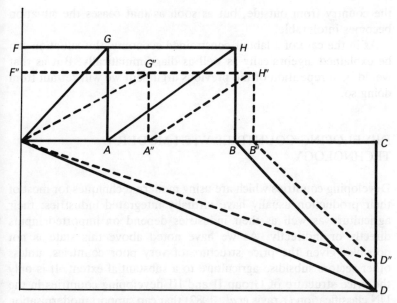

Figure 8.3 Medium-term macroeconomics with decreasing commodity
prices

ern commodities. The first does not use an imported commodity directly or indirectly as an intermediate commodity, while for the production of the last some direct or indirect input of the imported commodity is essential. As in the case of a labour-constrained economy, the higher the demand for exports the less remains for the production of wage goods, and the employment of labour and, hence, the total production with the available techniques of production, depend on the extent of the effective availability of the labour force.

As in the previous case, the production of wage goods per unit of land available for the production of the wage goods cannot be increased using traditional techniques of food production. Modernising the technique requires the use of imported inputs; this increases the cost of production in international currency; this increases the wage rate, resulting in the export commodities being unable to compete for the market with the countries that still use traditional techniques for the production of the wage goods. Thus the demand for foreign exchange increases while the export goods become less competitive in the international market. This situation can remain fairly tolerable so far as there is sufficient net transfer of resources to the country from outside, but as soon as that ceases the situation becomes intolerable.

As in the case of a labour-constrained economy, this situation can be explained algebraically as well as diagrammatically. But as that would be a repetition of the previous argument we will refrain from doing so.

DEVELOPING COUNTRIES WITH MODERN TECHNOLOGY

Developing countries which are using modern techniques for most of their production usually have virtually integrated industries; their agriculture as well as their industries depend on imported inputs directly or indirectly. As we have noted above this state is not possible, given the price structure of very poor countries, unless other sectors subsidise agriculture to a substantial extent. It is only the price structure of Group II and III developing countries in the UN classification (Kravis *et al.*, 1982) that can support modernisation of agriculture; once that price structure is achieved, the macroeconomic structure can be approximated as follows.

Unlike economies with traditional wage goods production techniques, these consist of only two sectors, one producing commodities for export and the other for internal consumption and investment, including the production of wage goods; there is no sector producing wage goods by traditional techniques independent of the world economy and prices. Figure 8.4 represents this situation, and is adapted from Figure 8.1 by omitting the traditional sector.

Here *OA* represents the number of people employed in export commodity production and *AB* those in the production of commodities for internal use. *AG* is the net amount of foreign exchange earned. The tangent of angle *GOA* gives the rate of net foreign exchange earnings per person employed in the export industry. The tangent of angle *HAB* gives the rate of the use of imports in the production for internal use per unit of labour employed in that sector. The total output of that sector is given by the line *BD*. The remaining labour force *BC* is not absorbed by formal economic activity and thus represents the unemployment. Until the time there is persistent unemployment, the basic wage rate for labour would not rise above 'subsistence' level. Let it be given by the tangent of the angle *BOL*. Then *BL* will be the output of wage goods and *LD* of capital goods and goods consumed out of non-wage incomes.

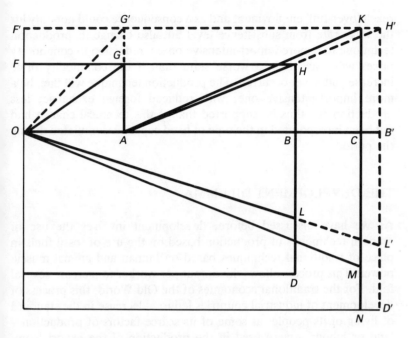

Figure 8.4 Macroeconomic representation of foreign
exchange-constrained economies

An increase in commodity price increases the foreign exchange
availability to *AG'* from *AG*. That will enable employment in the
sector producing for the internal market to increase from *AB* to *AB'*
and the output from *BD* to *B'D'*. However, if *B'* is to the right of *C*,
where *OC* is the total available labour force (as shown in the Figure
8.4.) there should be (a) some structural or technical change increasing the rate of import dependence of local production from the
tangent of *BAH* to the tangent of *CAK*, and (b) the wage rate may
rise from the 'subsistence' level.

Thus the increase in the world price of the export commodity
increases employment and production within the economy; when the
commodity prices decrease there is an opposite effect. However, a lot
of capital created in times of prosperity becomes just unutilised
capacity. When there is unutilised capacity, there is hardly any
incentive to invest, so the situation of the capital goods industry will
be much worse than if there had been an interlude of high commodity
prices.

If, during the period of high commodity prices, the country could reach 'over-full' employment and as a consequence could not only lift the wage rate from subsistence level but also change its production technique to a more import-intensive one, a reduction in commodity prices will leave it in a worse state than if the commodity price increase had never occurred. The production technique will then be a more import-intensive one, with reduced foreign exchange; less production can thus be supported than if this technical change had not been incorporated in the type of fixed capital accumulated during the period.

THE DEVELOPMENT DILEMMA

As we have discussed before, development involves the use of modern techniques of production based on the use of fossil fuels in place of traditional techniques based on human and animal muscle power. This process allows the output per worker to increase several fold. For the traditional economies of the Old World, this process of development of industrial countries led to a decrease in the standard of living of its people, as some of its scarce factors of production – land or labour – were used in the production of the export 'commodity', and therefore the amount of wage goods that could be produced by traditional techniques with the remaining scarce factor became proportionately reduced. The production of export commodities was established there, on the basis of wage goods being provided by traditional sectors, so capacities have been increased so much that their world price is usually so low that even bare subsistence wages cannot be paid if wage goods are produced with modern techniques. However, only modern techniques of wage goods production allow increases in the productivity of the scarce factor of production: these countries are caught into the underdevelopment trap.

The developing countries of newer settlement use modern production techniques for the production of wage goods. However, they are not self-sufficient in the production of the necessary intermediate goods; they have to find sufficient export opportunities that can support labour even at 'subsistence' level as imported inputs are used for the production of even wage goods.

Thus both types of developing countries require imports for their development; the second type requires imports even to keep up current production. Every developing country that wants to speed up its development and/or wants to be better prepared for its defence is required to increase its exports to acquire the necessary extra foreign exchange.

THE 'FALLACY OF COMPOSITION' AND THE BARRIER TO THE INCREASE OF REAL WAGE RATES IN THE LONG RUN

To increase foreign exchange availability, every such developing country will try to increase its exports – that is, to shift point A to the right in Figure 8.1–8.4 above. They mostly project the benefit of their efforts by assuming constant export prices (even World Bank experts going around advising individual countries on how to restructure their economies use a constant price assumption in setting the cost/ benefit ratios of their recommended policies). However, as all the developing countries are in a similar situation, this will lead to the world supply increasing faster than demand, especially if most of these countries are getting financial assistance for this increase in capacity. This will lead to a fall in the world price of the commodity in question, nullifying part of the effort. Thus an action which is good for one, if others do not act similarly, becomes doubtful in results if others also act in the same way. This 'fallacy of composition' is largely ignored by the policy-makers and their international advisors. This makes the line OG in Figures 8.1–8.4 a curved rather than a straight-line. To take account of this aspect we have modified Figure 8.1 above in Figure 8.5.

This shows that when exports increase from the output of labour OA to OA', net exports per unit of labour engaged in the export industry falls from the tangent of the angle GOA to the tangent of angle $G'OA$. This has a twofold effect on the economy: one due to additional labour AA' employed in the export industry, and the other due to proportionally lower increase in labour employed in the modern sector for internal use as foreign exchange availability does not increase proportionately.

This also reduces the production of wage goods from CD to CD', reducing the average 'real' wage rate of the economy. Even if the wage goods' demand of the labour engaged in export industry is partly met from imported goods, the real wage rate of that labour will also fall, because of the reduction in the value of their per labour output in the foreign currency.

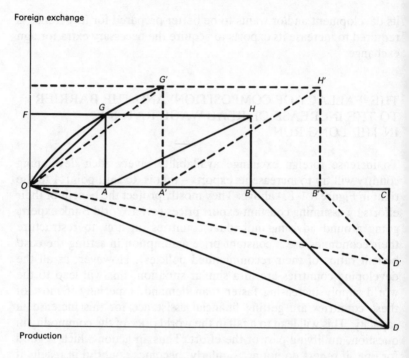

Figure 8.5   Changes in wage rates with increasing exports

Ordinarily, the real wage rates of formally employed labour cannot be reduced beyond a certain level. This level can be further reduced to some degree in a totalitarian regime. As most of the developing countries try to increase their export earnings as much as they can, in the long run they tend to increase exports until their wage levels are reduced to this level. No wonder that in the pursuit of this aim many such countries find themselves saddled with totalitarian regimes and a bare subsistence level of wage rates.

With these dynamics, it is highly improbable that these labour- or land-constrained developing countries would be able to raise their wage rates so high as to transform the price structure in such a way that modern techniques of producing foodgrains become economically feasible.

Similar considerations for the import-constrained developing economies having all production from modern fossil fuel-using techniques will show that the fallacy of composition also prevents them from increasing their 'real' wage rate on a long-term basis. Whenever there is a world commodity price rise, they may be able to increase their 'real' wage rate for a short time. But the increase in commodity prices generates a scramble for creating new capacity, until prices settle back to approximate the cost of production based on 'subsistence' level wage rates only.

Part IV
Macroeconomics of Developing Countries

Part IV
Macroeconomics of
Developing Countries

9 The Macroeconomics of Economic Subordination and Drain

ECONOMIC SUBORDINATION AND DRAIN

By the advent of the industrial revolution, Western European nations had already developed commercial relations with most of the countries of the rest of the world. A large number of these relationships were those of an imperial power's relationship with a subject nation, but they were qualitatively different from those of classical imperial powers like Rome. These were a consequence of expanding commercial capitalism rather than a politico-military complex. This gave them a characteristic commercial bias with manipulation of the market power as the main instrument of the relationship. This had a further interesting consequence. Even when the political empires ceased to exist the economic instruments forged remained effective and could easily be transformed to suit a new geopolitical situation. This particular commercial capitalism was primarily interested in the imports of agricultural and mineral raw materials and the export of 'services' and manufactured goods.

In land-scarce subordinate countries, this involved the use of scarce land resources in production of the export goods without simultaneously increasing the productivity of the remaining agricultural land or import of the wage goods from outside; thus the total amount of the available wage goods in the country were reduced. Similarly, in labour-scarce country some labour force was withdrawn from the production of subsistence goods for production of export commodities without increasing the productivity of the remaining labour force or imports of the wage goods; this also resulted in the reduction of the wage goods in the country. In this sense, the exports of these countries were not for the betterment of the economic standard of the people of the country, as formulated in the traditional theory of international trade, but in the terminology of Dada Bhai Naoroji (1888) a 'drain' on the scarce resources of the countries concerned. It was an exchange of the output of the scarce resource of

139

the country for something which was either not in scarce supply or was demanded only for the luxury of few at the cost of employment of many. Below, we shall examine the way in which it transformed the macroeconomic character of these subordinate economies.

THE MACROECONOMICS OF A TRADITIONAL LAND-SCARCE ECONOMY

Formalising the above, let the country produce A agricultural goods, and M manufactured goods, before it becomes a subordinate country. Let rM be the agricultural raw materials used in the production of M. And let F denote the total demand of agricultural products on the farm itself for the consumption of the farm workers as well as for use as intermediate inputs in farm production. Let kM be the farm produce required for consumption by the earners in the manufacturing industry.

Total agricultural land is limited; therefore, A is fixed, it cannot be increased until the traditional technique of agricultural production is modernised. Let us value agricultural output of non-foodgrain crops as equal in value to the output of foodgrain in the equivalent area. On this valuation, the value of the agricultural product will remain constant until the technique of production of foodgrains is improved so as to be able to produce more food grain per unit of standardised land than was possible from traditional techniques. And use of modern methods in the production of non-foodgrain crops only make them cheaper rather than increasing the total value of agricultural produce. Thus,

$$F + rM + kM \text{ is less than or equal to } A \qquad (9.1)$$

As the agricultural land is the constraining factor, we expect the sign of equality to be effective. Therefore,

$$M = (A - F) / (r + k) \qquad (9.2)$$

$[k + r]$ will be less than 1 by the amount manufacturing uses non-agricultural commodities as intermediate inputs and the earners in manufacturing consume the goods of non-agricultural origin.

For simplicity, let us assume F to be a fixed proportion of A. This condition will be approximately satisfied if the requirement of agricultural labour per standardised unit of land is the same for all the crops. Then $(A - F)$ can be written as bA, where b is the difference between unity and that fixed proportion. Then,

$$M = \{b/(k+r)\} A \qquad (9.3)$$

Thus the total output of manufactures as well as of the agricultural wage goods is determined as soon as we know the total arable land A, the coefficients of the agricultural inputs in the production, and the propensities to consume the agricultural goods.

THE MACROECONOMICS OF A SUBJECT OR INDEBTED ECONOMY

After the country becomes a subject country, a tribute becomes payable, though more often than not it is disguised under the nomenclature of various charges for services performed. For illustrative purposes, we shall deal only with the case where the tribute is directly collected as additions to land revenue. Let the tribute be taken out of the country in the form of agricultural goods. Let the amount of the tribute be D. And let the primed symbols denote the quantities after the tribute has started to be collected. Of course, A will remain unchanged, but due to decrease in the income of agriculturists by the amount D, the use of agricultural goods by the agriculturist will decrease to F'. Thus, in this new situation,

$$F' + (k + r) M' + D = A \qquad (9.4)$$

$$M' = \{A - D - F'\} / (k + r) \qquad (9.5)$$

These, together with equation (9.2) gives,

$$M - M' = [F' + D - F] / (k+r) \qquad (9.6)$$

As the income of the agriculturist is decreased by the amount D, his consumption of agricultural goods decreases by an amount less than D, as the income elasticity of consumption of agricultural products will ordinarily be less than 1. So assuming that the intermediate goods required for the agricultural production remain the same

$$D > (F - F') \tag{9.7}$$

Hence,

$$M > M' \tag{9.8}$$

Thus, though the tribute is taken in terms of the agricultural goods only and is collected from agriculturists, in a land-constrained economy it reduces the manufacturing production also, and thus creates extra unemployment. This may be considered a multiplier effect of the external drain. It is immaterial that the tribute is disguised as the administrative charges, or the repatriation of the salaries of the persons employed there or as any other charges for the services rendered. As long as agricultural raw materials are exported without corresponding imports of the wage goods, its macroeconomic impact on the subject economy will be the same. This will have similar effects even if the exports are for *servicing of the debts or so-called 'aid'* borrowed for industrial development, which does nothing to increase the availability of wage goods within the country but has to be serviced in terms of the agricultural products.

Thus, we see that in a subject economy experiencing land constraint, when the tribute is taken in terms of agricultural commodities, *the total reduction in the income of its inhabitants is more than the amount of the tribute.* Dada Bhai Naoroji called this extra reduction in the income of the subject country's people the 'internal drain', in contrast to the the external drain, which consisted of 'non-requited exports or non-commercial exports' which brought no 'equivalent returns' in the form of imports.

THE MACROECONOMICS OF LAND-SCARCE DEVELOPING COUNTRIES WITH A TRADITIONAL PATTERN OF TRADE

The traditional pattern of trade of the industrialised countries with the under-developed world has been the export of manufactured goods from industrialised countries in return for agricultural and mineral raw materials from the under-developed countries. This has been speciously justified on the ground that the under-developed countries have an abundance of labour and are scarce in capital, and raw materials are labour-intensive products. This argument completely overlooks the land scarcity of the developing countries. We can analyse the implication of this omitted constraint in terms of the simple model developed above.

Let D^* be the amount of the agricultural goods that are exported in return for the manufactured goods imported from the industrialised country, and F^* be the agriculturalist's demand for agricultural goods. Then, the supply of agricultural goods to local manufacturing industry is given by,

$$A - F^* - D^* \tag{9.9}$$

where A represents, as before, the total agricultural production. This should be equal to the demand of agricultural product from manufacture. Therefore,

$$(k + r) M^* = A - F^* - D^* \tag{9.10}$$

where M^* is the local manufacture in the new situation.

As the income of agriculturists does not change, F^* should be equal to F, then

$$M^* = [A - F] / (k+r) - D^*/(k+r)$$
$$= M - D^*/(k+r) \tag{9.11}$$

Thus,

$$M - M^* = D^*/(k+r) \tag{9.12}$$

As $(k + r)$ is less than 1, this shows that as a result of the imports of the manufactured goods, reduction in local manufactures is more than the amount of imports. As the output of the agriculture remains the same, the total *national product declines by more than the amount of the trade*. This results in the corresponding decline in the useful employment in the country.

All this decline is concentrated in the manufacturing sector. As a result the under-developed country turns into a predominantly agricultural country, in spite of the paucity of suitable land in relation to the labour force. Alternatively, it is termed as an over-populated country, where according to some development economists it should cut down the reproduction rate of the population by family planning techniques.

THE MACROECONOMICS OF LABOUR-CONSTRAINED UNDER-DEVELOPED COUNTRIES

Most of the countries of Sub-Saharan Africa serve the industrialised world as providers of mining products and plantation crops. The latter are grown on the most suitable area cleared of natives and based on the cheap labour of the native population. Though the best land was occupied by the colonisers, there was practically no dearth of the land suitable for cultivation; the extent of the economy was limited only by the availability of labour. Labour had to come out to work on mines or plantations not only through the inducement of new types of consumer goods, but also to earn some cash to pay the taxes or tribute which were levied by the ruling powers and which had to be paid in their currency. It is only by the use of cheap local labour that these mines and plantations could compete with similar products of the New World, based on slave labour.

The cheapness of the labour was due to the fact that no essential consumption good required by the labour was imported or made from an imported commodity, and therefore the cost of living was independent of the exchange rate. So until the time that wage goods were locally produced from indigenous materials, the international value of wages was immaterial to the production cost of the export commodities.

As labour was the real bottleneck to the economy, the production of wage goods depended on the number of labourers engaged in its production. Total production would of course decrease in almost the same proportion as the proportion of labourers withdrawn from their production to produce export goods in the mines or plantations. So the effect of this type of subordination of the economy is the deterioration of the natives' standard of living. At the macro level, this availability of wage goods put an effective upper limit on the extent of the exaction of this type of tribute, as well as on the export possibilities.

Thus, if the total labour is designated by N, and per capita product in the traditional wage goods sector is v, then the total output of the traditional wage goods sector will be vN. If the employment in the modern export sector is $N(e)$, then the product of the traditional wage goods sector is reduced to

$$v[N - N(e)] \qquad (9.13)$$

The standard of living may be more or less taken as the traditional standard of living in that society. So we may assume that the consumption of the traditional wage goods of the workers employed in the modern export sector is kept the same – v. This implies that the average consumption of the remaining labour force remains only

$$v[N - 2N(e)] / [N - N(e)] \tag{9.14}$$

With this reduced income, it is not expected that they will be consuming modern imported goods on any scale; the problem will be of day-to-day living in that condition below subsistence level. At that effective wage rate they will of course not go out to work as wage labour. Even working for themselves at that level below poverty line implies working with lower efficiency; this may further reduce the output of the wage goods.

We have not so far taken account of the fact that the land in the country may be of differing quality. In that case, the subsistence wage may be considered the income of the farmer working on the 'no-rent' land. Then the total amount of rent in the country will be available for employing people on production of export commodities, if the standard of living of all the farmers can be reduced to the level of the marginal farmer. However, in a labour-scarce economy, the employment of the people in export producing commodities will decrease the labour available for producing wage goods. With the increase in the production for exports, the production of wage goods will decrease. This will put an effective limit on the production for exports. Further, if the export commodity is an agricultural product and if the best land for production of food commodities is used for its production, it will further reduce the wherewithal required for supporting the labour in export industries.

Thus, if $f(n)$ is the product produced by the land worked by the one who is in nth place in the order of the output produced, then $f(N)$ is the product of the marginal farmer, when the number of farmers is N. Let $F(N)$ be the total output. Then $F(N)$ will be equal to the sum of all individual outputs that is,

$$F(N) = f(1) + f(2) + \ldots + f(n) + \ldots f(N) \tag{9.15}$$

As the production of all other individuals is greater than that of the Nth individual, $F(N)$ will be greater that $Nf(N)$.

Then, the total rent will be

$$F(N) - Nf(N) \tag{9.16}$$

This can support $[F(N) - Nf(N)] / f(N)$ workers in export or modern industries, if all the rent can be taken out of the farmers, and the subsistence wage can be maintained equal to $f(N)$. However, taking some labour force out of agriculture to work in export industries implies that the number of farmers will be reduced to (say) L only. Then the total rent will be reduced to $F(L) - Lf(N)$. This will support only $[F(L) - Lf(N)] / f(N)$ labourers in export and other modern industries. The number of labourers that can be taken out of traditional agriculture for producing export commodities and manufacturing goods is thus given by

$$[F(L) - Lf(N)] / f(N) = N - L$$

and

$$F(L) = Nf(N) \tag{9.17}$$

This simply stipulates that the total production of traditional agriculture should be at least sufficient for the total population. Any attempt to increase the export sector or modern sector more than this will show itself in famine conditions.

Ordinarily, in the years of better crop yields the farmers build up stocks for consumption in lean years. But existence at a low level of subsistence means that in such years they will be able to consume a bit more or will suffer less deprivation; this does not allow the building of any stocks for the rainy days. So when a lean year arrives, one witnesses famine conditions. In the last two decades, such famine conditions in Sub-Saharan Africa have become too common for comfort even for the hard-headed international community.

For the existence of such a condition, it is immaterial whether the labour is taken out of agriculture for nation-building enterprises or national manufacturing or production for export. The only sufficient condition is that the labour productivity has not increased in agriculture. Only when we can increase that productivity in food production without increasing the price of food, can we successfully deal with this problem. If the price of food is increased in the process, it will make the subsistence wage higher, pushing up in its turn the price of the export commodity. Even then will the commodity be saleable in the international market? It is on the answer to this question that the satisfactory solution to this intractable problem depends.

IMPERIALISM IN NEW COUNTRIES

In the areas of the new countries, which were either vacant or which were cleared of the natives by the early settlers, the situation was different. In them hardly any traditional technique of production of wage goods survived; competitiveness in the world market depended on the use of the slave labour for production purposes. However, the wherewithal for their support had to be produced by the use of modern techniques of production. Being mostly colonies having international connections from the very beginning, they did not develop any independent economy for themselves; their wage goods production could not be carried out without the import of some crucial input(s).

Even after the abolition of slavery, production conditions remained the same. There was a direct or indirect input of foreign exchange in the production of almost every item. Thus the wage rate, etc. could not be divorced from the exchange rate of the currency. Though the upkeep of a slave may be at a subsistence level, it required a certain amount of foreign exchange for mere maintenance; the availability of foreign exchange thus put an upper limit on the size of the economy: we should more aptly call such economies foreign exchange-constrained economies.

Let E be the export earnings of the country. Let the direct or indirect imported inputs in the production of the export commodity be $I(E)$. Let the foreign exchange available for importing other intermediate goods or direct consumption and investment goods be equal to J, then

$$J = E - I(E) + `A'$$ (9.18)

where 'A' is the *net* 'aid' or loans, that is total 'aid' and/or loans received *minus* debt servicing.

Then, the total product available for domestic use will be an increasing function of J. And so will be the total employment in the economy. That is, if X is the total product available for domestic use in the country dX/dJ will be positive and so will be dZ/dJ, where Z is the total employment. The total employment will be determined on the demand side by the total production in the country and on the supply side by the production of wage goods. This production of wage goods depend upon the amount of foreign exchange, J, the wage goods producing industry is able to get hold of. In a pure market system it depends on how much of J is appropriated by non-wage goods producers or consumers with market power.

Let the terms of trade change to T. Then the availability of foreign exchange for intermediate goods, direct consumption, and/or investment will be changed to

$$TE - I(E) + 'A' \qquad (9.19)$$

The improving terms of trade and net 'aid' thus gives extra resources for conspicuous consumption, developmental investment and for expansion of production within the country. While deteriorating terms of trade as well as increasing debt servicing and decreasing 'aid' not only may result in the decrease in consumer imports or reduction in the development effort, but may even lead to the disutilisation of the capacity already created due to lack of foreign exchange for intermediate exports, and also large-scale unemployment, which may push a large section of people to a sub-subsistence existence.

THE DEMOGRAPHIC MYTH

We have seen above that as soon as a land- or labour-constrained self-sufficient economy is opened up for international trade, and goods produced through using a scarce factor of production are exchanged for services or for non-wage goods, unemployment will be created. Land producing wage goods can thus be diverted to the production of commercial crops only at the expense of the production of wage goods. And this reduction can lead only to the an effective reduction of the number of people that can be employed by the economy. Similarly in a labour constrained economy, the diversion of the labour force to the production of export commodities will only reduce the availability of wage goods. In this case, though, it will not create open unemployment, it will create conditions of malnutrition of the self-employed labour force always on the verge of famine. In the case of foreign exchange-constrained economies, any decrease of the availability of foreign exchange and/or the increase in luxury

Table 9.1   Population in relation to arable land in some countries

(i) Country	(ii) Population (million)	(iii) Arable area (million hectare)	(iv) (ii)/(iii)	(v) Fertilizer per hectare of arable land (100g nutrient)
Bangladesh	88.2	9.1	9.69	592
China	985.2	99.5	9.90	1692
Indonesia	151.0	19.5	7.79	947
India	689.0	168.3	4.09	504
Pakistan	87.2	20.3	4.30	736
Philippines	48.3	10.9	4.43	358
Egypt	41.3	2.4	17.21	3473
Ethiopia	32.0	13.9	2.30	47
Sudan	18.7	12.4	1.51	75
Nigeria	80.6	30.4	2.65	108
Germany (FDR)	61.6	7.5	8.21	4273
Japan	116.8	4.9	23.84	4566
Netherlands	14.1	0.9	16.66	7812
UK	56.2	7.0	8.03	3566
USA	227.7	190.6	1.19	993

Sources: 1. Population and arable land figures are for 1980, from FAO (1986).
2. Figure for fertiliser use from World Bank (1988).

consumption or investment will decrease the availability of foreign exchange for the production of wage goods, and thus lead to increase in unemployment.

Even the unemployed use up some national resources. In the case of land-scarce or foreign exchange-scarce economies, the decrease of the population will increase the national income of the country. The unemployed are expendable; their paltry upkeep depends on relatives, friends, and/or scavenging. We have a classical situation of '*over-population*'.

Table 9.1 gives the population in relation to the arable land for some land-constrained or famine-prone developing countries of Asia and Africa, together with that of some industrialised ones. Fertiliser consumption per hectare of arable land is also given as an indication of modernisation. However, that is an indication of modernisation of agriculture as a whole rather than the foodgrain sector, and mostly the modernisation in developing countries is that of the export sector rather than the wage goods one. In some cases it may thus give misleading indications. We see that in Egypt fertiliser inputs are at similar levels as in industrialised countries; however, that is primarily for the export crop, cotton; the work-force is fed largely from imported grains, they are heavily subsidised to keep the wage rate low. When, under IMF advice, Egypt tried to cut the subsidy without a corresponding increase in the wage rates, it suffered extensive riots forcing the government to backtrack. Similarly most of the fertiliser is used on the coffee crop in Ethiopia and on cotton in the Sudan.

Agricultural output per hectare notoriously depends on the soil, climate and crop complex of the individual geographic area, and therefore the yield per hectare for two different areas cannot be strictly compared. However it is evident that in general the increasing use of modern inputs like fertilisers, pesticides, etc. can increase that yield by a significant amount. Of course, this must go hand in hand with complementary inputs like the development of suitable crop varieties, irrigation, etc.

It is clear that in the so-called 'Over-populated countries' the problem is not of high density of population but that of non-modernisation of agriculture. And the solution of this so-called demographic problem is not the reduction of the birth rate but finding an economic system that will allow that transition to modernisation in the country. It demonstrates the theoretical inadequacy of our profession that economists have translated the problem of the transition of under-developed countries into the problem of a demographic predicament. This suits both politicians and international experts, as their failures can be cleared in the mystique of the demographic myth.

10 The Wage Goods Constraint for Employment and Development

PRICES AND AVAILABILITY OF BASIC CONSUMPTION GOODS

That the prices of necessities in poor countries are cheaper than those in the rich countries at the prevailing exchange rates was the conventional wisdom among development economists for at least the past forty years; it was maintained that the comparison of per capita national income between different countries at the prevailing exchange rates might be quite misleading for representing the relative 'real' income enjoyed by the people of different countries. Some scholars tried to estimate their own 'real' exchange rates for the purpose, so that a better comparison of the purchasing power of different currencies could be obtained and thus a better indication of the relative poverty of developing countries. As a first approximation, a 'cereal' exchange rate was widely used; this was based on the premise that the exchange rate that equalised the cost of the basic consumption good like cereals across various countries better represented the purchasing power of the masses than the currency exchange rate. It might therefore be a better indication of the relative welfare of the countries in question.

On the other hand, from the early 1970s there was a growing realisation that developing countries were not able to satisfy even the 'basic needs' of their people due to the paucity of the necessary consumption goods in these countries. However, the implications of a scarcity of subsistence goods existing simultaneously with their low prices in developing countries was not adequately noted by development economists; nor was this phenomenon theoretically explained. In these countries the amount of low price necessities is far from being sufficient for its own population. Such a comparative low price indicates that it should be exported to countries where high prices of

151

that commodity prevail; this of course is out of the question, but its low price prevents a commercial imports of these essential stuffs.

UN STUDY OF PURCHASING POWER PARITY

These differences in the purchasing power of various currencies posed a practical problem for the international agencies like the World Bank, the International Bank for Reconstruction and Development (IBRD), etc. Their concessional loan policy depended upon the loan being given to 'poor' countries, and the definition of 'poor' depended on per capita income. If the per capita income of different countries could not be compared correctly, the whole basis of these operations became arbitrary. To examine this issue, the UN appointed a committee of experts consisting of Irving B. Kravis, Alan Heston and Robert Summers; they began by collecting detailed information about prices of consumer and investment goods and services for the year 1967 in Phase I. Phase III of this UN programme made an international comparison of purchasing power covering 34 countries for the year 1975, divided into five groups out of which the first two groups represent developing countries.[1]

Though these 34 countries are only a sample of the countries of the world, they are numerous enough to shed some light on the price structure that accompanies development. This classification of the developing countries is well suited to help in this process of understanding the working of the economies of the developing countries. It may be worth keeping in mind that there are wide differences in price and production structures within each group also, and similarly there must be individualities in the countries not in the sample. Even so, the general characteristics of these groups will give us some inkling about the nature of the economic compulsions faced by the developing countries.

In Table 10.1 we have given the average value of the quantities that could be purchased for one dollar in the USA for some of the consumer goods in these groups of countries (the cost in the local currencies has been converted into US dollars at the 1975 exchange rates). The average manufacturing wage rate in the corresponding countries has been taken from a UNIDO (1986) study and is based on national censuses of production. The average manufacturing 'real' wage rate is calculated from the same data by using the cost of living index from the UN study of purchasing power parity (Kravis, *et al.*,

Table 10.1   Prices of some consumer goods in developing countries

Commodity or sector	Group I	Group II	USA
1. Consumption goods	0.40	0.50	1.00
1a. Bread & cereals	0.35	0.57	1.00
1b. Clothing	0.59	0.60	1.00
1c. Footwear	0.43	0.49	1.00
II Fuel and power	0.65	0.82	1.00
III Average manufacturing wage rate			
(a) Nominal	0.08	0.11	1.00
(b) 'Real'	0.21	0.22	1.00

1982). From Table 10.1, it is clear that consumption goods are cheaper in developing countries; by and large, the poorer the country the cheaper are the basic wage goods. Cereal and bread shows this tendency most and then goods like footwear and clothing. However, modern consumer goods are no means cheaper in those countries.

SEMI-FEASIBILITY OF IMPORTING WAGE GOODS IN A DEVELOPING COUNTRY

Whether production of foodgrains within a country is sufficient to meet the demand of labour is crucial for industrial development. It is not only important if the country is able to import foodgrains from abroad; what is important is to find out whether the country has a potential for importing foodgrains in sufficient quantity for feeding a whole population. This depends on the export potential and the international price structure.

From Table 10.1, it seems that the poor developing countries should be exporting foodgrains, clothing and footwear to the developed countries, as the prices of these are so cheap compared to those in developed countries. This is in fact true for clothing and footwear. Their exports are limited by the willingness of the developed countries to allow these imports in their countries. However the whole economy seems to be out of balance for foodgrains; it is developing poor countries that are suffering from the foodgrains shortage, and it is there that the foodgrain prices are cheap. This shortage gets aggravated by attempts at industrialisation and development. With these price structures, what is the chance of commercial imports of foodgrains from developed countries to the developing ones? Why will somebody export foodgrains to get less than half the price in the foreign country than what he can get at home?

However, exports of foodgrains from developed countries to the developing ones are not uncommon. In low-income developing countries about 4% of the total foodgrain consumption was imported in 1977–9 (World Bank, 1980 p. 23). The proportion of imported cereals in the consumption of foodgrains and tubers in Sub-Saharan Africa was almost the same (3.8%) (World Bank 1981b). A large proportion of these imports were under a 'Food Aid' programme. Even commercial imports at the so-called 'competitive' price were at a much lower price than the consumers in the North American exporter countries pay. Even then, in many countries they are heavily subsidised; for instance in Egypt food subsidies are between 5% to 7% of GDP.

These imports primarily support a part of the urban population and labour which is needed in the production of export commodities. So, in a way, they support mainly the labour that is used in production for the developed countries. Thus the developed countries are able to get those goods at a much lower cost than would have been possible if they were required to support equivalent labour in their own countries. This method of support cannot be extended to the support of the bulk of the labour force in these developing countries in general, simply because ultimately the subsidies must be paid for by somebody, and the other sectors of the economy are themselves too poor to pick up the bill.

WAGE GOODS CONSTRAINTS FOR EMPLOYMENT AND DEVELOPMENT

For practical purposes, then, for most of the developing countries, we may take the short-term availability of foodgrains to be more or less given as equal to what the country is able to produce itself. We are back in the world of classical economics, where the Wage Fund Theory of employment and thus production prevails. The wage fund theory refers to economic statics; it tells us the amount of employment that can be sustained with the given wage fund or Ricardian 'Corn'. That in its turn determines the amount of economic activity that can be supported – that is, the amount of domestic product that can be created in the country.

In the development of the wage fund theory, there is an assumption that to employ a labourer a minimum real wage, called a 'subsistence' wage, has to be paid to him. A labourer, though unemployed is not available for hire at a lesser wage than this. So the behavioural assumption is that either a labourer works on a wage equivalent to at least the subsistence wage or he lives as a destitute, eking out a meagre living on the little that he can gather in so-called 'self employment'. This assumption may have been true for England and other European countries at the time classical writers were writing; then the labour market was notoriously filled with the army of unemployed and yet there was a limit below which the wage rate would not fall. This was not probably apparent when neoclassical writers were developing their theory, as at that time the wage rate in their countries was probably higher than the subsistence level. In general, when a wage rate is higher than subsistence real wage rates are expected to come down with rising unemployment. But there is a limit below which wage rates do not fall in spite of rising unemployment.

This has been found true in most of the studies conducted in developing countries. Nutritionists have tried to explain this on the basis of necessary replenishment of the physical energy spent in performing the required physical labour. For instance, Seckler writes:

> The specific problem I encountered was that in a highly under-employed and poverty stricken area of the hills – and I later found, generally throughout India – people will not work for less than Rs 5 a day. I thought it peculiar that people appeared to be willing to starve rather than work for this, under Indian conditions, not inconsiderable wage . . . It is clear that the physical energy expended in the physical work must be provided by food . . . Clarke and Haswell in their survey of the agricultural wage rates in subsistence economies, observed 'the strange fact . . . that, throughout all times and places we have information, the rural labourer, however poor, will not do a day's work for less than three kilogram equivalent' (in Sukhatme, 1982: 140).

Thus when the marginal labourer finds that the wage rate available to him is reduced below a subsistence level, he usually drops out of the formal labour force. He may linger on in the informal sector, as the working conditions in them will not be so regimented and he can put in less continuous physical exertion. In fact, he works (say) half time to get half the wages and that half time is distributed throughout the day so as not to exhaust him unduly.

However, when instead of marginal labourer an average labourer's wage is forced down below subsistence level by fiscal or monetary authorities, the reaction is often violent. There have been scores of food riots in the developing countries in the 1980s; they have been mostly caused by a government following the advice of the International Monetary Fund (IMF) for restructuring of their economy. An IMF package for restructuring almost always includes a reduction of the real wage of the labourer by fiscal means; these riots have therefore been nicknamed IMF riots. One wonders at the credulity of the IMF experts, who have such a blind faith in their theory of the possibility of reducing real wage rate to almost zero, that in case after case they go on giving such an impractical advice closing their eyes to the social misery and political turmoil to which it has again and again given rise. These theoretical blinkers can be attributed to their economic learning based on the underlying simple mathematics of differential calculus, in which complications arising out of the introduction of upper and lower limits to the value of a function have been avoided. And in their self-justification they term such complications 'non-economic factors', without realising that their theories were developed for different climes and places and are not at all applicable to the currently under-developed countries.

Even in developed countries where the wage rate is at a much higher level than 'subsistence', monetary and fiscal means could not reduce wage rates during the 1970s when these economies had to transfer real resources to the producers of internationally traded commodities. The whole burden of the transfer had to be borne by either non-labour factors of production or by unemployment; the rate of payment to the employed labour more or less maintained itself, though the mechanism of this was the organisation of the labour force rather than riots. It may be recalled that even in the Great Depression of the 1930s the 'persons who were fully employed throughout the 1929–33 period maintained their real income' (Baily, 1983). There the reason was, as pointed out by Keynes, that in the short run an economy working at a much lower level of capacity has its prices proportional to the wage rate. So the declining nominal wage rate brought down the price level with it, keeping the real wage rate unaffected.)

Thus, in the situation of high unemployment, the labour supply curve is horizontal in terms of the 'real' wage rate. With a limited supply of foodgrains, the amount of employment that can be sustained by an economy is effectively given. In fact, this limit is reduced when some citizens are able to take a larger share of foodgrains than that required by subsistence standards. This is the reason for the well-known fact that total employment could be increased during wartime by effective rationing which precluded some rich citizens from using or wasting the limited foodgrains resources of the country. The population of a developing country is thus effectively divided into two groups – those having employment and the destitute. The saving grace is that over the years a large proportion of the people at the margin go on changing their group and thus stay alive, though at a much reduced efficiency.

AUTONOMOUS EXPENDITURE IN A WAGE GOODS-CONSTRAINED ECONOMY

In a completely monetised economy which is not subject to any factor constraint the static equilibrium is maintained if planned investment is equal to planned savings. This condition, when translated into the situation which is characterised by a constraint on employment due to paucity of wage goods, becomes one that the labour employed in any new economic activity should be equal to the labour made unemployed in some other activity *plus* labour that can be sustained by the increase in the wage goods production. Any increase in employment due to developmental expenditure through construction of infrastructure, or industrialisation, etc. will be thwarted by the paucity of wage goods. This will show itself through the rise of foodgrain prices. This will increase the subsistence wage in monetary terms, thus subjecting the economy to inflationary pressures.

All the labour force will try to increase their monetary emoluments to protect their 'real' income; some at the margin will not succeed. Those not succeeding will fall into the category of the unemployed. Until the time the number of these unemployed effectively becomes equal to the number of persons getting new employment *minus* those getting employment due to the increase in the supply of wage goods, inflationary pressures will continue. We may designate this phenomenon as moving employment due to unsustainable developmental efforts, rather than 'employment creation', as the planners would like to call it.

This statement would be literally true if all the employment had been in the formal sector, where a person is either fully employed or unemployed. But when a person is working on his own account he may become under-employed and may have to curtail his consumption of essential goods. In a poor country with a substantial proportion of under-employed labour, the income elasticity of foodgrain would be quite high. An investigation of agricultural labour in India in the 1950s gave an income elasticity equal to 0.7. (Mathur, 1956). For richer rural people it was of the order of 0.55, while in urban areas it was between 0.3 and 0.5. For Kenya it has been calculated to be of the order of 0.6 (Sulaiman, 1989). Overall, for our illustration we may take it to be about 0.6 for developing countries. Then, simple calculations[2] will show that assuming a 2.5% rate of population growth, a 4% rate of growth in the availability of foodgrain would allow a rate of growth of only about 5% in the total disposable income of the nation. That is, about a 2.5% rate of growth in per capita income would be sustained by about a 1.5% rate of growth in per capita availability of foodgrains. Higher induced increases in national income through a development effort will lead to inflationary pressure.

MOVING UNEMPLOYMENT DUE TO AN UNSUSTAINABLE DEVELOPMENT EFFORT

We have seen that the development effort, if not based on the extra availability of wage goods, will put pressure on the prices of the wage goods in general and foodgrains in particular. As the price elasticity of foodgrain consumption is low, the consumption of foodgrains will decrease less than proportionately. This implies that a higher portion of income will be spent on foodgrains and other necessities, thus a smaller proportion of income will be available for spending on other goods. This implies a downward shift of the demand curve for non-essential current consumption goods. The demand for durable and semi-durable goods would be curtailed much more drastically as their purchases in many cases can be easily postponed.

However, a part of this reduction will be compensated by the newly created demand of the newly employed. But if the new employment is in only a part of the economy, (say) in a rural area, the pattern of the demand in that part may be different than the average. In such a case the extra demand generated would be for other types of goods than the ones for which the demand is being depressed. The increases in the prices of foodgrains, etc. will also tend to transfer income from the urban to the rural area. The consumption pattern of the rural areas is mostly quite different from that in the urban areas in developing countries; their structures of consumption reflect the traditional consumption habits of the poor classes, which have hardly any place for modern non-essential consumption goods. Even the clothes and footwear used by them are of different types, and any increase in their demand will not compensate for the decrease in the demand for those goods by the urban people.

The increasing price of foodgrains and other wage goods will put pressure on the wage rates in the whole of the economy; this will shift the supply curve upwards for all the industries. The net effect of these two shifts will be a reduction in the total production of these non-wage goods; this reduction will result in reduction of employment in these sectors (Mathur, 1959).

It may be worth recalling that to result in these inflationary tendencies, these developmental economic activities need not be financed only through deficit financing. If they are financed through orthodox financing it may be even more harmful, if the taxes are collected from those better off people whose consumption of wage goods does not significantly decrease as a consequence. In this case, hardly any extra wage goods will be made available for consumption of the newly employed through the instrument of taxation. However, this taxation will greatly reduce the effective demand for other goods. This extra downward shift of the demand curve for other commodities coupled with the upward shift of the supply curve due to increasing wage rate will lead to a much greater reduction of production and employment in other parts of the economy than if the development expenditure had been financed through deficit financing only.

EFFECT ON MARKETED SURPLUS IN A SEMI-MONETISED ECONOMY

In an agriculture where the variation in yield from year to year is large, the first priority of the farmer is to keep a large portion of his output as stock whenever he can afford it. Further, due to volatility of the prices from season to season a farmer will prefer to keep his savings in terms of his produce. In times of rising prices, the richer become somewhat speculators, and do not want to sell more than is essential for their immediate purpose. Their savings are thus immediately invested in the stocks of their produce and are thus not available to the general economy for economic development, etc.

In the short run, these farmers have fixed monetary requirements for necessary expenditure – payment of rents, irrigation dues, debt repayments, etc. – as well as purchase of some necessary usual household goods. With increasing prices of his produce, the farmer can meet these requirements by selling less of his produce than what he would otherwise have done; and as he is likely to resort to savings in kind, the produce going to the market tends to diminish with the increase in price. This results in a short-run backward-sloping supply curve for marketed surplus.

Mathur (1959), and Mathur and Ezekiel (1961) interpreted this behaviour 'as a reaction of an intrinsically non-monetised sector to the monetised world around'. This reaction of the non-monetised portion of the economy to the happenings in the monetised part implies that increases in the prices of the wage goods reduce their supply to the monetised sector; this reduction will lead to a further reduction in effective employment. So the final result of an increase in the developmental activity or autonomous demand beyond what is indicated by the increase in the wage goods availability will be the net decrease in the effective employment, which those schemes so fondly planned to increase.

Krishnan (1964) showed that increases in the monetary income of the foodgrain farmer occasioned by the rise in the foodgrain prices should increase his consumption of foodgrains as the income elasticity of demand for foodgrains is higher than price elasticity in developing countries. This also leads to a reduction of the marketed surplus. Krishnan carefully estimated these from the Indian data and found that with the observed price, increase in the private stocks ('saving in kind') is also involved. Detailed econometric studies by Mathur and Prakash (1980) and Ghosh (1983) have confirmed that both the above mechanisms were working in India up to late 1960s. After that, with advent of high-yielding modern agriculture a government policy of support prices and changing the emphasis away from the development expenditure for employment creation, other leading tendencies have taken over. India now considers that it has 'solved' its 'food problem', though about a third of its population lives below the 'poverty line' which is defined in a way that those under it are malnourished. Thus this 'solution' is the resultant of the development expenditure being less than that which can be sustained by present availability of foodgrains.

RECAPITULATION

The dynamic mechanism of the working of the wage fund theory in the modern market economy of a food deficient country is now becoming clear. An increase in the economic activity greater than is warranted by the short-run availability of wage goods increases their prices in general, and of foodgrains in particular. That increases the income of the foodgrain farmer. A part of this increase he considers as an enhancement of his permanent income; this leads to an increase in his consumption. Another part he saves in kind. This mechanism results in a backward-sloping supply curve for the market arrivals of foodgrains with respect to price. This reduction in the market surplus of foodgrains pushes up their prices further. The rise in the prices of foodgrains leads to a higher proportion of income being spent on foodgrain due to their low price elasticity. This leads to a reduction in the demand of industrial goods and services, which creates unemployment in these sectors. The consequent increase in subsistence wage rates make quite a few firms in marginal or informal sectors unprofitable, and this leads to their closure. The economy ends up with lesser employment than before as the wage fund is diminished in the process. The whole process results in a big shuffle between those living on a subsistence wage and those on the verge of destitution. This mechanism seems to be working in African developing countries at present as it was in India in the 1950s and 1960s.

11 Violations of Macro Constraints and Inflation: Different Types of Demand-pull and Cost-push Inflations, with Indian Illustrations

INTRODUCTION

Economic decision-makers are micro units like individuals, firms, financial institutions, various state agencies, etc. It is only a rare chance that the aggregate effect of their economic actions will conform with the macro constraints facing the economy. When they do not, the economy tries to adjust through disequilibrium, and the effects of various micro actions turn out to be different from what were intended. The final results are such that the macro constraints are satisfied, though the effects on various parts of the economy may be far from desirable ones. These are mainly influenced by price and employment changes. Price inflation makes for differences in nominal and real wage rates, and thus controls the demands of the wage earners. Differential price increases of different commodities also serve to deflect demand from the commodities using comparatively larger quantities of the factor constraining at the macro level.

In the economies where total output is limited by 'full' employment production, if the aggregate total demand is larger than total output, the economy will react with a general increase in prices, bringing down real wages; this is the classical inflationary situation. In the opposite case, where the aggregate demand is less than the full employment production, the adjustment will be done, as Keynes has taught us, by means of reduction in the total output, hence through creation of unemployment rather than through a reduction in prices. These are only two forms of possible adjustment; when there are other real constraints to the economy there will be other types. There

162

will similarly be other types of economic reaction when some factors of production stake a higher claim for themselves in the distribution of the national product than other cooperating factors are prepared to recognise. The mode of adjustment will be different according to the individuality of the factor that puts in a claim for higher share. Needless to say, all these involuntary adjustments lead to the frustration of the economic operators as their well-laid plans go astray. The most conspicuous of these are the ones by state regulatory authorities and planning organisations, as these lead to failure of national development policies. It is thus essential that these economic constraints, etc. are expressly taken into account before attempting to formulate national economic policies or plans; it may otherwise result in unintended economic hardships. This will not only slow down or even put back the clock of economic growth, it also may have highly undesirable socio-political consequences.

CLASSICAL DEMAND-PULL INFLATION

Up to the 1940s, the received economic doctrine talked only of one kind of inflation. This is best described by the textbook cliche 'more money chasing fewer goods'. This had been primarily the result of debasing the currency and/or deficit financing, and was sought to be explained by simple quantity theory of money. It was Wicksell (1934) who showed that this extra money could also be created by banks if at the current rate of interest the demand for investment (including hoardings) was more than the savings in the economy. The simple cure for this behaviour of banks was to increase the interest rate; this would curb investment demand as well as increasing the propensity to save.

The main indicator of this inflation was a general rise in prices. Further, the economy should have full employment so that the extra demand generated might not be capable of being satisfied by extra production. Inflation was alternatively perceived as an attempt by the sharer of a national cake to get such a portion each that the sum total of their shares was more than the national cake itself. Government's deficit financing should thus generate inflationary pressure only when the rest of national income receivers did not save the corresponding amount in terms of bank deposits or just currency notes. Similarly, when investors wanted to jointly invest more than savings there would be an inflationary pressure.

This traditional inflation is now termed *demand-pull inflation*, as there is more 'effective demand' for goods as a whole than supply, and the price rise results from the attempt of those whose demand is backed by monetary resources (through deficit financing or bank credit) to take hold of commodities not being given up by those who have earned their income through producing these commodities. They succeed only after bidding up the prices so much that the extra savings of the producers match this extra demand. This saving is a part of the 'forced' savings of fixed income receivers, the other part of 'forced' savings going to increase the consumption of those whose incomes increase due to this increase in the prices of commodities.

WAGE COST-PUSH INFLATION

After the Second World War, in the 1950s, economists realised that the inflation and unemployment were coexisting. This should be impossible in a traditional demand-push inflationary situation. With the unemployment in the economy, the extra demand should create more supply through a reduction in unemployment. It is only when full employment is achieved that higher demand will create inflationary pressures. When unemployment is prevailing the increase in prices can come when wage earners demand more wages than can be given at the prevailing price of the produce. In a pure competitive economy, where prices are determined outside the control of individual firms, this should result into the closing down of such a uneconomic firm. But banks are now prepared to accommodate the unit concerned if it can show that it would recoup the extra cost by increasing prices. Prices thus increase not as a result of demand–supply disequilibrium but by the shift of supply curve in an upward direction. These higher prices do not reduce demand as a whole as the income increases pari passu so as to be able to absorb the higher prices. It mostly starts with monopolistic industries who can increase their prices with impunity. When the trade union of one industry is able to push up the wages of its members, trade unions of other industries are induced to struggle for higher wages for their members too. Slowly wages are increased more or less in the whole economy, and so do prices without reducing the demand as a whole. A more or less general price rise is achieved without affecting the employment rate. This type of inflation is called '*cost-push*' *inflation*.

THE PARADOX OF THE INDIAN CASE

Neither of these two pure models fits the Indian case. Since the end of the Second World War, the general price level has risen about twelve times. With 1970–1 as base, the wholesale price index was 35.7 in 1947–8 and about 425 in May 1988. Throughout these years, labour was never fully employed. In fact, according to Plan documents there has been large-scale unemployment over most of this period, and even among those employed a large proportion had only part-time employment, thus finding themselves below the poverty line. In such a situation classical demand-pull inflation is ruled out.

Over this period, real wages have also not significantly increased. The organised sector of the economy hardly accounts for 15% of the labour force, so it cannot have a perceptible effect on general price level. Trade union power over the economy is rather limited; and that too has not been perceptibly enforced except in a few isolated sectors like banking and insurance. The observed changes of money wage rates have been completely explained by the need to regain the standard of living lost in consequence of the rise in the cost of living during this period; this rules out any wage cost-push inflation.

CONSTRAINED DEMAND-PULL INFLATION

Demand-pull inflation, as we have noted above, is caused by effective demand being more than the possible supply of commodities from the economy. In the neoclassical framework, this is possible only when the total labour force is employed. If any other factor of production is in short supply, it would be substituted by the factor which was not in short supply by moving along the production function. Until there is unemployed labour, labour is a factor of production not in short supply, and so is capable of being substituted for any other factor in short supply. This simple textbook microeconomics with continuous production functions ensures that the only bottleneck in fulfilling effective demand will be the labour force, and if the structure of demand is not the one suitable to this production possibility a movement on the smooth indifference surface will suitably modify it. Only when the total demand is higher than the full employment production capacity of the economy will demand-pull inflation emerge.

This textbook picture is a long-run one. Even if we have a smooth production function, it takes real time before capital goods, etc. corresponding to one point in the production function can be changed to those corresponding to another. And the indifference surfaces are far from smooth; there is hardly any substitutability between necessities of life like foodgrains with cloth or transport, etc. Thus, in land-scarce countries, the availability of foodgrains, for instance, can become a real bottleneck long before full employment is reached.

In such a case, the total availability of foodgrains will put an effective limit on total employment, which may be significantly lower than the full employment where everybody who wants to work is able to find some job. We shall call this limit '*effective full employment*'. In the case of effective demand being in excess of the supply of goods that can be produced at 'effective full employment', inflationary pressures will emerge.

The difference between this demand-pull inflation and the classical one is that firstly this inflation starts before full employment is reached; in fact it starts as soon as effective full employment is achieved. Secondly, the rise in prices should start with the commodity which proves to be the bottleneck. While in the general demand-pull situation all prices should rise almost simultaneously, in this case the prices of foodgrains will rise first if the availability of foodgrains is the bottleneck. Other price rises will follow only after the rise in the cost of living of the labourers due to rise in the foodgrain prices has forced wages up, and thus the cost of production of the commodities. This bottleneck-induced demand-pull inflation gives rise to the price of a commodity in short supply, and is followed by cost-push inflation for rest of the commodities to achieve the original relative prices. This makes the 'effective full employment' less than the full employment of the labour force.

THE LOGIC OF COST-PUSH INFLATION

When a commodity is in continuous production, the price at which it sells should be able to cover its cost of production. And if its total production can also be increased at short notice it will not be selling at much more than its cost of production. Such commodities are called 'fix-price' commodities (Hicks, 1974). The adjustment of their demand and supply is achieved by reducing or increasing their production rate so that the supply matches the demand at the price equivalent to the marginal cost of production. Most of the manufacturing industries are in this situation: most of them have also got quite a bit of unutilised capacity, primarily consisting of capital goods of older vintages yet not assigned to the scrapheap which can be put in service with a sudden rise in demand; this would increase the cost of production only at the margin. Increases in the demand should thus not affect these industries until their capacity to increase production to meet the increased demand is thwarted by the non-availability of labour to work the so far unused capacity.

However, such industries are sitting ducks for cost-push inflationary forces. Any increase in the cost of wages or interest rate, etc. they must pass on further down the chain to the ultimate consumer, just to be able to survive. This may reduce their total sales, but it will not put them in the red.

On the other hand, flex-price commodities are ones whose supply in the short run is more or less fixed and demand–supply adjustments are affected by price changes. Naturally their prices are the first to respond to demand-pull pressures. When their supply is absolutely rigid they may turn a simple demand increase into bottleneck-induced demand pull.

If all the commodities are fix-price commodities, the price of a commodity will be equal to wages of labourers, the cost of intermediate inputs, interest on bank loans *plus* returns on invested capital. Thus we can write

Price = (Price of Intermediate goods × Quantity of intermediate goods required per unit of output) +
(Interest rate × Price of bank financed stocks × Quantity of bank financed stocks per unit of output) +
(Rate of return × Price of investment financed stocks × Quantity of invested capital per unit of output) + (Wage rate × Number of standardised labourers working to produce a unit of output).

There will be one such equation for each commodity. The prices on the right-hand side consist of prices of other commodities, which would appear on the left-hand side in some other equation of the system. The price of the commodity on the left-hand side of the equation refers to the period when the output comes to the market while those on the right-hand side are those of the production period.

In an equilibrium situation the price of the same commodity is the same on both sides of the equation. If the wage rate increases that increase increases the output price on the left-hand side of the equation system. In next period those increased prices are fed into the right-hand side of the equation system; that further increases the output prices. This process will go on until all prices have increased proportionately in the same ratio as the increase in the wage rate. This will decrease the real value of the wage rate to the level at which the process started. So labour may have another go at increasing its wage rate. Then the process will be repeated. This wage-push inflation will go on until some other cost fails to increase in proportion to prices. For instance, the value of investment may not keep pace with the increases in prices. The accountants may calculate the profits on historical cost only; then the wage rate can increase at the cost of profit rate, and this will stop the wage cost-push inflation from going on.

NOMINAL INTEREST RATE-PUSH INFLATION

Given a wage rate, there will be an interest rate (and a profit rate) that will satisfy the price equation described in the previous section. The interest rate that equalises the two sides of the above relationship may be called the *real* interest rate. If the nominal rate of interest is put up above that rate, we can see from the price equation that output prices will be higher than input prices. When in the next period those output prices are fed into the cost of inputs the output prices will further increase. The inflationary process will continue until the nominal interest rate becomes equal to the real interest rate. This inflation can be termed *nominal interest rate-push inflation*.

A characteristic of this type of inflation will be that it will not lead to proportionate rise in prices of all the commodities, even eventually. As capital-intensive commodities will be more affected by this push than less capital-intensive ones, the increase in the output price will be proportional to the capital requirements per unit of production, and they are obviously different for different commodities.

(It may be worth distinguishing two effects of increase in nominal interest rate over the real one. The one described above may be termed the effect on the supply price; it tends to raise the supply curve. There is another effect of lowering of the demand curve that we can call the Wicksell effect. That works by reducing autonomous demand as the cost of investment increases. This is an important instrument in controlling demand-pull inflation. It is not widely recognised that this increase in the nominal interest rate tends on the other hand to stimulate cost-push inflation. That is why the so called 'soft landing' from an inflationary situation becomes so hazardous. A necessary condition of the existence of cost-push inflation is that the banks accommodate industry in meeting its higher cost of production, protecting themselves with the expectation of sales at the higher prices. When the demand curve shifts down, this expectation is not likely to be realised, leading to large-scale bankruptcies.)

IMPORT-PUSH INFLATION

For simplicity of exposition, we have not included the cost of the imported intermediate goods in the price relation given above. Including that, we can see that a rise in the cost of imported goods will put an upward pressure on the prices of various commodities. If labour is able to protect its real wage rate and interest rates as well as the profit rates remain the same, this will imply an increase in the prices of all the commodities in the same proportion as the increase in the cost of the imported goods. If the imported goods price again adjust to keep their real enhanced value, we will have another bout of price rises and so on, until somebody gives in.

RECAPITULATION

We have seen above that both recognised types of inflation have to be further subdivided to be able to explain inflationary conditions prevailing in different parts of the world and at different times. Their respective repercussions on the economy are tabulated in Table 11.1.

INDIAN EXPERIENCE OF DEMAND-PULL INFLATION WITH FOODGRAINS AS THE BOTTLENECK

Table 11.2 gives the wholesale price index as well as the foodgrain price index for India from the financial year 1955–6 to the financial year 1981–2 with the year 1970–1 as the base (= 100). It also gives the

Table 11.1 Different types of inflation

---

1. Demand-pull inflation

A *General demand pull*
Cause
: Autonomous demand – government and private sector credit autonomous expenditure more than savings at full employment level of production.
Price rise
: General; inflation neutral.
Employment
: Full.

B *Constrained demand pull*
Cause
: One factor of production acting as a bottleneck for extra production with effective demand exceeding the potential output producible with that bottleneck with available technology.
Price rise
: First in the commodity directly affected by the constraining factor; if that commodity is part of subsistence wage, then subsequently all prices affected by the subsistence cost-induced wage push; inflation neutral eventually.
Employment
: Full in the industry directly affected; partial employment in the rest.

2   Cost-push inflation

A *Trade-union induced wage push*
Cause
: Some trade unions by their power succeed in increasing the wages of their members; other trade unions with lesser muscle succeed in getting their members' wage increased in the catching up process.
Price rise
: General price rise starting with the industry where this wage push activity started; inflation neutral eventually.
Employment
: Partial.

B *Subsistence cost-induced wage push*
Cause
: With the increase in the prices of subsistence goods like foodgrains, wages increase in poor economies where wages are at subsistence level.
Price rise
: General and proportional; inflation neutral.
Employment
: Partial.

C *Nominal interest push*
Cause
: Nominal interest rate higher than real.
Price rise
: Differential price rise, with higher rise in industries having higher capital coefficient; inflation *not* neutral.
Employment
: Partial.

D *Import push*
Cause
: Increase in the cost of imported inputs.
Price rise
: Differential price rise, with higher rise in import intensive commodities; inflation *not* neutral.
Employment
: Partial.

Table 11.2   Foodgrain and wholesale price indices for India
(1955–6 to 1981–2) (1970–1 = 100)

(i) Year	(ii) Foodgrain price	(iii) Wholesale price	(iv) (ii) as % of (iii) (1955–6 = 100)	(v) % increase foodgrains	(vi) % increase wholesale
1955–6	35.2	40.8	100.0		
1956–7	45.0	46.5	112.2	27.8	14.0
1957–8	47.8	47.9	115.6	6.2	3.0
1958–9	51.2	49.8	119.1	9.1	4.0
1959–60	49.2	51.7	110.2	–4.0	3.8
1960–1	49.3	55.1	103.7	0.2	6.6
1961–2	48.4	55.2	101.6	–1.8	0.2
1962–3	51.0	57.3	103.1	5.4	3.8
1963–4	55.7	60.9	106.0	9.2	6.3
1964–5	70.4	67.5	120.8	26.4	10.8
1965–6	74.6	72.7	118.9	6.0	7.7
1966–7	88.4	82.8	123.8	18.5	13.9
1967–8	110.4	92.4	138.5	25.0	11.6
1968–9	97.2	91.3	123.4	–12.0	–1.2
1969–70	100.7	94.8	123.0	3.6	3.8
1970–1	100.0	100.0	115.9	–0.7	5.5
1971–2	103.4	105.6	113.4	3.4	5.6
1972–3	119.5	116.2	119.1	15.6	10.0
1973–4	141.9	139.7	117.7	18.7	20.2
1974–5	195.8	174.9	129.7	38.0	25.2
1975–6	174.1	173.8	116.6	–11.1	–0.6
1976–7	152.7	176.6	100.2	–12.6	1.6
1977–8	170.4	185.8	106.3	11.6	5.2
1978–9	172.6	185.8	107.6	1.3	0.0
1979–80	185.4	217.6	98.7	7.4	17.1
1980–1	216.7	257.3	97.6	16.9	18.2
1981–2	237.4	280.6	98.0	9.6	9.1

foodgrain price index as a percentage of the wholesale price index, as well as the yearly change in both.

From Table 11.2 we see that in the first year of the start of real planning (1955–6), foodgrain prices increased by about 28%, while the increase in wholesale prices was only so much as would be due to the foodgrain prices being their constituent. By 1958–9 it was 45% higher while wholesale price increase was a mere 22%, mostly accounted for by the rise of food prices. However, the relative price of foodgrains to wholesale price was only 2% higher in 1961–2 compared to 1955–6. One cycle of inflation was over, when non-foodgrains prices recouped their relative position (which they had lost through bottleneck-induced demand-pull) through cost-push.

Out of these four years of rise in foodgrain prices, 1956–7 was the year of the start of the second five-year plan with its massive emphasis on employment creation. It not only created employment in large-scale construction and other activities but also created vast amounts of effective employment through rehabilitation of cottage industries in general and handloom industry in particular. However, that employment was responsible for a significant increase in foodgrain demand. The extra demand did not create extra employment but only bottleneck-induced demand-pull inflation as foodgrain supplies could not be increased even in the medium term. The extra demand did not shift to other commodities to create equilibrium, but only tended to squeeze their demand as the employed persons found that after spending on food they were left with less money to spend on other products. It is only after the ensuing cost-plus increases in other sectors restored purchasing power that normality was restored.

The next big push in prices was in the year 1964–5, again to the extent of about 27%. That year was the year of a record harvest up to that time, so any suggestion that the price rise was due to the deficiency in the supply of foodgrains merely shows the bankruptcy of such analysis. 1964–5 was the year bearing the full economic impact of Chinese skirmishes in the Himalayan border; this led not only to large-scale mobilisation but also to consequent heavy construction work of border roads and other military installations, etc. The extra employment generated by the conduct of the war and these activities naturally led to bottleneck-induced demand-pull inflation, the bottleneck being again the foodgrains etc. Again it did not show much spillover into manufacturing.

The third upsurge in foodgrain prices was that of 1966–7 and 1967–8. This started even before the equilibrium ex ante could be established. This again was the aftermath of the Indo–Pakistani War. However, this was compounded by the effect of an unprecedentedly bad harvest in independent India. The fourth upsurge was between the period of 1972–5, the period of Indo–Pakistani clashes that led to the independence of Bangladesh. By 1976–7 that cycle had also run its course. The price ratio was almost the same as that in 1955–6.

The index of foodgrain price/wholesale price ratio (with 1955–6 as 100) was as high as 119 in 1958–9, 120 in 1964–5, 138 in 1967–8 and 130 in 1974–5; it came down to 101.6 in 1961–2, 100.2 in 1976–8 and has continued below 100 since 1978–9.

We have seen above that all the big inflationary bouts in post-war India were led by the foodgrain prices. During such bouts manufacturing prices hardly showed any effect of demand-pull inflation; they mostly increased because of the cost-push effect of wage increases consequent on the increase in the cost of living. However, manufactures slowly recouped their terms of trade over time. If we go to column (iv) of Table 11.2 which gives the foodgrain price index as a percentage of the wholesale price index, we can see the shocks that have pushed the price of foodgrains up, and how over the years manufactures have been making attempts to catch them up. They completely succeeded in their attempt after the first and the fourth shock; their attempts to regain their terms of trade after the second and third shocks were interrupted by the onset of new bout of bottleneck-induced demand-pull inflations.

CHARACTERISTICS OF BOTTLENECK-INDUCED DEMAND-PULL INFLATION

In these two decades of Indian economic history, an inflationary demand did not lead first to the full employment of the economy before creating general inflation, but increased the economic activity until the achievement of 'effective' full employment determined by the availability of foodgrains at much less than full employment capacity; almost the whole of the inflationary weight of extra-exogenous demand thus concentrated on foodgrain prices. Manufactures, on the other hand, experienced cost-push inflation in the short run. However, that did not change the terms of trade in agriculturalists' favour in the long run. As the wage rates in the manufacturing sectors could not be depressed below the prevailing almost subsistence level, manufacturers had to increase their prices to compensate for it and regain their long-run viability. They were thus able to regain the lost ground during a less inflationary period. It is well worth remembering that during this whole period the economy also suffered from endemic unemployment (Prakash, 1986).

This illustration of the Indian experience makes clear the difference between ordinary demand-pull inflation and bottleneck-induced demand-pull inflation. While in the former all prices increase almost simultaneously, in the latter only the price of the bottleneck commodity increases in the short run due to inflationary pressures. The prices of other commodities in the short run increase afterwards as they are affected by cost-push inflation. However, in the long run the prices will be changed in the same way as in classical demand-pull inflation. This will coexist with unemployment as extra demand can induce only that much extra supply which can be produced by 'effective' employment, which in turn is determined by the available quantity of a bottleneck factor such as suitable land for cultivation of foodgrains. The smooth substitution along a production function and/or along indifference surfaces of the neoclassical economic theory just does not seem to work.

INTEREST COST-PUSH INFLATION IN INDIA AFTER 1975–6

The above-mentioned characteristics of Indian inflation of being foodgrain bottleneck-induced demand-pull does not seem to work after 1975–6. After that inflation has never been more than of the order of 20% or so. And, much more importantly, it seems to be led by the rise in prices of manufacturing rather than of foodgrains (the 11.6% rise in 1977–8 seems to be just a swing after a precipitate fall in foodgrain prices of two earlier years). By 1979–80, the prices of foodgrains relative to wholesale prices were at the same level as in 1956–7, or 1961–2 or 1976–7. In 1979–80 and 1980–1 inflation was led by the prices of manufactures to the extent of about 18% per annum and the rise in foodgrain prices followed, that too at a lesser rate.

From 1974–5, foodgrain prices were drifting on the low side until 1978–9. After that they were mostly administered prices. The government is continuously purchasing the cereals at support prices; there is no demand pull working on them.

However, between 1974–5 and 1978–9, when foodgrain prices drifted downwards to 88% of what they were in the peak period of 1974–5, the wholesale price index as well as that of general manufactures moved up by about 6%. This can be construed as a slow correction by manufactures after their terms of trade *vis-à-vis* agriculture had been rudely disturbed in 1974–5 by the foodgrain bottleneck-induced demand-pull inflation consequent on the war of Bangladesh's independence. However during the same period, the prices of machinery and transport equipment rose by 17%, those of metallic products by 22% and those of non-metallic mineral products by 31%. This was a new phenomenon. From 1970–1 to 1974–5 the price increases in all these groups were in concert; from then on they started to diverge sharply. By 1982–3 the prices of general manufactures had increased only by 60%, those of machinery and transport equipment by 78% and those of metallic and non-metallic mineral products by 105% and a whopping 129% respectively.

It is clear from this that the inflationary forces operating from 1974–5 onwards were acting differently on different industries. They were so weak on foodgrains that producers had to take vital support from the government to be able to maintain some sort of parity with general manufacturing after it had lost vital ground; general manufactures kept the middle ground in the inflationary league, while non-metallic mineral and metallic products had to increase their prices out of all proportion. During this period the whole of industry was running quite a bit below capacity. There was unutilised capital (capacity), unemployed labour and the economy was suffering no crucial bottlenecks like the availability of foreign exchange of foodgrains. Demand-pull inflation either in its 'general' form or 'bottleneck-induced' form is therefore ruled out, and there is no evidence that technical change affected only general manufacturing industry, making its product cheaper in comparison with heavy goods industry.

Inflation which is not demand-pull should be cost-push. Ordinarily we understand the cost-push inflation where wages have been pushed up in a partially employed economy mostly as a result of a concerted action organised by trade unions. However, no such signs were visible in India. With a large-scale reservoir of unemployed labour, the success of a concerted action of trade unions is hardly likely to be successful. Further, it is well known that a rise in wage rates will increase prices proportionately; as Keynes has taught us, the wage rate just acts as a numeraire and increases all prices proportionately.

However, if the nominal interest rate is higher than the real interest rate of the economy, there will be a cost-push inflation that will lead to a higher increase in the prices of commodities having a higher capital coefficient. With higher interest rates the costs of those industries which have proportionately more interest-paying capital will increase proportionately more. This interest-paying capital not only includes working capital, but also fixed capital on which a dividend comparable to the current interest rate has to be paid. In India the heavy goods industry (non-metallic mineral products and metallic products) are highly capital-intensive. This model of interest push cost inflation therefore fits very well. This is the only model of inflation that can explain inflation existing simultaneously with unemployment, in an economy without bottlenecks and having differential price increases with the prices of capital-intensive goods increasing at a higher rate than other prices.

Interest rates in India jumped from 8.5% during 1971–3 to about 11% during 1973–5, to higher than 13% from 1975 onwards. This increase in the nominal interest rate was intended to curtail the demand-pull inflation which arose in the wake of the war of Bangladesh's independence. It succeeded admirably in its task; the prices of 'flex-price' commodities – that are determined through demand and supply calculus, like agricultural commodities or speculative markets of land, etc. – got rid of any inflationary pressure. But the prices of 'fix-price' commodities like manufactures started having cost-push inflationary pressures.

These pressures were not uniform, as would be the case with wage-push stresses, but were more acute on capital-intensive industries.

CONCLUDING REMARKS

If the sum total of micro decisions does not fit exactly into the macro constraints of an economy, it results in inflationary pressures and/or unintended unemployment of resources, which may frustrate quite well laid micro plans; different ways of discordance will lead to different types of inflations, etc. Without understanding the nature of each such type, an action programme to correct the situation may result in the drastic aggravation of the problem and may bring about unintended difficulties. In a developing country, it will lead to a reduction in the intended rate of growth.

Several types of inflationary pressures have been illustrated by the experience of India over the last thirty years. These types are not exhaustive in any sense, yet they depict sufficient variety to be useful in diagnosing inflationary problems in general, and those of developing countries in particular.

Mathematical Appendix

Let all the commodities be fix-price commodities, and let P be the price row vector; A is the domestic input–output coefficient matrix, L is the row vector of labour input coefficients, w is the wage rate. Then, we may write the price equation of fix-price commodities as follows:

$$P^{t+1} = P^t (A + r^t B) + W^t L + r^t K + f^t M \qquad (A11.1)$$

Here r is the interest rate, B is the matrix of stocks that are revalued with price changes and K is the row vector of capital at charge which is not subject to revaluation. Thus B will include all the working capital and that portion of fixed capital that is yearly revalued via some system of inflation accounting, while K will include that fixed capital which is not so revalued. M is the vector of imported inputs and f the price of currency in which imported inputs are designated.

If the economy has no cost-push pressure, the prices of $(t + 1)$th period would be equal to the prices of the tth period.

$$P = P^{t+1} = P^t = P(A+r B) + wL + r k + fM \qquad (A11.2)$$

w will be the wage rate, r will be the natural real interest rate, and P is equilibrium price structure. The solution of the above will be

$$P = \{wL+rK+fM\} * [I-A-rB]^{-1} \qquad (A11.3)$$

If K and M are zero – that is, if all capital is revalued with price changes, and there are no imported inputs – then from equation (A11.3) P will be proportional to w. Thus if w is increased to w' it will proportionately increase every price by the factor w'/w.

Let interest rate be increased to $r + r'$, then the cost of production will become.

$$P (A + rB) + r'PB + wL + rK + r'K + fM$$

$$= P + r'PB + r'K \qquad (A11.4)$$

This should be the equal of P^{t+1}. Thus not only will P^{t+1} be greater than P, but the increase in the prices of the hth commodity will be greater than the ith, if the value of capital required per unit of output is greater for the hth commodity than the ith. This shows that when the nominal interest rate is more than the natural interest rate, there will be the cost-push inflation and the commodity having higher capital at charge per unit of output will experience a higher increase in price than the one having a lower amount of capital at charge. *The inflation thus produced will not be neutral.*

The existence of capital K which is not adjusted to price changes will of course moderate the inflationary pressures, but at the same time the firm will not be covering its real cost but will in reality be eating into its capital base. Sometimes the money illusion works, to the cost of sophisticated accountants and financial managers.

Part V
The Microeconomics of Developing Countries

Part V
The Microeconomics of
Developing Countries

12 The Role of Scarcity Value and Market Price

ECONOMICS AS A RELATIONSHIP BETWEEN ENDS AND SCARCE MEANS

Economics has been defined as 'A study of human behaviour as a relationship between ends and scarce means which have alternative uses' (Robbins, 1935). Human wants are more or less unsatiable; with scarce resources they cannot be fully satisfied. As resources have alternative uses, they can be used to satisfy different wants, or combinations of them. The possibility and repercussions of this choice is the subject matter of economics. The choice is optimised by choosing various commodities that can be produced from the available resources in such a way that no other combination of commodities that is also feasible is preferred to the one chosen.

The resources that are necessary for production, and determine its extent, are called 'factors of production'. Traditionally, they are classified in the three categories of Labour, Land and Capital. Each of these categories may contain various non-substitutable factors of production; for instance, there may be a quality of land suitable for production of rice on which wheat cannot be produced. These two types of land are then in effect two factors of production; the availability of one does not help in the production of the commodity for which only the other is suitable. Similarly, there can be a skill necessary for the production of a commodity which may not be substitutable by any other kind of labour; the labour possessing that skill is then really a separate factor of production, at least in the short run, until the other labour can be trained in the required skill. Examples of this specificity among capital goods can similarly be found.

Apart from these three well recognised categories, other resources can limit production. For instance, in a country having no fossil fuel as a natural resource the availability of trading conditions that will allow it to import the necessary fuel may determine the extent of production in the country, and thus the standard of living of its people; in such a case foreign exchange may be considered as a factor of production.

These factors of production are in the control of different persons or legal entities; in a free society, labour power is in the control of the labourer himself, he (or she) can freely hire his labour power to anybody he pleases. Mostly, he will hire it to the highest bidder, but considerations of stability or tradition may induce him to hire it to a reasonable bidder though that bid may not be the highest one. In a slave owning society, however, the labour power of the slave is in the control of the slave owner; it is the slave owner who decides where the labour power of the slave is to be used. Similarly, if land is in the control of the land owner, he decides to whom he will rent out the land, and at what rent. The owner of capital decides the use of his capital goods, etc. etc. As regards foreign exchange, it is the exporter who gets it in exchange for his commodities, and it is his prerogative to decide the manner of its disposal. Of course in all these activities, the state may intervene. The state's function may be merely regulatory; at the other extreme the state may completely take over the function of the private owners of these factors of production.

VALUE OF SCARCE MEANS AND GENERAL EQUILIBRIUM SYSTEM

Every resource or factor of production is valued according to its scarcity in relation to its demand for production purposes. The income of the owner of a resource is the product of its price and its quantity owned by him. If he possesses more than one resource, his total income will be the sum of his income from each of them. A person purchases different goods and services in accordance with his income; the cost of production of these goods and services is the sum of the amount that has to be paid to purchase the amount of the factors of production directly or indirectly required to produce them. If profit is taken as the amount required to purchase the expertise of the person controlling the enterprise, this expertise may be considered as another factor of production. The price of these goods and services will then be equal to the cost thus defined; if every income receiver completely exhausts his income in purchase of goods and services, total income will be equal to the total value of the goods and services produced. The price system ensures that resources are used for producing such commodities and in such quantities that the income receivers are prepared to pay the price for those commodities equivalent to the amount to be paid to their factors of production, and the commodities will be produced in the quantities in which they are demanded at such a price by those income receivers. These income receivers, in their turn, demand various commodities and services in such quantities as to optimise their economic welfare from the income of the resources under their command. In this way, the economic process ensures that scarce resources are used to satisfy the most effective wants of the resources' owners. In this determination, every person has a say proportional to the amount of the value of resources held.

Several preconditions must be satisfied for the smooth running of this system. The most obvious one is that all the income earned by the various owners of the factors of production should be spent on the purchase of commodities and services produced by their help. This is called Say's law; it was commonly supposed to be always satisfied by neoclassical economists, until Lord Keynes demonstrated that in the short run there was no necessity for it to be fulfilled. When people save in non-commodity terms – in terms of monetary units – and the corresponding investment in the economy is not forthcoming, there will be production for which there will be no demand at a price equal to its cost of production; this deficiency of demand will lead to unemployment.

Similarly, the resulting economic order has to be politically accept-able, otherwise it will create frictions hampering its smooth oper-ation. Even when it is functioning smoothly, it does not imply that the equilibrium thus attained is desirable; there may be an economic equilibrium coexisting with economic stagnation – not only there is no mechanism ensuring optimum growth, there is nothing to suggest that there will be any economic growth at all.

NON-SCARCE FACTORS OF PRODUCTION AND THE DIFFERENCE BETWEEN SCARCITY VALUE AND PRICE

It is clear that if any factor of production did not remain scarce, its 'scarcity value' would be zero; if something is not scarce, it is available without being fully used. An extra amount of that factor can then be used without reducing the production of any commodity that was being produced previously. If extra output of a commodity is produced by using only that resource, its cost to the community is nil and so its 'scarcity value' should also be zero. Thus resources like wind and water may be free in many rural societies. To an individual, his extra labour, after doing his factory or office duties may also be free. In such a case, 'do it yourself' products are cheaper as the direct labour involved in producing them has zero value.

However, a zero 'scarcity value' does not imply that a resource will have a zero market price; in an economy with surplus labour, there will be unemployment. This implies that the 'scarcity value' of labour is zero. However, it is not possible to employ extra persons in the economy without payment; the wage rate does not fall to zero in such an economy. A labourer must be paid a minimum amount to sustain himself; classical writers called such a wage the 'subsistence wage'. We are not sure how this is exactly determined. Nutritionists think that an unemployed labourer requires much less food to stay alive, but when he is working, he must have sufficient wage to be able to feed himself and his family. As an empirical fact one finds that even in the poorest parts of India or Africa you cannot get a labourer for less than the prevalent minimum rate in the area, even when there is large-scale unemployment. (For instance, see Seckler in Sukhatme, 1982: 140). These wage rates are found to be automatically adjusted during inflationary periods. If some wage rate or prices are higher than is economically warranted, inflationary periods give an opportunity to the market to correct them. This is achieved by such rates not increasing with the general rise in the nominal prices; the movement of these wage rates with inflation, even in a chronic unemployment situation, shows that their level is not a quirk but is determined in accordance with some underlying reality, which economists can ignore only at the cost of making their analysis irrelevant in practice.

Similarly, if a particular capital resource is unemployed (i.e. idle), the extra production made possible by its help has a zero cost of capital as far as the total economy is concerned; the marginal social value of capital is zero, and so is its scarcity value. Even then, its owners may require positive returns for its use. During a period of under-utilisation of capital, returns on that factor again do not necessarily become zero.

These wage costs or capital costs are reflected in the price of the commodity they help to produce. However, they are not real costs to the economy. As we have seen above, the scarcity value of the marginal labourer's produce – the labour's 'shadow price' and/or the price of marginal capital – is zero when he is unemployed. The resulting price system does not then represent the scarcity value of the commodities to the economy. *The scarcity value of a commodity is that given by the sum of the scarcity values of all the factors of production directly or indirectly used up in producing the particular commodity. While the price is the sum of the total payments made to those factors of production, whether they were scarce or not, whether their price represent their scarcity value or not.* A wedge thus develops between value and price.

THE CLASSICAL EQUIVALENCE OF VALUE AND PRICE

Classical economists like the Physiocrats, Adam Smith, and Ricardo did not distinguish between value and price. For them the scarce resource in the economy was land; income was determined by the number of workers used to produce output and they were paid at subsistence level, while the land resource was determined by the amount brought into cultivation by land lords. Wages higher than subsistence level were not contemplated in times of chronic unemployment. The simple nature of the economy also limited the idea of 'capital' to working capital, which was primarily made up of advances of wages to labour to sustain it in the period of production. Labourers purchased the goods required for their subsistence, and these goods were primarily the product of land. Ricardo, in fact, represented them by just corn. The total amount of such goods depended upon the land available for cultivation; as labourers had to be given their means of subsistence before the output of their toil was put on the market, there had to be sufficient goods available in the economy for this purpose. The stock of these goods was termed the 'wage fund'. The number of labourers that could be employed depended on this wage fund; this theory of employment was therefore designated the Wage Fund Theory. For most production, the only cost was the cost of employing labour, which meant not only the wages paid to them but also the interest paid on the wage fund 'stocked up' to provide real wages prior to production. This total cost was proportional to the labour hours used in the process of production; hence we get the celebrated Labour Theory of Value. In fact in the classical system the scarcity value of labour was zero, and therefore the cost of production determined by the payment of wages should have been the Labour Theory of Prices and the Land Theory of Value, as land was the scarce factor constraining production in the economy. However, in this particular case the two were proportional; the land theory of value therefore gave identical results to the labour theory of prices for the relative value or price system.

Suppose commodity 1 is produced by a amount of labour and commodity 2 by b amount of labour, and that is the only cost of production; then the price of commodity 1 in terms of the commodity 2 will be a/b. Further suppose that to maintain 1 unit of labour produce of k hectares of land is required; then to maintain labour sufficient to produce 1 unit of commodity 1 the produce of ka hectares of land will be necessary. Similarly, to maintain labour sufficient to produce 1 unit of commodity 2 kb hectares of land will be required. As land is the scarce factor, the proportionate amount of land indirectly embodied in the two commodities will determine their relative values. The value of the first commodity in terms of the second commodity will thus be $ka/kb = a/b$, the same as the price ratio. In this simplified case the labour theory of prices is identical to the land theory of value. Because the land theory of value was designated as the labour theory of value, considerable confusion in the subsequent discussion of value and price theories was created.

Under these simple circumstances, the situation is not changed even if the economy is organised on capitalistic principles – that is, charging an interest rate on stocks and a profit mark up on production. This is because there is no fixed capital and the working capital for production is only the advances of wage goods given to labour before output is forthcoming. If the rate of interest is r then the total interest in the production of commodity 1 one will be rka hectares' worth of produce and in the production of commodity 2 rkb hectares' worth of output. Further, let the profit rate be m times the cost of production. The price of commodity 1 in terms of the commodity 2 will be

$$[(1+m)\ (1+r)ka]\ /\ [(1+m)(1+r)kb] = a/b$$

which is the same as given by the labour theory of value.

A difficulty arises as soon as fixed capital is introduced. These capital goods are not generally in proportion to the direct labour employed in producing the individual commodities, therefore the cost of production for different commodities will be different in proportion to their labour costs. Let the fixed capital goods themselves be produced without the aid of further fixed capital; then their cost can be stated in terms of the amount of land they have directly or indirectly used up. Let this be c and d hectares for the fixed capital required to produce one unit of commodity 4 and 2 respectively. Then the relative price of the two commodities will be

$$[(1+m)\{(1+r)ka + sc\}] / [(1+m)\{(1+r)kb + sd\}]$$

where s is the service rate – that is, interest and depreciation rates combined on the fixed capital. This price ratio will not only be different from the ratio of the direct labour cost (a/b), but will also change with the changes in the value of the service rate s. We thus see that the rate of interest enters into the formation of relative prices.

THE NEOCLASSICAL EQUALITY OF SCARCITY VALUE AND PRICE AND ITS PRACTICAL FUTILITY

The scarcity value ratio of two commodities turns into the ratio of opportunity costs of producing two commodities when more than one factor of production is the constraint to production. The neoclassical paradigm of economics assumes complete utilisation of all factors of production; this absence of unemployment of any factor of production is achieved by the further assumption that the techniques of production change in such a way as to lead to the complete utilisation of all the factors of production. With the assumptions of perfect competition, full employment of all the factors of production, maximisation of profits and utility on well behaved smooth and continuous functions, together with no economies of scale in the production of any commodity, it can be shown that price ratios will be the same as the opportunity cost ratios (for an early formulation, see Haberler, 1936).

This neoclassical result may be applicable to an economy in a stationary state, which has time to adjust itself to an unchanging economic environment. Even if there is sufficient inducement, the adjustment of techniques of production to and in consonance with the availability of various factors of production takes time. To obtain these results, we have to be sure that the relative availability of different factors of production will not change in the meantime. Smooth production functions and smooth utility surfaces are gross simplifications, and so are perfect competition and non-increasing returns to scale that will ensure the absence of monopolies. The price signals that are supposed to drive the economy to this solution would work if the price structure were the same as the scarcity value structure to begin with. If not, the price system will give wrong signals, and there will be no incentive to change the technology in the directions assumed by neoclassical paradigm. For instance, in an unemployment situation, if the wage rate is zero, there is an incentive to employ as much labour as possible until all are employed and the wage rate becomes positive. However, starting from a position of unemployment, but with a positive wage rate, there is no incentive to change the technology towards achieving full employment even in the long run.

In the short run we can thus expect a divergence in the structures of opportunity costs or scarcity values and price structures. The price structure will of course guide the consumption pattern, but for many economy-wide decisions it is the opportunity cost that is more relevant. As it happens, in many cases it is a single bottleneck that is facing the economy at a particular time; then the simple 'scarcity value' calculations may be really helpful. Such conditions arise more frequently in the case of developing economies, where a wrong decision may cost dearly indeed since, being under-developed, they are much less resilient.

The concept of scarcity value is general and can be used when any constraint limits an economy. Paucity of capital will give rise to a capital theory of value, which will be more relevant to many developing countries where development is constrained by its non-availability. When foreign exchange is a bottleneck, the relevant theory will be a foreign exchange theory of value. Where labour is in short supply, we shall have a 'real' labour theory of value. The theory of value applicable for a country can change over time, as different factors of production in turn become constraints to growth. A country finding capital as the main bottleneck at one time may soon discover that its constraint has changed to foreign exchange, and when that is remedied it may be land or labour that is constraining the economy. In these different situations, different theories of scarcity value may be necessary for decision-taxers. The price system does not lead us in that direction as it does not reflect the opportunity costs in the economy. Even decisions about changing technologies towards better utilisation of all factors of production will thus not be guided by prevailing prices; only scarcity values will be able to quantify the opportunity cost of adopting such transformations.

DIFFERENCES BETWEEN SCARCITY VALUES AND PRICES AS A RATIONALE OF COMMODITY TAXES AND SUBSIDIES

We have seen above that prices are ones found in the market place, while relative scarcity values give the extent of the possible substitution of one commodity for another in the economy because of limited availability of some factor of production. Individuals in general can take decisions only on the basis of prices; they have no means of knowing scarcity values. Only state or similar bodies can calculate scarcity values and use them for their decision purposes. In a simple economy, with no fixed capital or complications of indirect factor demand, scarcity value calculations can be decentralised in a simple labour theory of value. (Indirect factor demands are those that come through the consumption of intermediate goods; they can be easily calculated if the production technique is sequential. However, when production of commodities is interdependent, the calculation of indirect factor demand requires a huge data base and sophisticated mathematical analytical techniques.) With the modern complicated, interdependent economy, the calculation of scarcity values is a job far beyond the capacity of individuals.

This gives a neat criterion distinguishing the sphere of public and private decision-making. The economic decisions that may best be taken on the basis of prevailing prices may be left to individuals, firms or similar bodies at the decentralised level. Decisions that require a knowledge of appropriate scarcity values may best be taken by a centralised body, which can not only collect and analyse the necessary information, but can also integrate it with its decision-making process.

It is not necessary that all activities for which decisions must be taken through scarcity value considerations should be undertaken by the central body itself; institutional or efficiency reasons may dictate a different course. In such cases there may either be a central directive or, better still, a subsidy and tax system that will so adjust the market prices of commodities that they may approximate to scarcity values. Thus for commodities having lower scarcity values than prices there may be commodity subsidies to correct the difference, and in the opposite case commodity taxes may be used to correct the indicative function of prices. Thus in a country having heavy unemployment, labour-intensive techniques may be subsidised. Regional grants may similarly tend to adjust the difference between price and scarcity values. This explicit formulation not only gives us an economic, as distinct from a social or political, rationale, but also provides us with a mathematical method of calculating the right amount of production taxes or subsidies different production processes, etc. should attract. This will also be a check on the distortions in tax or subsidies rates brought about by the actions of various interest groups or lobbies, whose submissions are at present the only guide for the authorities.

These may be distinguished from consumption taxes or subsidies, which are primarily intended to affect the quantity of various commodities consumed. We refer here to 'production' taxes and subsidies – production agents will be faced by a price system that indicates the relative scarcities of various factors of production in an economy.

SOME USES OF DIFFERENCES BETWEEN VALUE AND PRICE IN ECONOMIC POLICY

As pointed out above, there are many economic decisions where a distinction has to be made between sound economic analysis and decision-making. Below we give a few illustrations where this distinction has been or can be used; these are purely illustrative examples, and should not be regarded as exhaustive.

Division Between Consumption and Investment

The first analytical use of this distinction can be gleaned from Marx's analysis of investment and consumption. In his time, labour was abundant, in fact he speaks of a large army of unemployed labour ensuring that wage rates were kept at the subsistence level. The only constraining factor in his system was the availability of land, which limited the stock of the wage fund; this in its turn limited the number of labourers that could be employed in the economy. In accumulating capital, one extra person employed in the production of 'investment goods' would imply that one less person was employed in the production of 'consumption goods'. Under these conditions, the value of these two bundles of goods would be equal. Thus we have a *supply side* condition that the value of investment should be equal to the value of saving achieved in consumption. This is different from the *demand side* condition that the total cost of investment should be equal to the total savings in monetary terms. While in the former the individual items of the commodities used in the investment process and of the items whose consumption was given up because of the saving decisions should be equal in 'value' units; while in the latter they should be equal in 'price' units. The demand condition is necessary for the stability of the price system, while the supply condition is necessary to ensure the feasibility of planned investment.

Indian Planning Experience

Illustrations of these difficulties can be gleaned from the planning experiences of different developing countries in the post-1945 period. India's Five Year Plans, for instance, did not take account of this supply-side condition of investment planning. The bottleneck to employment there, as in most of the developing countries, was the availability of foodgrains. The two aims of planning were the maximising of the long-run growth rate of the economy, and the maximisation of employment in the country. The first aim was envisaged to be achieved by the establishment of heavy industry and the undertaking of comprehensive village development programmes, mainly to expand the agricultural sector. To achieve the second aim many consumer goods were reserved for handloom and village industries sectors. These in their turn should have rehabilitated the old traditional industries of India, giving employment to the millions of largely destitute workers in these traditional industries. The limitation of the amount of the foodgrains available in India was not taken into account, and this neglect of the supply condition resulted not only in the doubling of foodgrain prices during the five years of the second Five Year Plan, but also in the relative impoverishment of the newly created employed as well as of those who were previously enjoying the advantage of having gainful employment. The reduction in the availability of foodgrains in the urban areas would have created a major catastrophe but for the timely availability of US food aid; this enabled the government to supply foodgrains to the urban areas on a rationed basis and even then, the physical targets of the plan had to be substantially cut, having recourse to the subterfuge of fulfilling the plan in nominal terms, which of course were much smaller in real terms due to the intervening inflation.

Early Planning in the Soviet Union

The first Marxist government hardly appreciated the Marxist law of value. Instead of using it for the purpose intended, it tried unsuccessfully to mould prices in its shape. Euphoria for rapid industrialisation after the revolution, in a food-constrained economy, led to similar results as in the Indian case described above. The consequent drying up of the supply of foodgrains from the rural to urban areas is well documented; it resulted in two drastic consequences. First, Lenin's famous New Economic Policy (NEP) virtually abandoned the experiment of socialisation of agriculture. Second, the party's realisation that to achieve its economic objectives it could not rely on economic laws but had to use force on its own proletariat. This evolved into a 'dictatorship of the proletariat' – euphemism for a command economy. The ensuing planning exercise was not merely planning of government development activities, as in India, but a wholesale direction of economic activities in detail by a powerful bureaucracy; the whole character of communism changed as a consequence, and the human cost in dictatorial excesses and loss of human freedom is well known.

Sub-Saharan Africa

In the Sub-Saharan economy during the post-1945 period the major bottleneck has been the availability of labour. In the fervour of industrialisation and urbanisation, labour was withdrawn from agriculture; within agriculture also it was transferred from production of staple food crops to export crops. Productivity in the food crop production could hardly be increased, as it required heavy infrastructural investment; if anything, it decreased as increasing population rose and less productive land had to be cultivated with traditional techniques of foodgrain production. Between 1960 and 1979 the labour force in industry increased from 7 to 12%. The percentage of urban to total population increased from 11 to about 21%; that in agriculture decreased from 81 to 71% (World Bank, 1981: 178–9). Food production in the 1960s increased approximately at the same rate as rural population. In the 1970s the per capita food production fell by 9%; labour productivity in food production stagnated in the 1960s and fell in 1970s (World Bank, 1981: 46–7, 143). This implied that quite a few urban–industrial complexes had to be fed through imported food, and rural areas were subject to large-scale recurring famines.

The scarcity value in Sub-Saharan Africa had to thus be determined via a 'real' labour theory of value, and the implementation of industrialisation and development of the export industries should have been calculated on the possible savings of labour from food-producing agriculture. Instead, a calculation made through prevalent prices and availability of local and foreign savings led to a drastic supply-side imbalance. The neglect of the supply side determined through the value calculus has been partly responsible for throwing the sub-continent into its present horrific state, leading to untold human suffering and hardly any economic growth.

Oil-rich Labour-short Countries

The labour theory of scarcity value is also applicable in the oil-rich Middle Eastern countries. Their investment opportunities seem to be mainly limited by the availability of labour. The use of foreign labour for the purpose is creating a specialisation of labour on ethnic lines; this may make the economic functioning of the society crucially dependant on immigrant labour and create a sort of caste system or two tiers of citizenship in these countries. A labour theory would be able to give direction to the right division in investment and consumption activities for each desired level, or the mix of local and foreign labour in the population.

Latin American Development

Most Latin American development was an appendage first primarily to European economies and then to North American ones. The outcome of this process was that they hardly developed any production processes that did not use imported inputs, either directly or indirectly. When, in the post-1945 period, they consciously embarked on an economic development process, the constraining factor was foreign exchange; they were then operating within the foreign exchange scarcity theory of value. This supply-side value calculus was not integrated into their planning process; this resulted in astronomical rates of inflation in the 1960s, and much lower economic performance than that planned. In the 1980s, when the crunch came with the collapse of commodity prices and a burgeoning debt problem resulted in a slump in foreign exchange availability, not only did high rates of inflation revive, but the national product as well as investments fell drastically.

Choice of Techniques of Production

There are also important implications of the scarcity of wage goods for the choice of techniques of production. The total labour force that can be employed is determined by the availability of wage goods; the total amount of goods and services produced can be optimised if the least labour-intensive technique available is used for production. This result is in sharp contrast to the one arrived at by neoclassical theory. That theory asserted that the suitable technique of production was one which employed the total labour force with a given stock of capital, without taking into account the availability (or otherwise) of wage goods. With a country having unemployment, it would recommend that the most labour-intensive technique be used; with a given amount of production the largest amount of labour could thus be employed. The scarcity value theory would assert that employment is determined by the availability of the wage goods, and not by the techniques of production used; the function of technology is then to maximise the output for the given amount of labour, hence a need for the least labour-intensive technique of production.

Capital Theory of Value

It is a commonplace to say that developing countries require capital accumulation. If the labour force is employed using traditional techniques of production, the problem may be considered as that of the accumulation of the capital relating to the modern techniques of production. The earlier that the equipment necessary to employ that labour on modern techniques of production is accumulated, the earlier the country will become a developed country using modern techniques for all its production activities. In such cases, capital is the scarce factor of production. To take economic decisions regarding that, we require a capital theory of value – that is, a value system representing the scarcity value of capital. In most cases, when the economic situation over several periods is being considered, the bringing of the new land under cultivation or improving that currently available may be subsumed under capital creation activities.

In the post-1945 development literature, the concept of the 'capital–output ratio' was used to meet this situation. It was maintained that as the shadow price of labour was zero, the profitability of an investment project to the economy was given by the capital–output ratio rather than by the ordinary profitability ratios which guide the activities of private investors. So one function of the planning authorities was to rank competing projects in the order of their capital–output ratios; projects were then selected on the basis of having a lower capital output–ratio. It was, of course, not the only criterion of project selection; but once the desirable profile has been determined by the central planning body, detailed selection at the lower level was guided by this criterion (see, for instance, the literature associated with India's second Five Year Plan).

This approach was conceptually a hybrid. While making decisions on individual projects, the shadow price of labour was taken to be zero, but both output as well as capital was valued at the prevailing prices; it was not realised that this assumption would completely change the value calculus of the concerned variables. This logic directly leads to the capital theory of value.

Once a capital theory of value is adopted, the capital–output ratio of all the modern techniques of production will be the same. This condition alone will give a unique value system and that value system may be called capital theory of value. This system will help to weed out non-optimal techniques of production. As any technique of production, if revalued according to a capital theory of value, is not able to show the common capital–output ratio, it will show itself to be non-optimal. This will be a great help in decentralising planning decisions; the central authorities have only to give the shadow prices of commodities according to the capital theory of value, and leave the decisions of detailed technical choice to the men on the spot. However, it does not help in deciding which commodities to produce, which must be decided with reference to overall needs and balance.[1]

13 Implications of Adopting Modern Technology

INTRODUCTION

Economic development is basically the transformation of human and animal energy-based production processes into mechanical power and chemical-based production techniques. The countries which have successfully made this transformation in all the spheres of economic activities are classified as the 'developed countries'. This transformation has been the result of the advancement of scientific knowledge and know-how and its application to everyday economic life. However, it would not have been possible to realise this in practice if there had not been favourable international economic environments for its successful implementation. The colonial and imperial past of the last four centuries, as we have seen, played an important role in creating such favourable international environments for the present-day developed countries. But such international environments cannot be recreated for the present-day developing countries; we must therefore examine whether the present international economic structure can be conducive to transforming traditional techniques of production to modern ones in a developing country. If the answer is in negative, we must then look for the policy options that will make it feasible. Below we shall discuss the economic problems attending this proposed transformation; we shall discuss this separately for agriculture and for industry, because in the former the successful adoption of a modern high-productivity technology of production depends on bio-economic factors conditioned by the crop–soil–climate complex of the region, while in the latter it is primarily the transfer of electro-mechanical technology that is involved.

METHODS OF INCREASING AGRICULTURAL PRODUCTIVITY

Water Inputs

After the establishment of cultivated agriculture about 13,000 years ago, the first major effort of increasing productivity undertaken by human beings was the development of artificial irrigation systems. That gave rise to the first civilisations of the world in the Nile, Tigris–Euphrates and Indus Valleys; they have been termed as 'hydraulic civilisations' by Wittfogal (1956 among others) who derives their socio-political management system from this basic innovation. It is a sad fact of history that when Greeks conquered Iraq in the early centuries BC, they could not keep up the intricate irrigation system nurtured by ancient monarchs for about 4,000 years; this was due not only to their technological ignorance but also to their unwillingness to sink the resources required for its upkeep. Probably they were ignorant also of the long-run consequences of their inaction and so were indirectly responsible for the desertification and waterlogging of large tracts of land, decimating in turn a large proportion of the population that could not be any longer supported by the reduced food supply (Toynbee, 1934–54).

This clearly illustrates the high level of organisational and investment resources required to undertake and maintain irrigation works, even in ancient times. The World Bank study *Accelerated Development in Sub-Saharan Africa* (1981) observes,

> In spite of considerable investment in irrigation development, total cultivated areas hardly increased in a number of countries . . . Additions to the developed area were offset by others that had to be abandoned and require rehabilitation . . . In Sudan, extensive restoration is now being prepared in the White and Blue Nile pump scheme areas . . . Macroeconomic problems leading to a lack of foreign exchange, and hence of spare parts, fuel, and machinery, have been an additional contributing factor (World Bank, 1981: 76–7).

This clearly illustrates that not only the creation of an irrigation project but also their maintenance requires expertise and foreign exchange until the country becomes a developed one.

Irrigation can use either underground water or surface water from rivers or lakes. Early irrigation systems mainly relied on surface water, that could be either captured during the rainy season or tapped from natural sources; using underground water requires more energy, since the water must be lifted. When water is abundant, flooding of the land can be carried out, and crops like rice grown. For row crops (corn, potatoes, vegetables, etc.) the practice of furrow irrigation is commonly used. With the advent of cheap energy, many farmers began pumping water from underground and distributing it through sprinkler systems, an energy-intensive method.

Irrigation often also holds the key to cropping intensity. Where temperature permits year-round cropping, irrigation permits two or three crops per year; an assured water supply permits the use of better seeds, which have high responsiveness to fertiliser applications. However, it takes a great deal of capital to irrigate extra land, and the cost per hectare of future expansion will rise since the least costly sites will have largely been developed already.

In Sudan, due to special natural conditions and the effect of the existing large infrastructure, new areas can be developed at costs in the $5,000–$10,000 range, but generally the costs are much higher. Recent projects in Niger, Mauritania, and Northern Nigeria have all cost more than $10,000 per hectare in 1980 prices, some even more than $20,000 per hectare. Even assuming efficient production, a ton of rice produced in a modern irrigation scheme developed at $10,000 per hectare is estimated to cost not less than $600 per ton. But imported high-quality rice cost $400–$500 per ton in coastal countries of Africa in 1980; the kind of rice ('brokens') imported in Senegal, Gambia, and Mauritania – the largest rice-consuming areas in Africa outside of Madagascar – is 40% cheaper. Thus unless consumer prices of wheat and rice are raised by a very substantial margin, production has to be subsidised. Indeed these subsidies might easily surpass debt service for the irrigation infrastructure. Raising domestic consumer prices of cereals to the projected cost of locally produced substitutes will thus be indispensable if such schemes are not to lead to permanent large subsidies (World Bank, 1981).

The extended quotation from the World Bank Report above clearly illustrates why irrigated land is hardly used for food crops in Africa, which seems to be mainly devoted to export crops like cotton and sugar. However, the World Bank study, in recommending the raising of the domestic price by a very substantial margin, does not stop to ask how this will affect the wages of labour working in export industries – and thus the availability of the foreign exchange to service the enormous debt incurred in the process of making the African countries self-sufficient in food.

Chemical Inputs

Fertilisers have become one of the major means of raising agricultural productivity. It is estimated that a billion and a half people are now fed with the additional food produced with chemical fertilisers. However their use varies greatly in different countries. In 1985, their use in industrial market economies was reported to be 1,164 hundred grams of plant nutrient per hectare of arable land, the corresponding figure for Sub-Saharan Africa being only 91 hundred grams. Among developing countries themselves it is as high as 3,473 hundred grams for Egypt and only 10 hundred grams per hectare of arable land for Zaire (World Bank, 1988: 234). Per hectare, agricultural production almost follows the same pattern. Its index was 391 for Egypt and only 65 for Zaire in 1980, taking the land productivity of USA as 100. (FAO, 1986). It may be noted that though the US agriculturalists' productivity is among the highest in the world, the same cannot be said about its productivity per hectare.

Country averages of fertiliser use indicate average demand only. Fertiliser use is often concentrated in certain regions and on certain crops; in developing countries it is mostly export crops like cotton, sugar, etc. or plantations like coffee that get the lion's share of fertilisers and other chemical inputs. It is their price relationship with that of the price of fertilisers, etc. that mostly ensures for them the best returns on fertiliser costs as well as on the cost of irrigation projects.

The effect of fertiliser use on yields and economic returns varies considerably with the amounts applied – depending, of course, upon soil, water and climate conditions, crop variety, and other similar factors. But basically the increases in yield follows the law of diminishing returns: the initial quantities of fertiliser normally produce a generous additional yield; on the application of additional quantities, the yield continues to rise but at a diminishing rate. On reaching high rates of application the yield increases more and more slowly, and eventually begins to decrease.

The farmer, of course, should not be concerned with the highest yield that can be obtained, but with the highest economic returns that he can obtain. The economic benefits of fertiliser use can be expressed as net returns – that is, when the additional cost is deducted from the value of the additional yield obtained by its use. The 'additional cost' is not only the cost of the fertilisers applied, but also that of pesticides and other purchased inputs that are a necessary accompaniment, and the cost of extra labour that may be required in other extra agricultural operations like weeding. With fertiliser inputs, weeds will also grow more vigorously and weeding may have to be done with more frequency and efficiency. Apart from all these extra operational costs there will be the cost of extra risk of production and marketing.

A rough but easily understood and useful measure for practical purposes is the 'value-cost ratio'. This is the value of the additional yield divided by the additional cost of the fertiliser. However, what value of this will be sufficient to induce farmers to undertake the use of fertilisers in a particular situation will have to be determined empirically; because this takes account of the major easily observable variables and other determining factors it leaves the farmers' behaviour to be inferred. For instance, a higher value–cost ratio may be required to induce farmers to use fertilisers in situation where the labour cost is higher and the risks are greater than where labour is cheap and the risks are covered. Trials in a number of countries have shown that value–cost ratios from 3 to 5 are common. A ratio of 2 to 2.5 seems to be minimum to attract farmers in developing countries to fertiliser use (Wierer and Abbot, 1978: 7).

DIMINISHING RETURNS TO FERTILISER USE

Net returns and value–cost ratios vary with the rate of fertiliser application. This is illustrated in Figure 13.1 below. In this output of the crop is measured on the Y axes while the X axis measures the amount of fertilisers applied per hectare. The curve OAB gives the yield of the crop per hectare for different doses of fertilisers. The line OC gives the ratio of the cost of fertilisers and their accompaniments to the price of the commodity produced. Let the line DF be parallel to OC touching the curve OAB at the point P. Let PQ be the line parallel to the Y axis touching the X axis at Q. Then the value of the incremental output of the commodity will be greater than the incremental cost of the fertiliser application until the rate of fertiliser application is given by a point between O and Q. If that point is beyond Q, the marginal cost of fertiliser application will be more

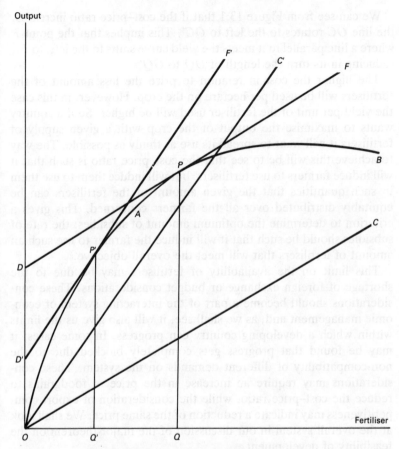

Figure 13.1 Net returns on fertilisers

than the marginal increase in the value of the product. The largest profit to the farmer will thus be when he uses *OQ* amounts of fertilisers on his crop; that will give him the largest net return on his piece of land.

From this figure, value–cost ratios can be easily derived. It will be seen that a higher value–cost ratio does not mean higher net return; the value–cost ratio is therefore not a measure to guide the farmer in determining the rate of fertiliser application, it gives only the lower limit at which a farmer can be induced to use fertilisers and thus gives a guide to the policy-maker. It is a rough measure, which can give an idea whether a farmer will apply fertiliser to a crop at all and can also tell that, given limited supply of fertiliser, the crops to which he will apply it.

We can see from Figure 13.1 that if the cost–price ratio increases, the line OC rotates to the left to OC'. This implies that the point P where a line parallel to it meets the yield curve shifts to the left, to P', reducing in its turn the length of OQ to OQ'.

The higher the cost in relation to price the less amount of the fertilisers will be used per hectare on the crop. However, in this case the yield per unit of the fertiliser used will be higher. So if a country wants to maximise the output of the crop with a given supply of fertilisers it will want to spread its use as thinly as possible. The way to achieve this will be to see that the cost–price ratio is such that it will induce farmers to use fertilisers, but will induce them to use them in such quantities that the given amount of the fertilisers can be equitably distributed over all the farmers concerned. This gives a criterion to determine the optimum amount of subsidies: the rate of subsidies should be such that it will induce the farmer to use such an amount of fertilisers that will meet the overall objective.

This limit on the availability of fertilisers may be due to the shortage of foreign exchange or budget considerations. These considerations should become a part of the interacting system of economic management and, as we shall see, it will also give us the limits within which a developing country can progress. In some cases, it may be found that progress gets completely blocked due to the non-compatibility of different demands on the system. These considerations may require an increase in the price of foodgrains to reduce the cost–price ratio, while the consideration of export competitiveness may indicate a reduction of the same price. We shall look at the overall system in our discussion of the major theorem on the feasibility of development.

Though the yield response function given in Figure 13.1 will be different in differing soil, climate and irrigation conditions, it may nevertheless be interesting to note the ratio of cereal price to that of fertilisers maintained in some countries. In United States, in early 1970s only 1.6 tons of wheat was required to buy a ton of nitrogen fertiliser (Brown, (1985): 33). In India, the ratio of the urea-based nitrogen price to the minimum support price of wheat has been calculated by Desai (1986: 257) as between 2.69 and 3.65 in the years 1977 to 1985. The same ratio for paddy varies from 3.32 to 4.44. In 1964–5 the cost of a ton of nitrogen in terms of paddy was 0.9 tons in Japan, 2.1 tons in Sri Lanka, 2.7 tons in the Republic of Korea, 4.4 in Taiwan, 4.5 tons in Philippines, and as high as 5.6 and 9.7 in Thailand and Burma. In Taiwan, Thailand and Burma, due to a remarkable suitability of the soil for rice cultivation, the government is able to earn revenue by administering these high ratios. Japan and Sri Lanka, on the other hand, subsidised the final consumers directly. Their farm price of rice was respectively 1.43 and 3 times the retail price in 1964–65. (Barker, 1977: 417). In Egypt, the consumer price for wheat was only 35% of the producer price in 1984 (Genazzini and Horhager, 1987).

FERTILISER USE IN DEVELOPING COUNTRIES

This economic law of net returns is responsible for the fact that in many developing countries, and especially in Africa, fertilisers are used mainly on cash and export crops, while they are little used on the staples for domestic consumption.

> In Senegal and Gambia more than 90% of fertilizers are used for groundnuts; in the Central African Empire almost all fertilizers are used for cotton and coffee; and in Kenya most nitrogen fertilizer is used for sugar, tea and coffee. For such staples as maize, cassava and plantains the value cost ratio is often below 2 because of the relatively lower prices for those products on the domestic markets. In the developing countries the role of ferti- lizers in the fight against hunger is still rather modest. Basic structural changes in the crop and fertilizer pricing systems seem to be required if the use of fertilizers for the production of domestic food crops is to be expanded to meet the need for larger food supplies . . . Experience in several developing countries shows that the farmer's demand for the fertilisers is highly sensitive to price changes. A 10% increase in the price of fertiliser has been found to cause an immediate reduction in demand which may be 5–10%. In the long run, if the same relative fertilizer and crop prices are maintained, the reduction may be two or three times as much (Wierer and Abbot, 1978: 10–11).

Little application of fertilisers in the production of cereal in Africa may account for the fact that in Africa between 1974–6 and 1981–3 fertiliser use per hectare has increased from 13 kg of plant nutrient to 19 kg, while the cereal yield per hectare has fallen from 1,005 kg in 1974–6 to 942 kg in 1982–84 (World Resource Institute 1986: 262, 264).

SUBSIDIES, ETC. FOR ADJUSTING PRICE RATIOS

To adjust to the desirable cost–price relationships, many countries adopt a policy of agricultural subsidies. The policy of farm support price in the United States of America, the European Community and Japan is one way of subsidising agriculture so that the output price's relation to cost may be kept at the desired level. This technique of subsidisation cannot be used by most of the developing countries as the international price of their export commodity puts an effective upper limit to the retail price of the foodgrain that can be charged. This implies that the fertilisers would not be used on food crops at the price they can be sold to the wage earners, some of whom are working in the export industries. Consequently, the governments of many developing countries have felt obliged to subsidise fertiliser use. The subsidy is often 30–50% of the would-be retail price; in extreme cases, it can be much more. While up to 75% of the price of fertiliser was subsidised in Tanzania in the mid-1970s, and 85% in Nigeria in the early 1980s, consumption of fertiliser per hectare of arable land in 1981 was only about 5.6 kg and 7 kg respectively (Lele, 1985, cited from unpublished World Bank data).

Subsidies can be given to fertilisers for inputs in the export crops until the export earnings are more than the import costs of the fertilisers themselves. Whether they can be given for food crops depends on the extra export earnings available for this purpose; the exercise then reduces to the allocation of export earnings, both in the short and long run. At the time of accepting any loan or aid which has to be repaid with concessional or non-concessional terms, it will be helpful if its repayment in terms of commodities to be exported is also decided upon. Otherwise the very logic of partial economic analysis with the current national and international price structure as the only guide may lead to debt crises, with uncalled-for losses to lending institutions of the developed world and development catastrophe for the indebted developing countries.

TECHNOLOGY TRANSFER IN INDUSTRY: TRANSFER OF EXISTING OR ALMOST OBSOLETE RATHER THAN APPROPRIATE TECHNOLOGY

An industrial technological transfer is mostly done to establish in the recipient country a more or less similar production unit to that in the original country. Though the basic technique of production remains the same, there might be some adjustments done to secondary processes like material handling, packaging or using a different fuel more suitable to the economic conditions of the recipient country and its factor endowments. The capital and input structure of the basic plant is expected to remain the same; this is due to the fact that the technological transfer is primarily the transfer of the know-how of the production process rather that of the fundamental scientific knowledge embodied in it. The knowledge base underlying the process is mostly freely available in books and articles, but the development of the practical ways of producing a good, construction of the suitable machinery, the standardisation of the processes involved, etc. is quite an arduous job requiring a high level of engineering and other relevant skills for a protracted period of time. Usually a large amount of expenditure is involved in the successful development of this know-how, and current factor price and cost structure is naturally in the back of the developers' minds . The know-how thus developed will be mostly that pertaining to the economic conditions prevailing in the country of its development at that time.

A firm or a country can transfer only that know-how which it possesses. If it develops a special technology appropriate to the economic conditions prevailing in the developing country, its cost is likely to be prohibitive, and there will be hardly any incentive for the firm to enter in this development process; developing countries also want to have 'on-the-shelf' projects, with well-tested technologies, they can hardly take risks with machinery of a completely novel design. However, for ancillary processes like material handling, packaging, etc. local well-tried methods can be easily substituted; these methods will naturally be more suitable to the factor endowments of the recipient developing country.

More likely than not, the technological transfer will be accompanied by the sale of the basic machinery and its appurtenances by the transferring firm; it may also have formal or informal contracts for providing several intermediate inputs required for the production of the commodity, as well as maintenance contracts on a continuing basis. These arrangements can be much better synchronised if the basic production processes, machinery, etc. are the same in the two countries.

ECONOMIC FEASIBILITY OF TECHNOLOGY TRANSFER IN INDUSTRY

There are three aspects of economic feasibility to be considered. First, whether the production of a commodity in the country through technological transfer will be cheaper than the import of that commodity. Secondly, whether it is capable of generating so many exports as to at least cover its foreign costs. Thirdly – and most importantly – how it will affect the overall foreign exchange situation of the country. In many cases, even when the cost of producing a commodity in the developing country is more than its imported cost, it is this last consideration that forces the recipient country to import the technology, as the projected rise in exports may be too small to allow a large-scale import of that and similar other commodities that may become necessary as the development of the country progresses. In such cases, the country may consider the age-old practice of imposing an import duty on the product commensurate to the difference in the legitimate cost of production and the imported cost. If such actions are not taken in time, the resulting balance of payment crisis can lead to progressive depreciation of the currency in the international market, thus giving protection to all production indiscriminately; this will correspondingly increase the cost of servicing in local currency any foreign debts incurred in the process of the technological transfer. Given that the traditional exports of these developing countries are of agricultural and mineral origin whose demand is not very elastic in the short run with respect to price, the increase in export revenue consequent to this depreciation of the currency is hardly likely to produce the extra foreign exchange that such a situation requires. The only way out, for long-term viability, seems to be that the goods produced through this technological transfer themselves become exportable. If even this more stringent second type of economic viability is ensured, it may not be necessary after all to impose the import duties. However, it may be that some commodities are viable in this second sense, while others are not viable even in the first sense, and to satisfy the balance of payment condition it may be necessary to impose import duties on these latter goods so that their foreign exchange deficiencies are covered by the extra export of the former goods. This is the logic of encouraging the exports of manufactures from the developing countries; we shall see below the extra cost that it imposes on the development effort as well as the constraints it places on the betterment of the workers' standard of living.

COST OF PRODUCTION IN NEW INDUSTRY

The cost of production of the new industry established as the result of the technogical transformation will be affected by the factor prices, tax structure, etc. prevalent in the recipient country. With techniques of production in these industries being more or less the same in different countries, the international comparative advantage mostly flows from the differences in the rates of factor payments. The economics of the envisaged technological transfers will also be affected by the extent to whether these transfers involve imported capital or imported intermediate inputs in the production process. In many cases, the technological transfer will also involve the sale of the basic and crucial machinery and its appurtenants, as well as a long-term arrangement for long-term supply of some crucial intermediate goods. A simultaneous technological transfer of the know-how of production of a commodity together with that of the production of all the intermediate goods required in its production, is a rarity; even technically it can be possible only for a big developing country that envisages near self-sufficiency in all types of production in the long run.

The imported intermediate goods will be more costly for the new firm than for the original as they have to bear the extra cost of transportation, trade, insurance, etc., apart from any monopolistic or oligopolistic profits of the supplying firm. The same is true for the imported machinery, etc. The extra costs due to transportation, etc. are calculable, but the mark up due to the monopolist supplies is very hard to estimate.

To get an idea of this, Bhagwati (1967) tabulated the differences between the high and successful bids in competitive tendering for some projects financed by the IBRD and the IDA; he found that 'the percentage of potential excess cost, measured as the ratio of difference between 'high bids' and 'successful bids' to 'successful bids', was on average 49.3 per cent. As for the monopolistic pricing, he quotes Mahabubul Haq (1965) as follows:

> The quotations offered by suppliers are often higher if the suppliers know that it is a tied credit and come down considerably

once it is made clear that the supplies will be financed against cash or untied credit. . . . One of the amusing examples in the recent experience of Pakistan was that of Atlas Copco type compressors under French credit. The French suppliers offered certain quotations which, when checked against the quotations received from the Pakistani agents for Atlas Copco, were found to be 33 per cent to 47 per cent higher for various items.

On the other hand, the labour costs and the cost of the completely indigenous inputs is likely to be substantially less. Similarly, the building and other construction part of the fixed capital would be much less costly, as plant will be mainly built using cheap local labour and materials. Interest rates prevailing in developing countries will be of the same order as in the developed ones.

The International Financial Statistics Yearbook of the IMF gives the interest rates for the countries having readily available information. Among the countries reported, one finds that between 1975 and 1985, central bank discount rates were below 8% for Japan, Austria, Germany, Spain, Switzerland, and Malaysia; below 10% for the Netherlands, Norway, Nigeria, India, and Pakistan, while for countries like the USA, the UK, Canada, etc. they were (in the 14–16% range in several years IMF, 1986: 103).

The burden of making the technological transformation feasible thus falls directly or indirectly on the wage rate. If the manufactured goods produced as a consequence of technological transfer are to be exported, the wage rates should be much lower than when the feasibility requirement is to produce them only at the lower cost than imports. If the arrangements leading to the establishment of the industry requires a long-term commitment to export for capital servicing or purchase of some intermediate goods, this low wage rate should be maintained in the long run: this is contradictory to the aim of increasing the standard of living of the working people as an aim of the development process itself.

TECHNOLOGICAL LAYERS AND TRANSFER OF KNOW-HOW

As Joan Robinson (1956) and Salter (1960) have vividly demonstrated, the know-how of technology is primarily embodied in equipment: the equipment or fixed capital embodies the technology of the time when it was newly installed. This technology remains more or less the same until the equipment embodying it is scrapped. 'Embodied technological progress' in the economy comes about by the installation of new equipment – embodying better techniques. At a particular moment of time equipment installed at different past dates will be simultaneously working – having, of course, different productivities.

This mechanism has been described by Galbraith (1952) as follows:

> The incentive in the typical American industry, does not in fact work in the direction of maximum output at lowest prices (as it would seem) to the man steeped in the preconceptions of the competitive model. The market power of the individual firm is used to obtain prices that are higher for an output that is smaller than would be ideal. However there is a major compensation for much of this inefficiency, and that is technical change . . . In the industry that is shared by a relatively small number of large firms, the convention that excludes price competition does not restrain technological innovation. This remains one of the important weapons of the market rivalry . . . whilst imitations must be assumed and expected the convention which limits the price competition also ensures that the returns to the new product from cost reducing innovation, will accrue to the innovator for a period of time. The power that enables the firm to have some influence on prices ensures that the resulting gains will not be passed on to the public by imitators (who have stood none of the cost of development) before the outlay for development can be recouped. In this way the market power protects the incentive of technical development.

However, it is not necessary to assume that there must be a monopoly power to prevent the equipment pertaining to old techniques of production from becoming obsolete immediately with the occurrence of a new technological innovation. The very fact that new technology requires an accumulation of corresponding capital will give a lease of life, for the time being, to the equipment pertaining to the older technique of production – that is, up until the time as as much new capital is accumulated as is required to produce the amount of the commodity that can meet its total demand.

With the opening of the horizon of technical transfer to the developing countries, this capital of older vintage which was on the verge of obsolescence in its own country can be passed on; sometimes the old equipment itself can be reconditioned to be passed on as virtually new, and even where this is not possible the capacity to manufacture that equipment incorporating the obsolete know-how can be used to supply the equipment to the developing countries before it is scrapped.

The range of productivity within an industry may be rather large. The author has analysed the range of productivity of firms within an industry as revealed in the 1982 *US Census of Production*; for the purpose the Census authorities were kind enough to retabulate the data productivity group wise for each industry. The results were startling, as the best group of the firms had less than half the cost per unit of production than the worst in most cases (Mathur, 1989).

This has implications for both the exporter and the importer of technological transfer. The technical transfer has hardly cost anything for the exporting country, in fact it becomes a profitable exercise as it is able to sell its obsolete equipment at a higher price than it would have got at home. It can also ensure a long-term market for the export of intermediate goods required in the production of the commodity. For the importing country, the production of the commodity becomes naturally more costly than it need have been; as exporters, in pursuance of competition with other nations, may slash the export price of a commodity to its production cost with the most efficient equipment, the country importing the technology, to match its production cost with the import price, may have to reduce its labour cost to a very substantial extent. Mostly, in such cases, the only way to sustain the technical transfer is by heavy protective duties; sometimes, we have the spectacle of imported intermediate inputs costing more than the import price of the manufactured commodity itself. This situation militates very much against any possibility of a successful achievement of development.

WAGE SACRIFICE FOR MANUFACTURE FOR EXPORT: SOME INDICATIONS

We have seen above that to be an exporter of manufactures it is necessary that the wage rate in the country should be sufficiently low; this is necessary to absorb the extra cost of production of a transferred technology and of the developing country being often saddled with a technology on the verge of obsolescence. But how low is 'sufficiently low'? By the very nature of things, we do not have any direct measure which can quantify this crucial parameter for development. We can get an indirect idea of the dimensions by looking at the developing countries who manufacture for export. The average wage rate of several countries has been published by UNIDO (1987), collected from the census of manufactures of individual countries. Collating them with the percentage of manufactured exports as given in the *World Development Reports* of the World Bank (1987 and 1988), we get the following picture.

Of 82 countries whose wage rates were reported by UNIDO for the year 1985, 20 had wage rates less than 10% of the US wage rate. For 14 out of these 20, the proportion of manufacturing exports to total exports was higher than 25%, for another 4 it was increasing between 1985 and 1986. Only two, Ethiopia and Ghana, may be considered to have such a low wage rate without attempting to export manufactures.

Out of 25 developing countries having more than 25% of their exports as manufactures, 14 had a wage rate less than 10% of that of the USA. If we have 16% as cut off point, 19 will fall in that group. The remaining 6 are the countries whose exports of manufactures have hardly any backward linkages within the country; they mainly serve as offshore centres for final processing and packaging as well as distribution centres for multinational and their affiliates. As such, some of the cost-increasing situations applicable to technological transfers are not applicable – for instance, the transfer of near-obsolete technology will be harmful only to the multinational involved, and there will be no gain in selling equipment costly to one's own subsidiary or to a contracted firm that works like a subsidiary, so even a lower difference in the wage rates is sufficient to make this type of production profitable. These countries are Hongkong, Singapore, Korea, Mexico, El Salvador, and Israel, and even then all of them have wage rates less than 30% of that of the USA.

[The 14 countries having more than a 25% share of manufactures in their exports and having less than 10% of the US wage rate as their average manufacturing wage were Bangladesh (2.38%), Brazil (9.03%), Central African Republic (10.20%), Dominican Republic (5.46%), Guatemala (10.13%), Hungary (6.09%), India (4.46%), Pakistan (5.21%), Philippines (5.98%), Poland (7.10%), Sri Lanka (2.96% in 1980), Thailand (8.73%), Uruguay (9.70%) and Yugoslavia (8.39%); figures in brackets are their wage rate as a percentage of the US wage rates.

The five other countries having their wages less than 16% of US wage rate were Turkey (15.00%), Tunisia (13.29%), Morocco (12.70%), Zimbabwe (15.8%), and Malaysia (12.74% in 1980).

The four countries having their wage rate less than 10% of the US wage rate and increasing their share of manufactures between 1985 and 1986 were Indonesia (3.85%), Kenya (7.53%), Madagascar (6.38%) and Tanzania (5.05%).]

SOME CONDITIONS FOR SUCCESSFUL TECHNOLOGY TRANSFER

We can thus surmise that developing countries that propose to develop their manufacturing industry on the basis of technological transfer from developed countries should ensure that the extra short-term or long-term export commitments that the process involves are capable of being met from traditional exports. For this planning purpose, these exports should be valued at their long-term prices. Further they should be prepared to protect these new industries from the competition of more efficient plants in the developed world.

If traditional exports do not provide sufficient foreign exchange, it may be necessary to export the outputs of the industries established through the process of the technological transfer. This seems to be possible only when the nominal wage rate prevailing in the economy is less than about 10% of the US wage rate. (In very favourable cases developing countries having wage rates even up to 16% of US wage rate have successfully exported manufactures.) Only this high margin in wage cost seems to meet the cost disadvantages inherent in the strategy of technical transfer from developed countries. In general the country will not be able to increase the standard of living of its working people until it has got export commitments that cannot be met by its traditional exports at their long-term price.

However, there is an exceptional class of countries, whose manufacturing exports mainly consist of products in whose production some labour-intensive stages have been carried out, and /or which work as the distribution centres for the region. We have seen that such countries have been able to increase their wage rates even up to 30% of the US wage rate. With the increase in their wage rates, the value of these firms as cheap processors or distributors will decrease, and with their present production structure they can hardly become economically independent developed countries.

The countries which try to industrialise on the basis of low nominal wage rates in terms of international currency, will have to manage their price structure and exchange rate in such a way as to be able to provide at least subsistence real wage rates. A 1982 UN study on purchasing power parity found that the low-wage countries have prices of wage goods, in particular foodgrains, substantially lower (Kravis *et al.*, 1982); this allows a sort of subsistence wage to the labourer. But the lower nominal prices of foodgrains makes the modernisation of the agriculture much more difficult, if that requires imported capital and current inputs. It does not matter if the production of wages goods does not require any imported input; but that puts an effective limits to development. Alternatively, the agricultural sector can be subsidised by other sectors; there is an effective limit to this type of strategy also, which will come much sooner in case of smaller countries.

14 The Economics of Technology Transfer

INTRODUCTION

We have seen that to initiate development technological transfer is a must. The success or failure of the development effort depends on the terms and the modalities of the technical transfer itself. On that depends whether the country can transform itself into a fully fledged developed country, or become an appendage to the developed world or, in the terminology of Gunnar Myrdal, participate only in the 'backwash effect' of the growth of the industrialised world – that is, to suffer a drain on its resources as the developed countries become richer and richer. We have seen that before the Second World War, quite a few countries had graduated into the membership of the exclusive club of the developed countries, now formalised as the OECD. However, after the Second World War the international economic order became so organised that not a single country entered the elect group. During the 1970s, high hopes of achieving this transition were entertained for some countries, but with the collapse of international commodity prices in the 1980s and the surfacing of the 'Third World Debt' problem, all those hopes shattered. Below, we shall look into the theoretical possibility of achieving technological transfer in a present-day world bereft of economic colonies and empires. We shall also see some of the pitfalls that may occur during the process.

LEWIS'S MODEL FOR THE ISOLATED DEVELOPMENT OF THE MODERN SECTOR

Following Lewis, (1954) we shall assume that a self-sufficient enclave of a modern sector is established in a developing country. The technology in that enclave is the same as that in the reference developed country. To fix our ideas, we shall work with a simple hypothetical arithmetic example.

Let the efficient technology of the industrialised country be given by the following input – output, labour and capital coefficients:

214

$$\bar{A} = \begin{array}{cc} : 0.15 & 0.25 : ; \\ : 0.15 & 0.25 : ; \end{array} \quad \bar{L} = : 0.4 \ \ 0.15 : ;$$

$$\bar{B} = \begin{array}{cc} : 0.0 & 0.0 : \\ : 1.0 & 2.0 : \end{array}$$

(14.1)

This implies that there are two commodities in the economy. For producing 1 unit of commodity 1, 0.15 units of commodity 1 and 0.15 units of commodity 2 are required as intermediate inputs. Similarly, for producing commodity 2, 0.25 units of commodities 1 and 2 go as intermediate inputs. Apart from that commodity 1 requires 0.4 units of labour to produce 1 unit, while commodity 2 requires 0.15 units. Further, to establish 1 unit worth of production capacity for commodity 1, 1 unit worth of commodity 2 is required to be kept in stock, say as machinery. Similarly for creating 1 unit capacity of commodity 2, 2 units worth of commodity 2 is used as capital for the industry.

Let the prices in the developed country be

p_1 and p_2

respectively, and wage and returns on capital (interest rates) be w and r respectively. Then, as the prices of the two commodities should cover their cost of production, the following equations should be satisfied.

$$0.85 \, p_1 = 0.4 \, w + 0.15 \, p_2 + r \, p_2 \tag{14.2}$$

$$0.75 \, p_2 = 0.15 \, w + 0.25 \, p_1 + 2 \, r \, p_2 \tag{14.3}$$

Further, let $p_1 = 1$; $p_2 = 1$.
Then, solving the equations, we get $w = 1.38$ and $r = 0.15$.

(The wage rate is in terms of either commodity, as both are priced as 1 per unit.) Here r includes not only the interest rate but also the depreciation rate; let the interest rate be 5% and the depreciation rate be 10%.

For the developing countries, let the price–wage–interest rate be denoted by primed symbols. As the complete technology is transferred to it, the technical coefficients will be the same there as in the developed country. However, the wage rate may be taken as one-fifth of that prevalent in the industrialised country. The assumption is that wage rate should be sufficient to draw as much labour force as desired from the traditional sector that is existing concurrently. And let the wage rate be in terms of commodity 1, which is supposed to represent consumption goods. On this assumption the wage rate will be given by $w' = 0.28\, p'_1$. Then, solving equations (14.2) and (14.3), we get

$$r = 0.288, \text{ and } p'_2 = 1.68\, p'_1 \tag{14.4}$$

We may note that the reduction of wage rate not only increases the value of r but also changes the relative prices of the two commodities. Out of this we take depreciation at the rate of 10%; the net returns to capital will then be 18.8%. If that is all reinvested, it will imply an 18.8% growth rate for the modern sector of the economy. There should be no constraint to this growth as the extra labour and land required for extra production of the modern sector will be coming from the traditional sector. As a consequence, the traditional sector will shrink by the requisite amount. Transactions in the traditional sector will be on a conventional barter basis and so the price formation in the modern sector will not disturb its working. Further, as savings will be equal to the investment there will be no imbalance.

At this rate of growth, the modern sector will be about 100 times its initial size in mere 27 years. As it depends for its growth on the absorption of labour and land from the traditional sector, we can expect that all the labour force of the traditional sector will be absorbed in the modern sector within a few decades. When that happens, the opportunities for further investment will become limited to the natural growth of the labour force. The extra demand for labour should increase the wage rate until it reaches a level equal to that of the developed countries. Then savings will be reduced to the level that can be absorbed by the investment for the natural growth of labour; the developing country will be transformed into a developed one.

ESTABLISHMENT OF A MODERN SECTOR THROUGH LOANS

This is the optimistic story. The condition for success is that the modern sector should have come as a gift or, which is the same thing, the investor should himself have migrated to the developing country. If it has been installed through a loan, the servicing of the loans will have to be taken into account. In the above hypothetical example, assume that the modern sector has been established through loans from the developed country; then the servicing of the loan may be of the order of 15% of the capital, consisting of 5% of interest and 10% of repayment per year. This will reduce the net investment income to a mere 3–4% – just sufficient for net returns but which will hardly be able to absorb the natural increase in the labour force. Further, as capital goods will have been imported in the first place, their cost will have to bear the transport and trading costs involved. If we put these at say 30%, the loan will be 30% higher. Thus the 18.8% of the original capital cost available as returns in the above example will be only 14.5% of the loans taken. This will be required for servicing the loans. There is hardly any chance of the growth of a modern sector in the economy of the developing country on such a basis.

ESTABLISHMENT OF A PARTIAL MODERN SECTOR

In the above example, let the modern sector in the developing country set up plants for producing the commodity 1 only, in which they were found to have comparative advantage, if it establishes both industries, the price of commodity 1 in terms of the commodity 2 will be less in the developing country than in the developed, because of the lower wage rate there.

The developing country will then import commodity 2 by exporting commodity 1 to the developed country itself; on both these transactions there will be trade and transport cost. Then, as commodity 1 is exported from and commodity 2 is imported into the developing country,

$$p_1' <= p_1 (1 - t_1); \text{ and } p_2' >= p_2 (1 + t_2) \tag{14.5}$$

where t_1 and t_2 are the proportionate transport and trade costs for the two commodities respectively. Here primed prices, wages, or returns represent those of the developing country while non-primed ones those of the developed country.

As commodity 1 is produced in the developing country, its price there should meet its cost of production; hence

$$0.85 \, p_1' >= 0.4 \, w' + 0.15 \, p_2' + r' \, p_2' \tag{14.6}$$

This implies that,

$$0.4 \, w' + (0.15 + r') \, p_2 \, (1 + t_2) <= 0.85 \, p_1 \, (1 - t_1)$$

Assuming, $t_1 = t_2 = 0.33$; and as $p_1 = p_2 = 1$,

$$0.4 \, w' + 1.33 \, r' + 0.20 <= 0.57 \qquad (14.7)$$

Let us assume that $r' = r = 0.15$, then $w' <= 0.43$. This implies that w' is less than or equal to $0.31 \, w$.

Thus the wage rate in the developing country has to be *less than one-third* of that in the developed country if the technology transferred to it is the same as that used in the industrialised country itself, and if it chooses to pay for its foreign exchange requirements by means of the exports of its manufactures produced by means of this transfer.

In the case of newly developing countries that work like offshore processing centres to the developed countries like Hongkong, Singapore, Taiwan, Korea, etc.), their export industries are effectively processing units for multinationals; as such they are transferred the latest technology for that part of the processing that is performed there. They come in the category exemplified above; they can hardly hope to be able to improve their standard of living much more than what they have already achieved, or become themselves a part of developed world.

IMPLICATIONS OF TRANSFER OF LESS EFFICIENT TECHNIQUES

Ordinarily developing countries are the exporters of agricultural and mining products and in return import manufactured goods. However, a limit to their development by this route is quickly reached as the availability of land and minerals starts forming the bottleneck for further growth. The way forward is progressive industrialisation of their economy; this involves the progressive transfer of the production techniques of different commodities. This transfer is accompanied by the sale of the relevant capital equipment at the start of the new capacity creation in the developing country, and usually the regular sale of some intermediate inputs afterwards.

To meet the extra foreign exchange requirements, the industrialising developing countries will export the output of those manufacturing industries to the developed world. This condition, as we have shown above, imposes certain constraints on the price and wage structures of these countries.

However, in many cases the technology transferred to the developing countries is, as we know, of the older vintage, which is on the way out in the developed country itself. The wage implications for that are more drastic. Let the production technique for commodity 1 transferred to the developing country have the following specifications.

Flow coefficients = : 0.15 : ; Capital coefficient = : 0.00 :
: 0.20 : : 1.25 :

and Labour coefficient = 0.45

The price equation in this case will be

$$0.85 \, p_1' = 0.45 \, w' + (0.20 + 1.25 \, r') \, p_2' \qquad (14.8)$$

Assuming as before, $t_1 = t_2 = 0.33$, we get as $p_1 = p_2$,

$$p_1' = (1 - 0.33)p_1 = (1 - 0.33)p_2 = (1 - 0.33)p_2' \, / \, (1 + 0.33)$$
$$\text{or, } p_1' = 0.50 \, p_2' \qquad (14.9)$$

Substituting this in (14.8), and assuming servicing charges to the capital to be 15%, we get, $w' = 0.17$ units of the commodity 1. If commodity 1 is the consumption good, it implies that the wage rate in the circumstances is only 12% of the wage rate in the developed country, which was 1.38 units of commodity 1.

Thus, in this case, if the country has to export goods produced from the imported modern technology, and if it has to service the foreign debt incurred while establishing its modern producing facility, its wage rate would be only 12% of that in the developed country in real terms. This is on the assumption that no depreciation fund is created within the developing country itself; thus when the life of the invested capital is over, it may have to borrow again to be able to keep the facility in working order.

However, if it found that 12% of the industrialised country's wage is too little for the developing country in real terms, it is not possible to modernise the developing country without some sort of subterfuge. One of the methods usually adopted is to build the modern sector as a parasite on the traditional one. The wage goods from the traditional sector may be taken away by exchange of the product of the industry. Mostly the traditional sector would not have the requisite demand for this commodity at that price. In that case, the major part of the wage goods will have to be acquired through appropriate taxation.

In cases where the traditional sector is not large enough to be able to bear this heavy burden, a policy of modernisation of agriculture can be attempted, made economically feasible through a judicious subsidisation policy, if extra goods can be exported to procure the import of inputs in modern agriculture (say, fertilisers). This may generate output worth more than the required real wage. However, to induce the producer to use those imported inputs in production process it is necessary not to distort the relationship between the prices of imported inputs and prices excessively. In this situation either the output will have to be heavily subsidised or imported inputs will have to be subsidised to the same extent. As we shall see subsequently, both these methods have been tried in different developing countries.

It will be interesting to look at the price structure which this situation will create in the developing country. The price of imported goods will be about 33% more than that in the industrialised country; that of output of the local modern industry will be about 67%, and that of wage goods about 40% of the corresponding price in one developed country. Nominal wage rates have turned out to be 12%, but real wage rates are of the order of 20% of those in the developed country. This will imply that the cost of services will also be of the same order. Compare these with the price structure of the poorest countries found in the (1982) UN study of the purchasing power parity noted in Chapter 1. There Table 1.1 gave the wage and prices of various commodities in different groups of countries. In the poorest group (group I), the price of consumption was found to be 40%, of producer durables 130%, clothing, tobacco and furniture, etc. between 55 and 80%, the nominal wage rate 8.4% and real wage rate 20% that of the USA. These are likely to have been generated by some process similar to the one described above.

These results have far-reaching implications. They signify that developing countries that adopt the strategy of industrialisation via technological transfer and which involves a continuous earning of foreign exchange by export of their produce cannot increase their wage rate beyond a certain proportion of the wage rate in the developed countries; in other words they will always remain underdeveloped countries until these conditions cease to prevail. The above examples are artificial created for pedagogical purposes; to get a feel of the real dimensions of the problem involved we indicate below a rough idea of the difference in productivity observed between different firms of the same industry in USA; the importance of this depends on the substantial differences in the best practice technology from the least efficient one in developed countries.

We get an idea of the extent of low productivity that can result from the transference of less efficient techniques from a pilot study of US Manufacturing industry for the census year 1982; the aim of the study was to find out the differences between the best and the worst technology in each industry. The preliminary results of that study were startling (see Popkin and Mathur, 1989). From that study, we found that the vast majority of industries (68%) have a coefficient of variation of unit output cost ranging from 0.151 to 0.245.[1]

Thus in the modal case we find that the least efficient technique cost per unit of output 137% of the average, while the most efficient one 63%. This implies that the cost per unit of the most efficient technique of production is only half of that of the least efficient ones.

CONCLUSIONS

We have studied two types of technology transfers, one where the transferring country transfers the most efficient techniques to the recipients; such was the case with the defeated countries after the Second World War. The recipient countries were Japan and West Germany; that enabled them not only to rebuild their shattered economy after the war but, unshackled by the burden of the old technology enabled them to go to the economic forefront of the developed nations. There has also been a partial transfer of efficient technology to some small countries that can become the processor of some labour-intensive part of production for the multinationals; that allowed such countries to go forward in the race for development ahead of other developing countries, though now they seem to be stuck as the level achieved.

Another type of technological transfer has been that of near-obsolete techniques to the developing countries. The economic necessities that are imposed, in shape of compulsory exports to pay for the privilege and the debts incurred in the process, have compelled these countries to export at any cost. To make that feasible wage rates had to be depressed sufficiently, in turn forcing the prices of wage goods to a low level; this implies that modernisation in such cases will not proceed to all sectors.

We thus see that the the technique of development through technical transfers is not likely to lead to the graduation of the developing countries into the 'developed' world, if this implies a compulsion to exports. In such a case, if the transfer provides an opportunity for the industrialised countries to transfer technologies becoming obsolete in their own countries to the developing countries, the wage rate in those countries is hardly likely to increase to more than 10% of that of the industrialised world.

This seems to be an economic law independent of the local institutional framework. Post-communist countries like Poland, Hungary and Yugoslavia, as well as the free market economies having democratic or dictatorial regimes, all seem to be equally constrained by this restriction to growth through the technique of technological transfer, the economic cost of which has to be paid for through subsequent export creation.

Appendix: Feasible Price Structure and the Range of its Variation

BOUNDARIES OF PRICE STRUCTURAL VARIATIONS

In order that a producer may continue to produce a commodity, the commodity price should be able to meet its cost of production. This implies that the price of a commodity should be more than or equal to the cost of raw materials, and intermediate goods, both those produced within and outside the economic system. Further, it should meet the processing costs, and wage costs, as well as the interest and normal returns on the invested capital or normal profit. Only that will allow the producer to remain in business.

Thus if there are n commodities and services, and p_i is the price of a unit of commodity i, then p_i should be greater than or equal to

$$[a_{1i}p_1 + a_{2i}p_2 + \ldots\ldots + a_{ji}p_j + \ldots + a_{ni}p_n] + vM_i + rK_i + wL_i \qquad (1)$$

where a_{ji} is the amount of j th commodity used as input in the production of one unit of i th commodity; and M_i, K_i, and L_i are the inputs produced outside that economy, capital at charge and the labour units used up in the production of one unit of i th commodity. v is the rate at which outside inputs are purchased in terms of numeraire that is taken as commodity number 1. Further, r denotes the rate of returns to the capital (including interest etc.), and w is the wage per unit of labour.

We shall have n equations like the equation (1) above – one for each of the n commodities. These set of equations would set effective upper and lower limits to the price that any commodity can command. If the price is too low, the equation relating to the feasibility of the production of that commodity would not be satisfied, while if it is too large it will make its use as an input in the production of other commodities non-feasible. However, this upper limit does not apply to those luxury commodities that are not used as an input for any other commodity. Their price can be as high as the market would bear.

This price system can be written in matrix notation as follows:

$$P[I-A] > \text{or} = vM + rK + wL \qquad (2)$$

where P is the row vector of prices, A is the Leontief Input-Output Matrix representing the domestic inputs per unit of outputs, M is the row vector giving outside inputs per unit of production of various commodities, and K and L are capital and labour row vectors respectively. All terms on the right hand side of the equation (2) are positive. First we shall look into the implications of the right hand side being greater than zero and then introduce the effect of their being positive.

From eq 2, we get $P[I-A] > 0$ (3)

We want to find out the relationship between prices of i th and j th commodities viz between p_i and p_j. Let us partition the vector P and the matrix A into two sets. Let P^1 denote the vector (p_i, p_j); and P^2 denote the remaining part of the vector P. Let A^{11}; A^{12}; A^{21}; and A^{22}; be the corresponding partitions of the matrix A. Then the equation (3) can be written as

$$[P^1\ P^2] \begin{pmatrix} 1 & (I-A^{11}) & -A^{12} \\ 1 & & \\ 1 & -A^{22} & (I-A^{22}) \end{pmatrix} \begin{Bmatrix} 1 \\ 1 \\ 1 \end{Bmatrix} > [0\ 0]$$ (4)

This gives the following equations,

$$P^1 (I - A^{11}) - P^2 A^{21} > 0 \text{ and}$$

$$P^2 (I - A^{22}) > P^1 A^{12}$$

$$\text{or, } P^2 > P^1 A^{12} (I - A^{22})^{-1}$$ (5)

From the first equation we get,

$$P^1 (I - A^{11}) - P^1 A^{12} (I - A^{22})^{-1} A^{21} > 0$$ (6)

$$\text{or, } P^1 [I - \{A^{11} + A^{12} (I-A^{22})^{-1} A^{21}\}] > 0$$ (7)

The matrix within curly brackets is the sum of positive matrices, and therefore is itself a positive matrix. Let us call it as matrix C. Then equation (7) becomes

$$P^1 [I - C] > 0$$ (8)

Expanding, this gives,

$$p_i (1-c_{ii}) - p_j c_{ji} > 0 \text{ and}$$

$$-p_i c_{ij} + p_j (1-c_{jj}) > 0$$

$$\text{or, } [c_{ji}/(1-c_{ii})] < p_i/p_j < [(1-c_{jj})/c_{ij}]$$ (9)

This clearly gives the range between which the ratio of the price of the i th commodity with j th can move. If this ratio becomes less than the lower limit or more than the upper limit, it will not be possible for the producer of one of the commodity to even meet the cost of the intermediate goods required for the production of that commodity. By means of the procedure similar to the above, we can find the range in which any price ratio should remain so that the production of the respective commodities remains feasible.

Recalling equation 2, we find that the right-hand side should not only be greater than zero, but also greater than labour cost, the return on capital as well as the cost of intermediate goods purchased from outside the system. How does this effect the range of variability of the price ratios? First let us see the effect of the requirements to purchase intermediate goods from outside the system, as they are necessary inputs. As the first commodity is the numeraire, their cost can be accounted in terms of p_1. So from cost point of view, as in equation (1) p_i should be greater or equal to

$$[(a_{1i} + vM_i)p_1 + a_{2i}p_2 + \ldots\ldots + a_{ji}p_j + \ldots + a_{ni}p_n] + rK_i + wL_i \quad (10)$$

Thus the equation (2) can be written as

$$P (I-A') >= rK + wL \quad (11)$$

where input-output matrix A' is the expanded matrix A, where the elements of the first column have been enhanced by the addition of the vector vM. It may be noted that each element of A' is greater than or equal to the corresponding elements of the matrix A.

Analysing equation (11) in the same way as above, we get, corresponding to eq (8), the following,

$$P^1 [I - C'] > 0 \quad (12)$$

where C' is similarly derived from the matrix A' as C was derived from Matrix A. It will be seen that each element of C' is greater or equal to the corresponding element of C. This gives us the range of the ratio between the prices of i th and j th commodity as follows:

$$(c'_{ji}/(1-c'_{ii})] < p_i/p_j < [(1-c'_{jj})/c'_{ij}] \quad (13)$$

As each element of C' is greater than or equal to the corresponding element of C, equation (13) indicates a lower range to the possible movements of the price ratio than equation (9). In general we can say that a positive value on the left-hand side of the equation (2) will reduce the range of variation of the price ratios. The greater is that value, the more will be the reduction in that range. Thus if there is a minimum wage specified the range would be further reduced.

The range specified above is to be considered as technologically given. No economic manipulation would allow the price ratios to transcend it. Any attempt to do the same would only disrupt the economy either by creating inflationary or deflationary pressures or bankruptcies closing down certain essential industries. Within this range the value of the price ratios would be determined by the economic conditions determining the rates of factor payments.

DETERMINATION OF APPROPRIATE PRICES

If we assume that all extra income is absorbed in the profits, we can have the sign of equality in the equation system (2). This gives us

$$P = \{vM + rK + wL\} [I-A]^{-1} \tag{14}$$

A being the input-output matrix, the matrix $[I-A]^{-1}$ have all its elements as non-negative by a well known theorem on Leontief matrices. This means that the value of P can be written as the sum of the three components $vM[I-A]^{-1}$; $rK[I-A]^{-1}$; and $wL[I-A]^{-1}$. Of these the first one is exogenous, that is outside the working of the economy. However the other two will be affected by the rate of return or wage rate the economy chooses to give itself. Really, as soon as either the rate of return or the wage rate is determined the other can be derived as a residual. There is only one decision, therefore, to be made at the level of the economy. If the economy tries to make both decisions independently, that will lead to either inflationary or deflationary tendencies.

In a developing economy, we may have to determine only the minimum wage rate. Then whatever profit rate comes out is to be reinvested in development. The priority should not be to have a given profit rate as that may either depress the wage rate to a morally, socially and politically unacceptable level and/or create inflationary pressure that may nullify most of the development efforts.

Thus this methodology will give a schemata for determining an appropriate price system for the economy.

Part VI
Strategies for Development

15 The Role of Subsidies and Import Controls in Modernising Low-income Countries

INTRODUCTION

Developing countries traditionally earn their foreign exchange through the export of primary commodities, which may be agricultural- or mineral-based. The foreign exchange earnings of the developing countries as a whole from this are, however, limited, due to the low price elasticity of world demand for the primary commodities. An individual country may try to increase its foreign exchange earnings by increasing its exports of these commodities, but as soon as other countries also try to do the same, the price of the commodity is likely to slide down so as to frustrate the efforts of all of them. So if the development process requires extra imports for investment, etc. it may have to be paid by the exports of non-traditional commodities, which can in most cases be only manufactured goods. The situation remains the same even if the development process is supported by international aid, as the loans available have to be repaid with interest, and that requires the availability of foreign exchange.

To be able to export manufactured goods, the developing country should have a sufficiently low labour cost. The basic technology of production of these goods is by and large the same; mostly, the production facility in the developing country is established through technological transfer rather than new fundamental research incorporating intermediate technology. With technological transfer, more often than not, the appropriate machinery is also exported to the developing country; this will mostly come from the same production line as that used in the developed country itself. If the output of the industry thus established is to be exported to the developed country itself, the developing country should provide substantial savings in the labour cost; these savings should be able to cover not only not the inconsiderable transport and trading costs, but also the cost of imported energy and minerals required for modern manufactures.

Bangladesh, India, Pakistan, and Philippines are some of the developing countries in which the proportion of manufacture in exports is half or more. UNIDO (1986) gives the average industrial wage in these countries in the year 1975 in US dollars; they are found to be 3.23%, 5.76%, 4.89% and 6.97% of the average US industrial wage respectively; this gives some idea of the cheapness of the labour cost that is necessary to achieve this extent of manufacturing exports from these countries.[1]

Low wage rates are not only required for exporting manufactures, but also for exporting the many primary commodities where low domestic wage rate gives an edge in international market. One such commodity is cotton. Egypt, which is one of its main exporters, had a wage rate less than 10% of that of the US in 1975. Similarly the exporters of rubber, Indonesia and Thailand, had wage rates about 4% of that of the USA in 1975. The Philippines has also adjusted its wage rate so that it can export sugar at world prices. To be able to export sugar, Mauritius had a wage rate less than 10% of the US rate and so on.

The UN study on the International Comparison of Real Gross Product (Kravis *et al.*, 1982) found that the standard of living of the labourers in these countries was not low as indicated by these figures; the prices of the necessities of life in these countries were much cheaper than in the USA. In 1975, the price of bread and cereals in India, Pakistan, and the Philippines was only 32.6%, 27.0%, and 44.8% respectively of the US price. Under a 'Bread and Cereal' standard for international comparison, their wages were 17.67%, 18.11%, and 15.56% rather than 5.76%, 4.89%, and 6.97% respectively of the US wage rate.

A very low wage rate in terms of an international currency (say dollars) in a developing country is sustainable only if the wage goods production in that country do not require any imported products such as raw materials or intermediate goods. Then the local cost of labour becomes independent of the exchange rates of the country. The international price of exports become more or less independent of the local wage rate, provided producers are able to attract (or coerce) sufficient goods from the traditional sector to be able to pay the labour force in terms of the wage goods produced in that sector. The difficulty with this economic mode is that very soon the traditional techniques of production reach an upper limit to their output due to the labour or land bottlenecks faced by the country; the solution is to increase the productivity of the scarce factor of production. That productivity increase can be achieved only by using modern methods of production which replace labour power by fossil fuel power in the process of production, and also use man-made chemicals in place of the biological processes of agriculture to increase the productivity of the land.

The problem with the adoption of these processes is that they require foreign exchange, not only for the purchase of machinery, etc. but also for the current inputs of energy, fertilisers and other inputs required in production with modern technology. When the cost of the production of wage goods become dependent on the exchange rate, the nominal value of the wage goods in international currency can hardly remain that low; this in turn will tend to reduce the marketability of export goods. This 'Catch 22' situation, where the road to development requires more imports and the very process of development tend to reduce exports, effectively bars these countries from the development process, and their efforts in this direction can only be counter productive. This dilemma many developing countries have tried to overcome by wage goods subsidisation.

DEVELOPMENT THROUGH JUDICIOUS SUBSIDIES AND TAXES

For a detailed study of the wage goods subsidisation process, we have selected two countries, Egypt and India. Egypt's main exports, apart from a recent surge of oil, are cotton and textiles, thus it is one of the countries which has to subsidise the modernisation of agriculture to maintain its edge in the market for traditional commodity exports. India depends for its extra export earning on increasing its manufacturing exports, and has already reached a broad level of industrialisation sufficient to be classified by the World Bank's *World Development Report* (1987) among the developing countries who are exporters of manufactures.

The question to be probed is how these countries have achieved such development of the modern sector in the face of the basic dilemma posed above. And why are they not able to increase their industrial wage level in spite of these achievements?

THE CASE OF DIRECT SUBSIDIES: EGYPT

In Table 15.1, we first give the average manufacturing wage rates reported for Egypt for the years 1975 and 1980.

Table 15.1 Average manufacturing wages in Egypt

	1975	1980
In Egyptian pounds (EL)	423.4	1,031.8
In dollars ($)	1,082	1,474
Average US wage ($)	11,096	16,406
Egyptian wage as % of US	9.75	8.98

Table 15.2 Price, cost and prices of foodgrains in Egypt

(i) Year	(ii) Consumer price index	(iii) Producer prices per ton EC ($)	(iv) Egypt (EL)	(v) Egypt ($)	(vi) Egypt as EC% (v)/(iii)	(vii) EC ($)	(viii) Consumer prices per ton Egypt (EL)	(ix) Egypt ($)	(x) Egypt as EC% (ix)/(vii)	(xi) (ix)/(v)
1970	40.9	106.7	33.3	76.6	72					
1975	59.6	169.9	46.7	119.3	70					
1980	100.0	291.3	83.3	119.0	41	512	22.3	32	6.3	26.9
1981	110.4	251.8	83.3	119.0	47	435	41.3	59	13.6	49.6
1982	126.8	240.6	83.3	119.0	50	421	41.3	59	14.0	49.6
1983	147.2	228.3	93.3	133.3	58	400	41.3	59	14.8	44.4
1984	172.3	200.5	120.0	171.4	86	355	41.3	59	16.6	35.0

Table 15.3 Food subsidies in Egypt

	1980	1981	1982	1983
Total food subsidies (m EL)	1,703	1,473	1,332	2,005
As % of GDP	9.8	7.3	5.3	6.8
Cereal subsidies (m EL)	880	877	916	1,156
% of food subsidies	51.7	41.7	68.5	56.3

The average Egyptian wage was thus about 10% of that of the USA. We see from Tables 15.2 and 15.3 that not only does Egypt keep the price of cereals at about 15% of that of Western Europe, but that its method of achieving this aim is open subsidy; the cost of production is about three times than the consumer price, but open subsidies are used for bringing the consumer price to the level required. About 7% of GDP is spent on food subsidies and the gross domestic savings were about 15% during this period. If the resources devoted to subsidies could have been devoted to investment, the rate of economic development of the country could have been substantially higher. It is crucial to understand, why this has not been possible, in spite of continuous pressures exerted by the IMF, the World Bank and other donors.

Tables 15.2 and 15.3 have been taken from a study by Genazzini and Horhager (1987).

This data also shows that the low price of cereals found in low-wage countries cannot support more modern productive agriculture, and as we know the traditional techniques of agriculture cannot provide the base for economic development; so the countries like Egypt, India, Pakistan, etc. provide direct or indirect subsidies to cereal production. However, these subsidies must come out of the income of some other sector – usually from savings. This may be one of the reasons for the slow rate of growth.

INDIRECT SUBSIDISATION: INDIA

Development Based on Squeezing Traditional Agriculture

India is geographically a big country. Before the Second World War, the Indian Union consisted of what are now the three countries of India, Pakistan and Bangladesh. In such a big country, the traditional wage goods producing sector could be squeezed by taxes, etc. sufficiently to provide the wage goods for the modern industrial sector. As the wage goods sector was working on traditional techniques it did not require any inputs from the modern sector, and the wage rate, which was dependent on the prices of wage goods, also did not depend on the price structure of the modern sector. However, there was an upper limit for the production of wage goods through traditional means, due to the availability of land; this implied an upper limit to the number of persons that could be adequately fed and clothed. In the whole of the Indian Union, between 1900 and 1944, food production remained the same, reducing the per capita availability of food to 73.5% of that at the beginning of the century. This was in spite of the fact that area cultivated increased by 18%. This was taken up by commercial crops, in which production increased by about 60% over this period (see Mukherjee and Sivasubramonian, 1958). Although this implied widespread unemployment and destitution, it could support a modicum of industrialisation; the Indian Union was producing textiles, iron and steel, simple machinery, railway engines, coaches, and other equipment, chemicals, etc. even before the Second World War.

Over the whole of this period the land productivity for production of the food crops declined slightly (85% at the end of the period) as lower and lower productivity land was transferred to the production of food crops. For commercial crops, like tea, jute and cotton, there is a clear evidence of increasing yield rates; most of the research efforts were concentrated on them, and they were the main beneficiary of modern inputs. Food was being produced by traditional techniques, and its producers were being squeezed to provide cheap wage goods; in this there seems to be some resemblance to the relationships between food and commercial crops in Africa today.

Subsidising Agriculture

Squeezing of traditional agriculture had its limits; for further development it was necessary to increase the production of wage goods. This, of course, could not be done without the use of modern chemical-based agricultural techniques. As these inputs had to be imported or manufactured from imported raw materials, the price of wage goods cannot be kept immune from international prices without massive subsidisation. The strategy used was to introduce improved land-saving agricultural techniques of production, while containing the per unit costs of production by a complicated system of incentives and subsidies. This allowed an increase in the availability of agricultural wage goods in low wage countries without increasing the wage cost of industry. Not only did traditional export goods thus remain competitive in the international markets, but new manufactured commodities could be exported for foreign exchange earnings on the basis of low labour costs.

However, there are real costs to this strategy. Subsidies to agriculture must come from some other sectors; these industrial sectors, though gaining from cheap labour, have to pay for the subsidy through general taxation and other resource mobilisation methods, and this obviously cuts into resources for other aspects of development. The new industries that grow up in the process of the development are faced with a low wage economy, and therefore do not give sufficient attention to labour productivity in their management; the resulting inefficiency of labour does not allow the economy to reap the full benefits of the subsidies, further depressing the wage rates.

The subsidies will give the price advantage only to foreigners purchasing the exports of the country. Over time, with the reduction of necessary imports for development, this subsidy can be slowly removed and the economy will then have made the transition to the developed economy. However, this inefficiency fritters away the indirect gains of the subsidy and makes the transition more and more difficult.

The annual rate of growth of industries and services in India during the 1965–80 period was 4.4 and 4.8% respectively, in comparison to 7.6 and 6.4% respectively for the developing countries as a whole (World Bank, 1987: 204–5). Some part of this modest growth may be due to this transfer of resources between sectors. We shall illustrate some of the ways in which this subsidy is given; we shall discuss the case of India in more detail, as it is the most conspicuous country adopting this strategy and its experience may be useful for some countries which could increase the size of their market by some common market-type arrangements.

Irrigation Subsidy

The use of irrigation technology to enhance land productivity has a hoary tradition in India as in many ancient civilisations. Before the Second World War, it was more or less a self-financing activity of the government; now it has become one of the chief vehicles for subsidising agriculture, thus helping to keep the cost of necessary wage goods down.

As an illustration, we have taken the average of irrigation subsidy for North Western states of India where the agricultural yield rate has been highest in the last two decades. This have been calculated as operational and maintenance expenses plus depreciation and interest rate at 9.44% (combined) *minus* gross receipts. They have been found to be of the order of 25% of the price of wheat paid by the state procurement agency to the farmer (calculated from Gulati, 1987). The new irrigation works are usually financed through long-term government securities; the interest payment and its redemption is taken care of by general government expenditure, allowing the irrigation department to give a substantial subsidy without declaring it as such.

Electricity Subsidy

In India there is a huge subsidy on electricity for all consumers, hidden by accounting subterfuges. Agriculture gets a further subsidy over and above that; for instance, for the Gujarat state of India. Kothari and Dadi (1975) have calculated for 1972–3 the cost of electrification as follows:

	(Million Rs)
Interest and depreciation charges on Gujarat Electricity Board capital at 12% (combined)	253.5
Operating cost with repair and maintenance	168.2
Total	421.7

However the revenue of the electricity board was only Rs 150.3 million. It is obvious that the electricity board was trying to meet only its current cost through the electricity tariff. For a capital-intensive industry like electricity, this implies a general subsidy of the order of 65%, due to differential rates of electricity charges to different types of consumers; Kothari and Dadi (1975) found that the charges for agriculturists were 84% of the average charges. Farmers were thus paying only about 30% of the cost of electricity. For another state of Tamilnadu for the year 1982–3 Shankar and Hema (1984) gave the average cost per kwhr of electricity as Rs 0.63 while the rate charged for big farmers was Rs 0.15 and for small farmers only Rs 0.12, giving electricity price for farmers between 20 and 25% of its cost of production.

However this does not give any idea of the subsidy per unit of output. In Punjab, electricity charges are roughly estimated to be of the order of 4% of total expenditure; if we can generalise the Kothari–Dadi estimate of capital cost versus the average subsidy to the farmer, this comes out in the order of 13% of the cereal price.

Credit Subsidy

Agriculture gets finance from the nationalised banks in India on preferential terms. Gulati (1987) has estimated it as the difference between the weighted rate of interest charged by financial institutions from agriculture and from retail trade, which was 4.5%.

Fertiliser Subsidy

Fertiliser subsidies are one of the means of inducing the farmer to use modern methods of production. The production elasticity of its relative price to that of the price of various foodgrains has been estimated in the region of –0.4 (see for rice Radhakrishna and Indrakant, 1987; for wheat Sirohi, 1984). Fertiliser subsidy in 1984–5 was 50% of the price of the fertilisers charged to the farmers though it was only 27% in 1983–4. Thus if the subsidy had not been there, production of foodgrains would have been about 18% less (Radhakrishna and Indrakant, 1987).

It is estimated that, on average, for every tonne of fertiliser (nutrients) put into the soil there is an increase of 7 tonnes of foodgrains (Government of India, 1985–6) Fertiliser costs per tonne in India are equivalent to about 3 tonnes worth of wheat[2] (Desai, 1986). Fertiliser thus costs between 30 and 50% of the value of the incremental production of foodgrains; that will make the value of the fertiliser subsidy about 20% of the extra foodgrains produced.

Foodgrain Subsidy

Foodgrains are procured at a guaranteed minimum price announced beforehand. This is an incentive to the producers to increase production, with an assured margin. Prices that are considered remunerative to the producers may not be affordable by the poor, especially after the costs of transport, handling and charges of retail are added. Hence, there develops a gap between the two, which is bridged by foodgrain subsidies. However, the beneficiaries are largely in the cities as the government distribution system is mainly concentrated there. The wage structure in the organised industries and the public sector is closely linked with the prices of consumer goods. Higher food prices would, therefore, increase the cost to the urban and industrial producers of goods not only for home consumption but also for export; this subsidy is directly designed to protect that sector from the consequent price increases.

The issue price of the major foodgrains have been about 20% higher than the procurement price paid to the producers; the excess cost of distribution through the public distribution machinery is borne by the government in the form of the food subsidies: during the last few years, it has been around 30% of the procurement price of rice (Radhakrishna and Indrakant, 1987). It may be of the same order for wheat. Government supply of non-rice foodgrains in 1981–3 was reported at the annual average of 7.39 million tonnes. The corresponding subsidy was Rs 3,545 million, giving the subsidy rate as about Rs 480 per ton. The average procurement price of wheat was Rs 1,360 per ton in Punjab. Assuming the same for all procurement and assuming most non-rice to be wheat, the subsidy rate comes out approximately as 35%.

Collating the above rough estimates, we see that direct and indirect subsidies, etc. are responsible for the reduction of the price of foodgrains by about 40–45%. Some other details have to be studied if the total subsidisation of food grains is to be assessed. For instance, there is a semi-subsidy in the shape of an almost negligible excise tax on diesel oil in comparison to the tax on petrol. As tractors as well as the trucks used for transport of produce use diesel oil only, this helps to keep the prices of agricultural products down. Further, there is a small excise tax on agricultural machinery which works in the opposite direction by increasing the capital costs of agricultural transformation.[3]

However, for our purpose we need not go into the minutiae of these incentives. It is sufficient to note that through its subsidies and other incentive schemes India could keep the price of its foodgrains for urban labour as if there had been no modernisation of agriculture, and thus retain the competitiveness of its exports in international markets, as well as the scope of increasing exports on the basis of cheap labour costs. Even then, the economic feasibility of adopting these costly land-intensive cultivation practices by farmers was determined as if the price of the foodgrains was almost double its actual level.

LIMITS TO PRICE ADJUSTMENTS FOR GROWTH

We have seen that India has pursued a strategy of adopting land-intensive agricultural production while keeping the price structure of the economy the same as it was when traditional methods of food-grain cultivation were practised. This strategy worked well, allowing a whole fabric of modern industries to be established. The foreign exchange required for the process was earned, and the necessary wage goods were produced, through this ingenious scheme of uncoupling the supply and demand prices of agriculture. But this strategy has its price, and its limits; it is necessary to appreciate both before any further progress can be made in adapting such a strategy to changing circumstances or applying the lessons and experiences to new situations.

The financial core of the Indian government's industrialisation strategy has been to provide industries with cheap electricity and cheap labour through cheap food. It has also given them protection from world market forces by erecting a tariff wall around the country, well beyond their 'infant' stage. This is in addition to generous investment incentives and finance provided both for industrialisation and for supporting small-scale and cottage industries in the name of social expenditure to protect the weak. (It may be noted that this social expenditure makes non-agricultural items of wage goods available to labour at the traditional prices and thus supplements the effects of agricultural subsidies in lowering the nominal wage rates.)

The wherewithal for all this largesse is collected primarily by means of high direct and indirect tax rates in the form of custom and excise duties. This not only gives the requisite protection to the industries concerned, but also transfers investable funds into the hands of the government to be invested, or given as subsidies or even to increase unproductive government expenditure. The major consequences of such a strategy are as follows.

RESTRAINING OVERALL INDUSTRIAL GROWTH

As already pointed out, the annual growth rate of Indian industries was dismal during the 1965–80 period at 4.1%, as compared to that of all developing countries at 7.6%. In 1985 the proportion of its industrial output in GDP was 27%, while for developing countries as a whole it was 34%. The growth of employment in industries was at the rate of 2% per annum during the 1980s. This is less than the rate of growth of the population, which is of the order of 2.5% per annum. With this strategy there is hardly any prospect of industries absorbing large chunk of the labour force in future; so the price paid for this development strategy in terms of the rate of growth has not been negligible.

Low Labour Productivity in Import Substitution

Protection given to import-substituting industries, implies that they have not been able to meet the international prices of manufactures in the protected market. Being oligopolistic industries, and having relatively cheap labour, they tend to employ many more people for the industrial technology they have adopted from developed countries than is warranted by international standards. Some of the advantages of subsidies, etc. are thus frittered away as inefficiency and labour productivity loss: even after the commodities have started production within the country, the price structure does not change to one pertaining to the modern technology that is being used.

This low productivity makes most of the non-agricultural intermediate goods as costly as if they were imported. With wages being determined by agricultural prices, which are only a fraction of international prices, this high price of intermediate goods make for comparatively higher prices of the goods required for the minimum comforts of life. We thus see from the UN Purchasing Power Parity study (1982), that while bread, cereals, meat, fish, footwear, gross rent, medical care, public transport, education and residential construction costs in India are less than a third of international prices, the cost of total consumption expenditure is 40%. The commodities that cost more than the average include clothing, oils, milk and milk products, beverages and tobacco, fuel and power, household furnishing, etc. These cannot be considered as luxuries; their comparatively high prices have lot to do with the selective subsidisation of agriculture and overmanning and other oligopolistic inefficiencies in intermediate goods industries.

High Capital Costs

The most disturbing spillover of this inefficiency has been in the capital goods industry. Though most capital goods are being produced in India with the help of 'cheap' labour, that advantage is not reflected in their prices. The UN study on purchasing power parity, Kravis *et al.* (1982), puts the comparative price of producer durables at 115% of the international price, while consumer goods are priced at a mere 40%. This implies that, on average, the machinery capital–output ratio will be about three times that in developed countries. The damaging implications for growth rates and the necessary non-wage incomes, and the extent of interest and depreciation in formation of industrial prices is obvious.

The implication for further growth of agriculture in the land constrained economy of India is even more critical. Bhalla (1979) has estimated that the incremental capital–output ratio for foodgrains is of the order of 4. Indian government sources still estimate that more than 30% of the population of the country remains below the poverty line. This implies a huge capital outlay before the country will be able to feed its population adequately. If the price of capital goods and foodgrains was in the same proportion as in the advanced countries, this incremental capital–output ratio would shrink to the order of 1.3 instead of 4. Then the achievement of the aim would become almost three times easier; probably, it would then not require any governmental help as it would become quite profitable for the farmers and businessmen to undertake the task unassisted.

The claim that the country is self-sufficient in foodgrain implies that foodgrain is sufficient to meet the effective demand. 'Effective demand' is the demand of foodgrains from those who have the money to purchase it; the very existence of a large number of people below the poverty line implies that effective demand is so low because a large number of people are unemployed or under-employed. As and when they get employment the effective demand will increase pari passu. The process will tend to stop only when nobody remains below the poverty line. In other words, the constraint on fully utilising the Indian labour force is still the land; there are technical means available to overcome that constraint, but the skewed price structure is an obstacle to removing it.

The Limit to Growth With This Strategy

With a cross-financing strategy, India has modernised part of agriculture by the adoption of land-intensive technology, simultaneously keeping wage goods prices at a level that could finance the export development that is so necessary for getting technology and capital goods from the developed countries. So the country has been able to use modern techniques of production in almost every branch of economic endeavor. However, a large proportion of the population of the country is still abysmally poor; India's rate of growth of GDP or industry is nothing to be proud of. And its strategy is running out of steam: a further increase in agricultural output not only requires huge amounts of capital investment but also increasing amount of direct or indirect subsidy. The Finance Minister in his 1986 budget speech opined, 'Food and fertiliser subsidies have now reached Rs 37 billion and have increased by over 40 per cent per annum in the last three years. Even with buoyant tax revenues, this order of increase is simply not sustainable. At this rate the total subsidies would exceed Rs 410 billion over the seventh plan period. To put it in another way, this amount would be sufficient to provide one deep tube well and one primary school building in each village of the country' (quoted in Desai, 1986: 250).

Clearly there is a dilemma. The subsidies given to part of the country to start the land-intensive cultivation are now being claimed by other parts of the country: that is the logic of diffusion of technology. However, the country cannot afford it; the industrial structure that has been developed is so inefficient that it cannot increase the pool from which these subsidies can be extended for development of other regions. The old pool is over-extended, and the alternative of reducing subsidies is creating unrest among the original beneficiaries.

Since 1984 there have been attempts to liberalise the economy further by reducing restrictions on imports and exports and trying to reduce the various subsidies, etc. However, this is treating the symptoms without looking to the underlying causes; with the current structure no fundamental changes can be achieved without reducing import demand and other reasons for exports. The result of these measures has been a sharp fall in the exchange rate of the Indian currency from Rs 10.56 per SDR in 1982–3 to Rs 17.12 per SDR in 1987–8. During this period the consumer price index also increased by 51%. The net result of treating symptoms alone has been to inflate the price level and correspondingly depress the exchange rate without any fundamental improvement in the economic situation.

The strategy is thus fast reaching an impasse well before the country can either diffuse land-intensive agricultural technology so as to leave nobody below the poverty line, as well as before industrial growth can reach its natural momentum. It has done its job in bringing the economy out of the under-development category but for its fulfilment it requires a radical *transformation*.

CONTOURS OF THE WAY FORWARD

It is thus clear that at this stage of development, countries like India have to normalise their price structure in order to proceed on the road to development. Only that normalisation will help to make agriculture naturally profitable and cure the inefficient use of labour in oligopolistic industries, as well as make the natural profitability of modern industry available for further development. However, this will reduce competitiveness in exports. There is hardly any reason why other than natural resource-based exports should command a cost advantage over developed countries when the technique of production has been borrowed from them. Of course, there should be significant scope for mutually beneficial exports to other developing countries, as most of them are small countries and thus hardly suitable for developing the whole range of modern industries on an economic scale. As India can produce the whole range of these manufactures it should not feel unhappy about switching to a more inward-looking strategy.

Another aspect of reducing the necessity to export is desisting from taking any foreign loans which have to be repaid from general export income; it does not matter whether these are on market terms or concessional ones like loans from the World Bank, IMF, etc. All loans or extra trade should be intrinsically barter-type, delineating in detail the extra export earning that will repay them. While making feasibility studies about that, the indirect subsidy involved in making extra exports possible, and its implications for other sectors of the economy, should be clearly spelled out. From the other end, the subsidies for various wage goods should be slowly removed, thus making labour costs more realistic.

Management of these two streams should take the country's economy a long way towards a suitable strategy of growth; the necessary adjustment will be quite painful, not only for industry but also for the government as and when labour ceases to be subsidised through the wage goods subsidy.

16 Partnership in Development?

THE DILEMMA OF AN INDIVIDUAL COUNTRY'S DEVELOPMENT: A RECAPITULATION

The process of 'developing' changes traditional techniques of production based primarily on human and animal energy, to the modern ones based on chemicals and fossil energy. These are responsible for increasing the productivity of labour manyfold, with the help of modern electrical and non-electrical machinery and fossil fuel-operated transport equipment. For this transformation, a developing country requires the implementation of such technology, an implementation which requires not only the import of know-how but also the import of the relevant equipment until the recipient country is advanced enough to produce it for itself. It also requires the import of chemicals and other intermediate goods before their own capacity for production is created. And, of course, it needs to import the raw materials and fuel, etc. not produced in the country itself. This really implies that until the time it is completely developed it will require a continuous stream of imports, and foreign exchange earnings will be a *sine qua non* for the purpose. The availability of loans from international or national agencies in developed countries for the purpose will result in long-term repayment commitments in foreign exchange, the sustenance of which, as we have seen, will help to keep the country under-developed.

For most developing countries, foreign exchange earnings depend on their traditional exports; each of them may think that by increasing exports they may be able to increase the availability of foreign exchange, but this concerted action only results in supply of the commodity outstripping demand in the international market, driving down the price of the commodity in turn. The resulting misery in the exporting country reduces the enthusiasm to expand the capacity of a now loss-making export commodity. The recouping of its price in the international market restarts the cycle, prodded by the desire for extra foreign exchange which makes further development possible. The development advisors' failure to appreciate this 'fallacy of composition' tends to keep the prices of internationally traded commodities

244

around the minimum supply price under present international economic conditions.

Present international economic conditions involve a subsistence level of living for most of the working force of the developing countries, and the mechanism outlined above ensures that their low level of living is not improved. A commodity price increase that could lead to an improvement will induce extra capacity creation and thus extra supply and price downturn in the long term.

On the other hand, if a developing country wants to earn foreign exchange by exporting the manufactured goods it has started producing as a result of induced industrialisation through foreign loans, etc. it has to keep the price of its manufactured exports sufficiently lower than of those produced in the developed countries in order to be able to meet the extra cost of transport, trade, etc. of the finished goods. Its cost of production will be enhanced by the higher costs of imported capital and intermediate goods, as well as from the fact that the technology transferred is probably one of the least efficient still in production in the transferring country. As the only countervailing item of cost available is the payment to labour, this strategy requires very low nominal wage rates indeed.

The maintenance of a low nominal wage rate implies a low price of wage goods in general, and basic food items in particular. This is no problem while these items are produced with traditional technology; however, that limits the total extent of production due either to the scarcity of the suitable land or to the availability of labour prepared to work on less and less productive land with traditional techniques only. A sizeable portion of this agricultural production is transferred for the consumption of labour working in the export crop or industry sectors. As the income elasticity of these subsistence wage goods is very low, this transfer is effected by a compulsory rent and/or sufficiently low emoluments for the labour working on these traditional techniques of production.

The strategy of increasing agricultural production by using modern methods of chemical and machinery-intensive agriculture requires the import of crucial inputs; this puts a lower limit to which the price of cereals, etc. can fall, which in its turn implies a higher minimum possible wage rate. This higher wage rate in its turn will tend to over-price exports for the international market, thus defeating the whole development effort.

Some countries have tried to overcome this dilemma by subsidising agriculture. But subsidies have their costs, and some other economic sectors have to pay them; this tends to reduce the growth of those sectors, the very engine of growth is jeopardised and self-sustaining growth becomes unachievable. This strategy can be used only by big countries who have sufficiently sizeable other sectors to subsidise agriculture, and even big countries find after a time that they cannot go the whole way of modernisation through this route as they reach a limit to what other sectors can be made to pay. They, then, lament the burden and appeal to the favourite scapegoat of over-population for their difficulties.

SOME NECESSARY CONDITIONS FOR DEVELOPMENT

It would seem, therefore, that certain conditions for the development of the under-developed world are necessary; six of them are noted below.

1. Financial arrangements should be so organised that economic projects financed through loans are not expected to bear the double cost of amortisation – one at the time of repayment of the loan and the other when replacing their depreciated capital stock. In industrialised countries the resources to start a firm are de facto loaned from the shareholders; they are never paid back. However, the owners of the shares can sell their shares whenever they please to willing buyers without involving the establishment in any way, so there is no strain of paying back the original capital on the firm. They only amortise for replacement when necessary through depreciation funds. A similar arrangement is necessary for the infant industries of the developing countries.
2. All intermediate and capital goods should be produced within the economy. We have seen that growth of industries vertically integrated within the economy is likely to have more chance of becoming economically viable in the long run. If necessary inputs are imported the general equilibrium conditions of the economy tends to distort the price structure in a way that makes long term development more difficult, as it almost always implies that products of some sectors are priced so low that it is uneconomic to modernise them. Even medium-term development seem to be jeopardised by fluctuating international prices of export commodities that usually bring in the foreign exchange necessary to purchase essential inputs.

3. The production of foodgrains should be at least as profitable as the production of internationally traded agricultural and plantation crops. This also implies that price relations between foodgrain prices and those of modern agricultural inputs like fertilisers, fuel and agricultural equipment, etc. should be similar to the ones prevailing in the industrial world. That would ensure that food production was modernised so that it was able to provide adequate sustenance to the people of the country.
4. The products of the mining and quarrying industry should command a price which gives sufficient purchasing power to the workers, enabling them to purchase foodgrains, etc. at the higher price indicated above.
5. Manufactured goods should command sufficiently large market not only to take advantage of all the possible economies of scale, but also to have sufficient competition to retain efficiency in the use of resources, avoiding monopoly profits for the few at the expense of general well-being.
6. Until there is complete employment, the new innovations should gradually be introduced so as not to force a large amount of undepreciated capital equipment into obsolescence, thus increasing the capital cost of the industrialisation process.

The first five of these requirements will be more or less satisfied if free migration of population as well as free entry of all goods produced in developing countries is encouraged by industrial countries, together with stable currency exchange rates. Then the problem of the development of the under-developed world will become similar to the problem of economic growth of outlying areas within a country. The requirement of slowing down the rate of obsolescence sufficiently is not satisfied in the developed market economies themselves; consequently it produces extra unemployment as well as lower life-time returns on the capital employed, but allows faster growth of productivity. However, investment funds for modernisation of traditional industries are in short supply in a developing economy, and this short-term under-utilisation of resources may put a great strain on its attempts at modernisation.

This is politically a tall order. There does not seem to be any economic, political or social interest in the industrialised world in this economic reorganisation. In fact, there will be short-term cost to them in terms of higher raw material prices, as well as more market penetration by developing countries; this will imply not only a temporary reduction in living standards, but also higher unemployment in the industrialised world, and free immigration will swamp the much higher standard of living that they at present enjoy.

A SOUTH–SOUTH COMMON MARKET

The other alternative is for the developing countries to work out a 'South–South common market', and then deliberately try to meet the requirements outlined above. This will require uncoupling the price structure within the common market from the price structure that is being imposed by the international commodity markets on the developing countries; this can be done by means of judiciously administered external tariff duties and subsidies, as well as generous internal subsidies and price support to develop essential agricultural and manufacturing industries. An intra-market regime of discriminatory tariffs, trade directions, quotas and indicative planning may be considered, to ensure both sufficient competition and mutually consistent resource allocation. These may be necessary so that the presently more industrialised countries in the South may not take undue advantage of the common market to play the same role as that the present industrialised market economies are playing on the world scale.

There is a well-defined mathematical methodology (Mathur and Hashim, 1979) to determine the dimensions of all these tariffs, subsidies, etc. which will lead to optimal allocation of resources in such a way that the gains for each of the participating countries are similar. This is designed to ensure that these may not be manipulated by vested interests and other similar elements. Most of the South–South common markets attempted so far have foundered on tariff details, which gave the impression that some of countries were gaining at the expense of others, or which required unacceptable sacrifices from some members in terms of their trading relations with the outside world.

Further, a common market of developed countries not only increases efficiency by sharpening competition, but also permits a bigger market for technological innovations to succeed, and thus promotes rapid technological change. The need of developing countries is different; it is to ensure that the industries necessary to provide basic needs as well as capital goods are established within the group. For the purpose, the format, rules, etc. of the common market have to be thought out afresh. For instance, to be able to have a total vertically integrated industry in a developing countries' common market, some industrialised developing countries may have to be persuaded to be a part of it. However, their inclusion may give them an unfair economic advantage, which may become a focus of resentment in other less developed countries in the market. The general pattern that is practised in industrialised economies may thus even be harmful for the aim of achieving development.

There should, however, be no illusions about the political difficulties of achieving this South–South common market in a politically and economically unfriendly international environment. It is well known that the groups which are economic losers from any new economic arrangement use all their direct or covert economic and political capabilities to thwart the arrangement in its infancy. Whatever the reasons, the sad fact is that such attempts have hardly met much success in the past; we have to consider whether we can find any less radical and more gradual way to get out of this development dilemma.

MULTILATERAL PROJECT-BASED PARTNERSHIP (MPP)

No new country can hope to join the ranks of the developed countries with the present international economic order. No developing country can extract itself from the toils of international finance, a necessary consequence of the attempt to achieve the technological transfer involved in the process of development. Unlike the nineteenth century, there are no colonies or dependencies that can supply cheap labour and where costly exports can be sold. It was the availability of cheap labour to produce land- and labour-intensive commodities and markets for the products of the then industrialising countries than was so helpful in the development of the present-day developed countries; even now the currently developing countries are performing a similar function.

As no country by itself is capable of becoming developed in the current international economic system, we have to see whether some multilateral arrangements can be devised that would allow a group of them to develop out of this poverty trap. UNIDO's *Global Report 1986* (1986: 159) opines, 'The countries of the South are fully capable of producing some of the capital goods needed by the other countries of the South. Not every country can have a fully integrated industrial structure, and a pooling of the resources and the capabilities through trade will be essential. This also means a pooling of the scientific and technical personnel to lead the South into a new Industrial Revolution and to adapt its advances to the special needs of developing countries'.

> Brazil and India and, to a lesser extent Argentina and Mexico have reached a considerable degree of self sufficiency in non-electrical machinery industry. This industrial branch, which manufactures industrial machinery and machines to make machines, comprises the heart of the capital goods industry . . . Further, Brazil, China (Taiwan), India, Mexico, and the Republic of Korea produce a full range of heavy electrical equipment (electricity generators, transformers, switchgears) as well as electronic goods, television sets and radios. Brazil, Argentina, and Mexico manufacture passenger cars, trucks and buses, and railway equipment; Brazil also has a substantial shipbuilding capacity. India is the South's largest producer of electric locomotives, followed by Brazil and Turkey. India, Argentina, Brazil, Cuba, Ecuador, the Republic of Korea, and Turkey are the major producers of railway wagons. Latin America is largely self sufficient in the metal product industry. Among the world's 34 largest steel producers are included Argentina, Brazil, Mexico, and Venezuela among Latin American countries, as well as the Republic of Korea, India, Turkey, and Taiwan. The non-ferrous metal industry is heavily concentrated in Latin America, which accounts for 70% of the output of the South. Chile is the largest producer of refined copper in the South, followed by Zambia, Peru, and Zaire. Brazil is the South's largest producer of aluminum, followed by Venezuela, India, Argentina, Ghana, and Egypt. Mexico is the largest producer of the refined lead and zinc in the South followed by Brazil and Peru, while the largest producers of tin in the South are Malaysia, Indonesia, Bolivia, Brazil, and Nigeria. . . . . The production of building materials (like cement, bricks, pipes, etc.) in the developing world is heavily concentrated in ten economies. Among them are Argentina, Brazil, and Mexico in Latin America, etc. (UNIDO, 1986: 76–91).

This extract from the UNIDO study shows that the developing world has created a capacity for producing almost all types of industrial products. Not only capacity, but the know-how to expand that capacity is available in profusion. That shows the possibility of development of most of these countries even if they rely only on different countries of the South. But the major question is how to overcome the dilemma pointed out above, which seems to be inherent in development with the present rules of the game.

MULTILATERAL VERTICALLY INTEGRATED COMMODITY DEVELOPMENT PROJECTS (MVICDP)

The international monetary and financial system has proved to be one of the major constraining factor on the growth of the developing countries. Any extra effort for development should try to bypass that system if it is not to be enmeshed in similar problems. This implies that separate long-term vertically integrated sub-systems may be envisaged for each commodity that is considered basic for development. This would be similar to the system practised by vertically integrated multinationals or Japanese conglomerates (called Zaibatsu), where the prices used in all capital and intermediate goods transactions are internalised while that of the final consumption good is determined by the market. The accounting exchange rate within the system is determined through internal economic conditions rather than by the exchange rate determined in the general market. As there will be only one commodity that will be finally sold in the market, all internal valuation should be theoretically made in the future price of that commodity. International markets for the commodity 'futures' are well developed; they are the markets where goods are sold for future delivery and contracts are made. These markets can provide a way out also for the participants who for some reason cannot wait for their share until the final production of the commodity comes to the market. These internal exchange rates between different inputs and services involved directly or indirectly in the production of the commodity should be settled between participating countries before the start of the individual projects. This will ensure that until the time the project is established on self-sufficient basis any uncertainty surrounding it will be of a technological rather than a monetary or financial nature.

Fortunately in the developing world there are countries which have not only a base of basic engineering, chemical, and biological know-how but also the raw materials required for production. They also have unutilised capacity for the production of electrical and non-electrical machinery, basic chemicals, fertilisers, etc. as well as the expertise in developing virgin land for modern cultivation. All these factors of production are under-utilised. There are countries having unutilised capacity to produce extra fuel as well as petro-chemicals without having effective demand for these products. On the other hand many countries have land resources which they are trying to develop but they have at present neither the technical know-how or the technical resources to develop them, and their price structure does not allow such developments to be an economic proposition. There is seemingly no way in which they can ensure a continuous supply of foreign exchange to import non-indigenous intermediate goods like fertilisers necessary for modern agricultural production.

Here is a chance for the development of a mutually fruitful partnership to see through individual vertically integrated comprehensive projects among participating countries. These projects should not require any input or capital equipment that cannot be provided by the participating countries themselves, and it is not necessary that the same countries should cooperate on all projects. But each project cooperation will have to be on a long-term basis, thus avoiding the rigidity of structure that is implied in existing or previous common market institutions. However, this introduces another rigidity in terms of irrevocable long-term commitments on the terms decided in detail at the very beginning, before the start of the project itself.

For its success long-term financing, marketing, and managerial arrangements must be agreed upon before the start of the scheme; the relative prices of all the commodities and the services involved in its execution should also be agreed. We can thus have a multilateral scheme for agricultural development between the following three types of countries. One may be a country in Sub-Saharan Africa having virgin land to be developed, requiring reclamation as well as agricultural area-specific research. Another may be an oil-producing country, which would like to produce much more oil than international market conditions permit, and which would also like to develop not only a new regular market for its oil, but also for products like petro-chemicals, fertilisers, etc. which it is capable of producing at quite a low cost. The third may be a country having a requisite engineering capacity together with the raw materials and other intermediate goods required for the production of the agricultural machinery, etc.; it may also have the expertise to develop new agricultural land as well as the requisite research establishment. A country like India which has developed its state agricultural self-financing universities, together with self-sufficient mechanical and electrical industries readily fits the bill.

For our convenience, we shall call these three types of countries *A*, *B* and *C* respectively. It will be to the long-term advantage of all three countries to develop modern agriculture in country *A*. Countries *B* and *C* may jointly invest and provide know-how in a reclamation scheme, and after that reclamation is achieved may also provide expertise to run the new type of agriculture for some time. The expertise will imply establishment of an agricultural university for the area which will train the local experts in the field and also develop suitable strains of crops and efficient agricultural practices. It will administer the farms until sufficiently trained local personnel are ready to take over; the condition will be that all the farming machinery, etc. is procured from country *C*, while there is a long-term contract to procure energy, fertilisers, pesticides, etc. from country *B*. These countries will also provide the expertise to run the scheme during the developmental phase. In return, both countries *B* and *C* will be paid for all their capital and current intermediate inputs and services, in the 'futures' of the commodity planned to be produced (that is, in certificates entitling them to an amount of share of the future produce of the farm). The payment rate may have to be negotiated before the start of the scheme, not in terms of the currency of any country but in terms of 'futures' of the agricultural commodity expected to be produced (so many tons of wheat to be provided for so much fertiliser next year, or so much wheat to be provided for so many years in return for capital goods sent, or so much of a 'wheat future' to be provided against the salary of experts sent, while their actual salary may be the responsibility of the country supplying them). These commodity 'futures' will be negotiable instruments; the receiving country can either sell them in the futures market or avail itself of the commodity when that is due. For the producing country, that will ensure that it will be paying the debt incurred in terms of the commodity being produced by means of the facility developed through the utilisation of that loan, and at a rate that is technically feasible. And it will know that the real terms of its debt will not change due to the movement of the international price structure. The market risk would not be borne by the weakest member participant, as is the case with the current international economic order. Of course the debt may be also conceived as equity, avoiding the repayment of the principal that strangles so many projects in the developing world started by the help of international loans.

Once the modalities of such a project are worked out in the framework suggested above, it will be clear that all the participating countries need not be from the developing world. Even industrialised countries can beneficially participate if they agree to have their returns to investment as well as the payments for the goods and services provided in terms of commodity futures. However as the most basic commodity for which such a scheme may be crucial will be foodgrains, industrialised countries which are surplus in that commodity may not be interested.

This type of contract can be an independent part of the economies of the participating countries; other parts of the economy may continue to run as before. However, the new contracts will be independent of the price structure prevalent in the rest of the economy, it will have its own price structure which will allow it to establish technically modern industry where the prevailing price structure was making establishment economically unviable. Such a scheme will also ensure that it is not trapped in the labyrinth of international finance and commodity markets which, as we have seen, has been responsible for keeping the developing countries under-developed. As the scheme bears fruit, its advantages will permeate other parts of the economy.

This type of contract will be for a predetermined period (say, ten to fifteen years), in which it is expected that the scheme will mature and be able to be managed by local expertise with the institutional arrangements thought best by country *A*. After maturity, the contract may be renewable according to the conditions prevailing; the services of the outside experts may no longer be necessary, and the contract for the supply of the farm inputs, machinery, etc. and their values may also be renegotiated.

One of the major condition for the success of such a scheme is that once its details are settled by the respective governments, it should be left to be run by an independent commission, not subject to the day-to-day pressure of participating governments. This expert commission should be allowed to run the scheme independently on the preagreed lines until the time limit stipulated. It should not only be taken out of the current economic arena, but of the current political arena also.

Similar schemes to that just illustrated can be devised in almost all the branches of productive activity. The main condition is that the country where the production facility is located pays for all the goods and services received by it in the futures of the commodity which the facility helped to produce. How much and when it is paid is decided beforehand. This will not only remove it from the vagaries of the international price fluctuations and financial upheavals, but also give an effective indication of its technical feasibility at the planning and negotiating stage itself.

SHADOW PRICE RATIOS BETWEEN INPUTS AND OUTPUTS

For mutually advantageous multilateral partnerships, the now thorny question is that of the determination of the value of various inputs in terms of the commodity produced. Theoretically, it should be provided by the general formulae of long-term price determination or cost-based price. In these formulae the basic assumption is about the appropriate interest rate to be used. For relative prices, the wage rate does not matter since it can be taken as uniform for all the production units; different skills can be rewarded at the established proportion of the basic wage rate. When choosing an appropriate interest rate, historical experience of the real interest rate in the present developed countries in their development phase should be kept in view. Further, different shadow interest rates may be chosen for the purpose of determining prices in different schemes according to their maturity period. The longer the maturity period of a desirable scheme, the lower should be the shadow rate of interest associated with it. As Galbraith (1958) has shown so vividly in *The Affluent Society*, public works tend to be neglected in a free enterprise market economy. These public works include not only roads, housing, etc. but also big comprehensive development projects like area development, land reclamation, or big river valley projects. In most of these countries they were undertaken as public projects outside the economic calculus based on the sheer gut feelings of politicians or administrators. If their costs are included in the capital costs of a scheme naturally its rate of return will be much less than otherwise. As in developing countries these infrastructural facilities are likely to be more or less absent, the scheme may also to have develop these and their cost will become a natural part of the outlay. In such cases, the relevant guide interest rate to take will not be the historical market real interest rate of developed economies, but one adjusted after taking account of all this necessary expenditure which an individual entrepreneur did not have to pay at that time.

However, as a first approximation, guidance may be taken from the prevailing structure of prices in the developed countries. For instance, capital formation in 1975 was about 1.9 times more costly in terms of cereals in the poorest group of countries than in the USA; in terms of tobacco, it was almost equal and for tea, coffee, etc. it was even less (0.84 times) (Kravis *et al.*, 1982: 190). No wonder that capital formation in these export crops in poor countries is comparatively much larger than in food crops. If the shadow price was pitched as nearly equal to that in the USA, capital investment in such poor countries would also pay.

However, price ratios differ between countries which have successfully transformed their agriculture in pursuance of government policy. For instance, in Japan where the government wants to pursue intensive agriculture, the price of fertilisers in terms of agricultural output is only 45% of that in the USA where extensive agriculture is the norm and there is no reason to encourage such an intensive agriculture due to availability of extensive land area (FAO, 1986: 41). It may be noted that in both these countries – in fact, in most of the industrialised world – it is the government rather than the market that determines the price of agricultural commodities. This implies that shadow price ratios should be chosen for each scheme according to the individual circumstances of the situation.

THE LONG-RUN EFFECT OF MPP

We expect that the first schemes under Multilateral Project-Based Partnership (MPP) will relate to the production of more wage goods; when those wage goods come to the market, they should not depress the price of wage goods in the country. As we have seen earlier, the price of wage goods in these constrained developing countries do not depend on the demand and supply calculus, but on the prices of the internationally traded commodities which the country exports. As the shadow price structure within MPP will be isolated from the rest of the economy, the market price structure in the country is not expected to be affected by it in the short run. However, this extra supply of wage goods will permit the employment of a larger labour force in both export-producing as well as modern development projects.

As more and more industries are developed, the price structure will approximate more and more to that of the developed countries.

This will be primarily due to the fact that all imported inputs are also priced in that way under the shadow pricing system. However, the exchange rate with the rest of the world will depend on the international commodity prices which the country continues to export, but the need to export to the developed world may also diminish if the populace do not develop a new taste for the imported goods. Only when the need to export to them to pay back international loans and their interest ceases will the exchange rate tend to approximate the purchasing power parity of the currencies involved. The country will by then be well on the road to development.

17 Foreign Exchange-constrained Developing Economies

DETERMINATION OF PRODUCTION, ETC.

In foreign exchange-constrained developing economies, imported goods enter into the production of almost every commodity, as raw materials or intermediate goods. They may not be entering as direct inputs but may be the inputs of some input entering into the production of that commodity. In such countries, the economy is so integrated with the international economy that without any imports it may be not possible to produce anything. Imports also enter directly or indirectly into the production of the essential wage goods. Thus to employ labour also implies the use of certain amount of foreign exchange. The availability of foreign exchange thus vitally affects every aspect of the economy.

On the decline of international prices of the staple exports of the country, the availability of foreign exchange will decline pari passu. As it enters into the production of most of the commodities, this will imply a reduction in the production due to the foreign exchange bottleneck. It depends on the individual economy how the scarce amount of foreign exchange is allocated between debt servicing, consumption goods imports and imports of raw materials and intermediate goods. A basic conceptual division is between the production of basic wage goods and other commodities. The larger the amount devoted to the production of basic wage goods, the larger will be the labour force that can be employed.

With wage as well as non-wage income out of the production decreasing and total production and employment also going down, there will hardly be any incentive for new capacity creation. Not only will the imports of new capital goods be affected, but also the national capacity for producing them will have a large disutilisation rate. This reduced activity will have a multiplier effect, reducing in its turn the demand of various commodities for consumption; reduced demand will thus help in the allocation of the scarce foreign exchange to various other uses.

However, it is not expected that the overall reduction will be correctly anticipated by all the entrepreneurs and they can plan to reduce their production accordingly. Further, there is hardly any likelihood that the reduced demand and reduced potentiality of production will match exactly. Quite a few of those experiencing a reduction in their income would have to dig in their savings, thus registering their demand in excess of income. In practice, though the decision on the amount used for debt servicing is a governmental one, the other allocative decisions are left, by and large, to market forces. The struggle in the market for the command over scarce resources is decided by the command over the monetary resources or credit of various parties, and this struggle shows itself in inflationary pressures: the greater the struggle, the higher is the rate of inflation. The way to ameliorate this situation is to institute some sort of rationing of the scarce resource, though this method creates other difficulties.

EFFECT OF THE COMMODITY PRICE CRASH IN THE 1980s ON LATIN AMERICA

Among the developing countries, the countries of Latin America and the Caribbean fit the description of 'foreign exchange-constrained economies'. There is hardly any traditional self-sufficient sector left; nearly all production uses imported inputs directly or indirectly. Their economies are so well integrated with the international economy that hardly anything can be produced with current techniques of production if all foreign trade is cut off. Obviously, with any change in world commodity prices, every aspect of their economy will be affected. In the 1970s when commodity prices were on the higher side, international lenders lent to these countries aggressively under the impression of a high repayment capacity; that money illusion was rudely shaken when commodity prices crashed in the 1980s.

The deterioration of the terms of trade should not affect the extent of production of the necessary wage goods in the countries not using imported inputs in their production, though this condition itself limits the extent of development it can achieve. However, for countries using the imported inputs in its production of necessities, it limits the total production possibility because of the reduction in the availability of foreign exchange.

The terms of trade of the non-oil primary commodities exported by

Latin America and the Caribbean in 1985 reached 79% of what it had been in 1980. The devastating results for gross domestic product and investment are given in Table 17.1. We see there that on the average the per capita GDP in 1986 was the same as that of nine years earlier (1977), and gross investment in 1985 the same as ten years earlier (1975). That is the average, but for seven countries the per capita GDP fell back to that in the 1960s and for nine countries gross investment was lower than any time in the 1970s. 'In Mexico, the government reported that the annual earnings of agricultural workers plunged from the equivalent of $412 in 1982 to $163 in 1984. Most professional salaries were cut in half. Peasants suffered from rising raw material costs and sinking farm prices. Labor congress, a confederation of government aligned unions, contends that the real union wages were being halved by 1987 from [the] 1982 [level]. They claim an unemployment of five millions out of the total labour force of 28.5 million. One industrial association estimated that a thousand manufacturing jobs eliminated weekly by the shrinking local market and the rising import competition – a result of the trade liberalization policy adopted in part to appease Mexico's creditors. The government is laying off thousands of skilled workers at sugar mills, truck factories, rail roads, etc. and other money losing enterprises. The Fundidora Monterrey, Latin America's oldest operating steel work, employing 6000 workers was closed' (Orne, 1987).

So the Great Depression for Latin American states has already arrived. In view of the theoretical considerations outlined above, these dismal results could have been expected. Table 17.1 gives the GDP per capita in 1986 as well as gross investment in 1985 for the Latin American and Caribbean countries as prepared by the Organisation of American States. The collapse of commodity prices and the sharp deterioration in the terms of trade of these countries meant a slide in both the per capita GDP as well as in gross investment. Table 17.1 also give the last year when it was so low. The implication is that all the progress in development achieved during the period has been wiped out due to this price collapse.

We have seen already that this deterioration of the terms of trade was not a fortuitous event but was a *necessary consequence* of the way the international commodity market is organised. This implies that this reversal of development was itself a natural consequence of the way the world economy is organised. Continuation of poverty seems to be a necessary condition of export promotion. And if during a temporary supply stringency in commodity market there is a decrease

Table 17.1 Per capita GDP, investment and wages in America

Country	Per capita GDP 1986 (in 1984 US$)	Year when first reached	Gross inv. 85 (million 1984 US$)	Year when first reached
A. *Latin American and the Caribbean*				
Argentina	2,062.3	1968	6,548.8	1959
Bahamas	7,397.3	1979	168.6	1985
Barbados	2,834.6	1970	234.3	1980
Bolivia	805.8	1963	591.5	1964
Brazil	1,970.2	1980	49,603.7	1975
Chile	1,884.3	1969	3,069.7	1966
Columbia	1,155.1	1979	6,654.3	1981
Costa Rica	1,693.4	1974	911.5	1977
Dominican Republic	1,205.9	1977	1,584.3	1978
Ecuador	1,201.8	1977	2,020.8	1975
El Salvador	759.8	1964	392.5	1964
Guatemala	1,186.4	1971	776.8	1968
Honduras	715.1	1972	562.5	1977
Haiti	309.1	1976	363.6	1985
Jamaica	1,652.4	1964	560.6	1956
Mexico	2,093.4	1978	34,865.0	1974
Nicaragua	798.4	1953	608.3	1973
Panama	2,225.7	1981	757.9	1971
Paraguay	1,738.8	1979	1,358.1	1979
Peru	1,106.5	1970	2,603.3	1966
Trinidad & Tobago	2,492.4	1977	1,714.3	1979
Uruguay	2,252.6	1976	545.1	1959
Venezuela	2,410.9	1964	8,955.6	1968
Regional average	1,765.0	1977	131,641.8	1975
B. *North America*				
Canada	13,680.0*	1985	15,286	
USA	16,690.0*	1985	16,406	

Note:
* GDP per capita of 1985 in 1985 US $

Source: OAS (1987).

in this poverty, it gets reimposed with a vengeance as soon as normal conditions return.

We may also recall that in the development strategy dependent on 'aid' in the form of long-term loans, the development of commodity exports becomes a must for the developing country; this triggers the mechanism which keeps commodity prices so low that poverty becomes a necessary condition of export promotion. Is there any way out from this well-intentioned but usurious international relationship?

IMPORT SUBSTITUTION INDUSTRIALISATION (ISI) OF LATIN AMERICA AND THE CARIBBEAN

The consequences of the dependence of the economy on the availability of foreign exchange were feared sufficiently in Latin America in the 1950s and 1960s and led governments to adopt Import Substitution Industrialisation (ISI) as a means of achieving growth. As Werner Baer writes, 'The ISI wave in Europe and the United States occurred in the middle and second half of the nineteenth century. It is well known fact that in this early ISI process governments played an active role in encouraging and protecting the development of the infant industries. Another characteristic of the nineteenth century ISI is its "national" character. Although in some countries finance for infrastructure investment was obtained from abroad, industries were for the most part in the domestic hands. In [the] Latin America of [the] fifties and sixties, the principal policy instruments used to promote ISI were protective tariffs, special preferences for domestic and foreign firms importing capital goods for new industries; preferential import exchange rates for industrial raw materials, fuels, and intermediate goods' (Baer, 1972).

Two major distinctions between the successful ISI of the nineteenth century and the unsuccessful one of the last three decades emerge. One is that the ownership of the firms was in 'national' hands in the earlier ISI; those who gave 'foreign aid' themselves migrated, and there was hardly any debt service charge to the creditor country. Secondly, whatever was being produced was almost wholly produced in the new country; ISI then implied not only the fabrication of the final product but also that of its raw materials and intermediate inputs.

Latin American ISI was mostly foreign loan-financed, loans which were supposed to be serviced not from the export of the items to be produced by their help, but from the proceeds of traditional exports. This implied that a smaller and smaller proportion of the foreign exchange generated by the traditional exports was available for imports of the intermediate goods and the raw materials of the industry so established. This did not matter much during the 1970s as export commodity prices were high. That even produced a scramble for lending by international banking community to establish (thinly-disguised as ISI) assembly plants for the final consumer goods, as well as to governments for establishing capital goods industries based on imported intermediate goods. This obligation of debt servicing not only took away a big chunk of the savings that were necessary to be reinvested for continuing growth, but also reduced the availability of foreign exchange for running the economy.

The second difference about Latin American ISI was that the country did not care to have import substitution of vertically inte-grated industries as a whole. This mode of ISI did not reduce the import dependence of the economy as it was intended to do; it only made the running of the economy more difficult in times of scarcity of foreign exchange, in the manner described above. 'In some cases, where the initial thrust of ISI was on final consumer goods industries, a built-in resistance to backward vertical integration developed. That is, firms which established themselves in the first ISI period pressured governments not to develop domestic intermediate and capital goods industries' (Baer, 1972). In the oligopolistic market, firms were taking the advantage of protection of the final product and preferen-tial treatment of intermediate goods' imports to manipulate not only higher profits but also a bigger chunk of the foreign exchange re-sources. This could be achieved by transfer pricing in a multinational or with tacit agreement with local company having a long-term contract for imports of the intermediate goods, maintenance, etc. We thus find that for Latin America as a whole the import coefficient did not come down from about 10% throughout these decades.

Another contributing factor to final assembly-type ISI is that the final stages of production are usually labour-intensive and give much larger returns per unit of capital invested; so they get the largest advantage of 'cheap' labour: witness the growth of offshore final processing facilities in Hong Kong, Singapore, etc. for US firms which import the final product back into the USA. If the product uses a considerable amount of imported inputs on which there is no tariff, or on which the tariff rate is lower than that on the final product, then the effective protection the final product gets is higher than the nominal tariff – the margin available for the domestic value added is higher than the difference indicated by the nominal tariff. All this advantage is lost as soon as backward integration is attempted.

It is thus ironic that the net result of ISI has been to place the Latin

American countries in a new and more dangerous dependency relationship with the more advanced industrial countries than ever before. In former times the decline in export receipts acted as a stimulus to ISI; under the new circumstances, 'a decline in export receipts not counterbalanced by capital inflows can result in forced import curtailments which, in turn cause industrial recession' (Baer, 1972).

The conspicuous exception to the above general tendency was Brazil, which tried to have an ISI strategy for the whole range of goods; its government was anxious to promote maximum vertical integration. The beneficial effect of that policy can be seen from Table 17.1. We see that for Brazil, the decline in per capita GDP was among the least in Latin American countries: in 1986 per capita GDP remained much as it was in 1980, even after a steep decline in the export prices of its major exports.

PRODUCTIVITY IN IMPORT SUBSTITUTION INDUSTRIES

In ISI, productivity has been in general on the lower side. Firstly it is well known that in the oligopolistic industries the difference between the efficient cost of production and the going price is filled by 'feather bedding', rather than by price reduction. Unless there is a preannounced scheme of tariff reductions over time as the industry becomes less and less 'infant', there is no incentive to plan for increasing productivity over time. Further, the smallness of many economies precludes the gains of increasing returns due to size which are usual in such industries, as well as those from the descipline and efficiencies of competitive environments. The attempt to introduce the latter by trying to have several firms producing the same commodities made the situation worse, by reducing the size of each unit of production.

Having said that, there is a basic difficulty in matching the productivity of ISI with the corresponding production facilities in the industrialised country providing the technical know-how. In modern times, unlike in the nineteenth century, technological advance is rapid. In industrial countries themselves, most of the industrial machinery becomes obsolete much before being worn out. (see Mathur, 1977, 1987 for a detailed discussion). 'Obsoleteness' implies that even the prime cost of the commodities produced by the help of obsolete capital equipment is higher than the market price of the commodity itself. Mostly, technical know-how which is on the verge of obsoleteness is transferred to the developing countries; as even the prime cost of production on that equipment was higher than the prevailing price, the total cost when the return on the capital as well as the depreciation charges are also included will naturally be much higher. No wonder that the productivity in import substituting industries is so low in the developing countries. With an obsolete technique, sometimes the import of the necessary intermediate goods may cost as much as the final commodity produced by the best technique in the developed country.

A lot of low productivity in developing countries stems from this phenomenon. This cost may have to be borne by developing countries as it is difficult to conceive that in a market economy any firm will part with its industrial secrets to establish import substituting industries in the developing world; and all technical know-how except that which is on the verge of obsolescence is an industrial secret. However, if the establishment of manufacturing is effectively as an offshore processing facility for a multinational, we can expect the introduction of the best technology. Not so when it is a part of the import substitution for a protected domestic market.

STEPS FORWARD

The economic situation of the foreign exchange-constrained developing economies is grim; there is no easy way out, and easy ready made 'solutions' are available only from ideologues of both right and left. If these are followed they are likely to leave the countries in even more of a mess. On the basis of the analysis given above, we list below some outline approaches that may be helpful.

Import Substitution Strategy

We have seen that the import substitution strategy has not delivered the goods in this century. But then nothing else did; after the Second World War not a single developing country joined the club of the industrialised nations, in spite of an international hullabaloo in shape of international institutions, development aid and the so-called 'commitment of the world community' to the cause. A similar period at the close of the nineteenth century saw the emergence of half a dozen such countries; all on the crest of import substitution strategies. We discussed above what went wrong; in view of that the following approach may prove helpful.

The import substitution strategy should be a vertically integrated one. It is necessary for success that attempts be made to produce intermediate goods for the industries already installed. However, the problems of economies of scale do not allow each small country to have such a self-sufficient strategy. This indicates that countries must bilaterally or multilaterally negotiate the establishment of complementary industries. These negotiations should have a long-term commitment of purchases and supplies with a mutually determined price formula which is independent of the vagaries of the international price anarchy. This is not 'all or none', like a common market strategy. Every small amount of this independence from the international suppliers will reduce that much dependence on the availability of free foreign exchange.

About the technical possibilities of meeting these requirements, the UNIDO *Global Report* (1986: 159) writes, 'The countries of the South are fully capable of producing some of the capital goods needed by other countries of the south. Not every country can have a fully integrated industrial structure, and a pooling of the resources and capabilities through trade will be essential. This also means the pooling of scientific and technical personnel to lead the South into a New Industrial Revolution and to adapt its advances to the special needs of the developing countries'. This report shows that the major countries of Latin America like Brazil, Argentina and Mexico are able to provide most of the capital goods for development or restructuring. It also lists other countries that can provide different types of goods. The necessity now is to have detailed negotiations to find out what other countries can provide in exchange for these capital goods, and when. To have any chance of viability a long-term perspective is necessary for organising such a mutually beneficial exchange.

Not only governments can move to remedy this drawback of the current ISI programme. *Business consortia* in different countries can enter into mutually sustaining arrangements; then they need not be confined within the group of developing countries only, a business consortium of developed countries may take part. It is a question of long-term production and sale agreements on terms that are independent of the unreliable international market situation and of producing all stages of the production of a commodity within the partner consortia. For instance, a chemical firm in Puerto Rico may produce fertilisers for use in another Caribbean country and a sister firm take in exchange some previously decided product from that country. So these two firms of Puerto Rico will form a business consortium to negotiate the mutually sustaining deal with a similar consortium of the partner country. This way a part of the process of development can be taken out of the political arena. It is in sponsoring this type of arrangements that *banks can take a leading role*.

Tariff Protection and Productivity

We have seen above that with the twentieth century's fast technological advance in manufacturing industry it is not possible to industrialise without tariff protection. It was not possible to do so even in the nineteenth century, and to explain the phenomenon the economists of the period developed the logic of the 'infant industry' argument. With fast technological advance that logic becomes an extended one; it is hardly possible to develop industries without its help. And this can be abandoned only when the innovative faculties in the developing countries develop to the same extent as in the current developed countries. It is remarkable to note that in spite of the abundance of the innovative activity in industrialised countries, developed industrialised countries like the USA, the EC, Japan and others heavily protect their manufacture to protect their employment and income. For them to lecture the developing countries on the virtues of free trade through the medium of the World Bank, etc. is nothing short of hypocrisy, and/or a thinly veiled attempt to keep the developing countries' market for their own industrial products.

However, the protective wall is conducive to substantial inefficiency; this is also one of the major obstacles in inter-developing country economic cooperation as no country is likely to enjoy purchasing costly products from any other country unless and until there is a visible *quid pro quo*. To deal with this difficult problem, an attempt may be made to quantify the 'infant industry' argument, on the basis of a sliding rate of protection, given in such a way that it will automatically go on sliding down over the years, until and unless there are grounds for new protection because of a significant technical advance in industrialised world; some such scheme may keep the local producers striving for productivity increases all the time.

It will also be conducive to create a larger market specially for goods having perceptible increasing returns to scale. These agreements may also be negotiated between different countries on the basis of groups of commodities; with suitable give and take it may be possible to have sufficiently large effective markets for almost every commodity. GATT rules allow tariffs for all outside imports if there is a free trade area, and that free trade area does not imply completely free trade, but only special preferences to each other.

No blanket solutions are appropriate, and doing away with all protection in the name of increasing efficiency will be suicidal for development. The partial economics taught by Marshall for small businessmen in a static economy cannot be applied to the national economic problems of general development; you cannot determine the efficiency of production of one commodity by comparing it with the cost of production in any other country at the current exchange rate. The long-term productivity of the economy as a whole has to be considered, together with the effect on the availability on foreign exchange of any action about an individual commodity. The moving general equilibrium combining the techniques of input–output and linear, non-linear and integer programming analysis may give some useful results, but all partial economic analysis will have to depend either on a ceteris paribus or some other ideological proposition like free trade or perfect competition, etc. to give any conclusion. Such slipshod analysis may have a very high cost in terms of the well-being of the people involved.

Employment and Wages

When an economy is faced by a foreign exchange constraint, the extent of employment and wages depends on the availability of wage goods. The production of wage goods will be constrained by the allocation of foreign exchange for the purchase of the intermediate goods for their production. The basic intermediate goods required for the production of agricultural wage goods are chemicals like fertilisers and energy sources; negotiations between different countries or business consortia for their availability on an effective barter basis are called for: once they are adequately provided, almost full employment at the minimum wage level can be achieved by suitable economic management of the economy on the principles taught to us by Lord Keynes. The non-agricultural part of the minimum wage goods will be efficiently supplied by the informal sector, that does not require much foreign exchange resources.

Making the Life of the Unemployed More Productive

However, even if the wherewithal is available, it will take some time before the unemployment level can be reduced to tolerable limits. Where land is not in short supply, there is a possibility that people can live at least as well as our forefathers lived in the pre-industrial revolution period; the problem is the organisation of property rights and the market. However, the state can temporarily override laws of property rights, as it does during war time, or if land is required for some public purpose. Then it can make it available to the unemployed or partially employed to eke out some extra supplementary production both for increasing welfare as well as to keep them out of the mischief that usually accompanies boredom.

Debt Repayment and the Latin American Payment System

Economic activity in these countries is directly related to the availability of foreign exchange. The collapse of commodity prices in the 1980s has made the creditor banks nervous and instead of having a net inflow of capital much higher than net payment of interest and profit abroad, these countries are finding that the situation has completely reversed; unless and until this basic situation improves, there does not seem to be any way out of the depression. Otherwise 'It will require even more severe wage cuts and further deflation and the tragedy is that this is the best that the more industrially successful countries of the south can hope for' (UNIDO, 1986).

To stop this bloodletting, in the short run, it may be necessary to make repayment of interest and capital on the outstanding loans in 'semi-convertible dollars'. The recipients may have to reinvest the non-convertible portion creating the requisite investment demand. Some sort of Latin American payment system may take up the administration of such a scheme, deciding the portion that may be made convertible every year. This would also give foreign investors a choice of the countries where they want to invest that portion of their repatriated capital which happens to be in non-convertible dollars.

Of course, the creditor banks will not exactly jump at this idea if the alternative is to get the whole repayment in convertible dollars. However, they have by now got used to the idea that they have to make some compromise on the legalities of this issue; this is evident in the fact that most of them are putting aside some amount to meet this contingency, and quite a few are selling their debts at a substantial discount. This opens up the possibility that the Latin American Payments Union may issue bonds of semi-convertible dollars and service debts by them; their market price in the industrialised world will determine the actual scaling down of the debts that will be necessary to meet this situation.

Of course, this implies a modicum of economic cooperation among these countries. These blocked dollars may be freely convertible into currencies of various countries in the group; this may also lead to coordination in the investment activities of different countries.

International Bankruptcy Law

Previously, the private bankruptcy laws were very severe; the debtor who could not pay his debts had to spend much of his life in servitude or prison. However as we grew more 'civilised', this practice became intolerable and the creditor's rights are now mostly confined to the property of the debtor and not to his person. With the debt crisis of the 1980s it is becoming evident that international jurists and legal experts should be looking into its international counterpart. At present, there is no accepted limit to which a debtor country can be pressed to service debts in foreign currency. That, as we have seen above, may bring economic misery to many who personally were neither responsible for the events nor were the risk-takers involved in any speculative undertakings. Even the countries involved may not have been irresponsible in taking on a debt burden which they now find difficult to repay due to world market conditions.

In the circumstances, a clear limit must be set to which creditors are entitled to demand the repayment in foreign exchange. Setting that limit should take account of its effect on the well-being of the people involved. Of course, servicing the loan in non-convertible currency may be taken on a different footing; we require an international expert committee to look into these complex issues.

Part VII
Appendix: Towards an International Trade Theory without Say's Law

18 Why International Price Structures Differ

INTRODUCTION

The important work of Kravis, Heston, and Summers (1982) not only gives estimates of the 'real' income of the various countries investigated, but also gives a detailed price structure of consumption and investment goods. They found these price structures to be fundamentally different, and neoclassical international trade theory is not able to explain the differences observed. It is intended here to propose a theoretical explanation of this phenomenon that not only does justice to the detailed information thus brought to light, but also is in agreement with the known economic history of the rich and poor countries of our planet.

THE CONVENTIONAL EXPLANATION: INTERNATIONAL PRODUCTIVITY DIFFERENCES

For explanatory purposes, Kravis et al. have reclassified the consumption and investment goods as tradeables and non-tradeables, and then advanced the following explanation: 'As a first approximation it may be assumed for purposes of explaining the model that the prices of the traded goods, mainly commodities, are the same in different countries. With similar prices of the traded goods in all countries, wages in industries producing traded goods will differ from country to country according to the differences in productivity – a standard conclusion of the Ricardian trade theory. In each country the wage level established in the traded goods industries will determine the wages in the industries producing nontraded goods, mainly services . . . Because international productivity differences are smaller in these industries, low wages established in the poor countries in the low productivity traded goods industries will apply also in the not-so-low productivity service and other nontraded goods industries. The consequences will be low prices in low-income countries for services and other non-traded goods' (quoted by Bhagwati, 1984, from Kravis et al., 1983).

This interesting explanation is further elaborated by Bhagwati (1984: 281): By extending the formalisation beyond the excessively limiting Ricardian framework of a single factor, . . . so that we can get closer to a more realistic and meaningful formulation . . . in a general equilibrium two factor model'.

Samuelson (1984) supports this explanation of 'exchange-rate-based estimator's downward bias' by 'productivity differentials' of the tradeable goods. He writes, 'Kravis et al. cite, in addition to Ricardo, such names as Viner, Harrod, and Balassa. The last two do assert the empirical likelihood of greater productivity differences in tradeable than in non-tradeable sectors.

273

Samuelson (1984) makes similar points and works out rigorously the relation between countries' wage levels, exchange rates, and Ricardian cost ratios' (1984: 270n.)

Samuelson (1984: 270–1) explains this phenomenon of productivity differentials as follows:

> Countries that are rich are rich because somehow they have been endowed with greater ability to respond to competitive challenges. In this case, from the fact that tradeable goods involve a country in more challenges, in challenges from all countries, we can deduce that tradeables generally should display greater productivity improvements in any fixed time epoch than nontradeables do and that the countries that have become rich should display their greater productivity differentials in the tradeables sector. Crude and obvious as this model is, it does provide a 'productivity differential' paradigm that is methodologically satisfying in a way that the general Ricardo–Viner theory does not pretend to be.

DIFFICULTIES WITH THE CONVENTIONAL EXPLANATION

Kravis *et al.* have defined 'tradeables' as 'All commodities except construction' (1982: 69) Services are defined as 'categories in which expenditures are on nonstorable goods' (1982: 22). The rest are defined as 'commodities'. Thus tradeables include all foods; all clothing, and footwear except repairs; fuels except electricity; household furnishings; drugs, medical supplies; automobiles and other personal transport equipment; books, stationery; toilet articles and other personal goods. Apart from these, it comprises all the commodity purchases of the government, as well as all producer durables (1982: 69). The detailed price indices for each sector are given in Table 18.1, which gives them for the six groups of the countries according to their national income. Because of the crucial relevance of this information to the topic, Table 18.1 has been repeated here from Chapter 1.

Once we look at the relative prices of tradeables in this disaggregation, all the simplicity of the conventional formulation breaks down. We find, for instance, that for the poorest group of countries (group I), while the price of bread and cereal is 35% of the international price (US price) of the same commodity, the price of transport equipment is 168%. Both commodities belong to the tradeables, whose average price is 60% for this group. Though not so extreme, many similar variations can be discerned even from this summary table.

The variation within the group of tradeables is too large for it to be treated as one group. Even the sign of the exchange rate-based bias is different for different goods. To construct a general theory on this foundation is precarious; in the circumstances, the above assumption of Kravis *et al.* that 'the prices of traded goods are same in different countries' may be taken as a big first approximation. However, it cannot realistically be made for 'tradeable' goods as defined by them. Unfortunately, they have not given the price relatives of the intermediate goods, which are the staple exports of most of the developing countries. However, looking at the price relatives of the

Table 18.1   Average price indices for groups of countries (1975)

	Real income group					
	I	*II*	*III*	*IV*	*V*	*VI*
Real GDP per capita **(US = 100)**						
Range	<15	15–30	30–45	45–60	60–90	>90
Mean	9.01	23.1	37.3	52.4	76.0	100
Price indexes (USA = 100)						
Tradeables	60.0	70.7	86.6	97.9	118.5	100
Of which						
Food	49.8	62.9	68.2	82.2	107.2	100
Of which						
Bread and cereals	35.3	56.7	55.0	58.1	97.2	100
Meat	44.4	67.3	72.7	93.2	127.2	100
Coffee, tea, cocoa	81.8	118.5	167.7	285.1	192.8	100
Tobacco	73.2	66.2	130.4	78.5	147.8	100
Clothing and footwear	55.7	59.0	79.8	100.5	126.0	100
Furniture, appliances	77.6	91.4	96.3	94.9	93.8	100
Transport equipment	168.4	163.5	226.2	162.4	149.1	100
Producer durables	130.1	105.6	135.8	116.4	125.8	100
Fuel and power*	64.4	82.1	81.9	99.1	151.7	100
Of which						
Liquid fuel	123.4	118.4	113.7	166.0	166.5	100
Non-tradeables	24.9	37.2	46.5	53.4	96.7	100
Of which						
Construction	46.0	52.2	72.8	78.5	115.8	100
Services	20.7	34.1	41.2	46.3	94.6	100
Of which						
Education	11.0	17.7	32.2	38.0	100.7	100
Medical care	27.5	29.7	35.9	33.2	62.0	100
Total consumption (including government)	40.1	50.1	59.2	69.1	102.8	100
Non-residential capital formation	109.0	95.6	118.7	107.4	131.5	100
Av. industrial wage rate**	8.4	11.0	26.0	36.9	77.5	100
Av. real consumption of industrial worker	20.9	22.0	43.9	53.3	75.4	100

Notes:
1. There are wide variations within each group, so the table is largely indicative only.
*   In this group electricity is included, which is largely non-tradeable.
**   Industrial wage rates have been calculated from UNIDO (1987) which has culled them from the industrial census data of individual countries, data is approximate, as not all the countries in the group reported.

Source: Kravis *et al.* (1982) Tables 6.8; 6.12; Appendix Table 6.3.

producer durables, which are mainly imported in the poor countries, and of simple manufactures which are exports of some of the newly industrialising poor countries, we can surmise that this approximate equality of the prices may be about 30%–50% either way for traded goods. For non-traded tradeables, the prices in poor countries are found to be as much as 65% lower in poor countries. Even then, they do not seem to make any attempt to export them, as they should under traditional paradigm. Thus they seem to forgo a fine opportunity of making a fast buck. In many cases their governments import foodgrains and subsidise them for the consumption of the local population.

In the 1980s we have seen a fast deterioration in the real wage rate in many developing countries – 'especially in Latin America.'[1] To assume that, somehow, their productivity in tradeables changed so fast seems a bit credulous. The theoretical explanation should not only explain one year's differences, but also sudden changes over the years. Another supplementary or alternative theoretically satisfying paradigm is called for.

IMPETUS TO EXPORTS FOR DEVELOPING COUNTRIES AND TRADED GOODS

Let us relax the assumption that all countries can produce tradeable goods with different productivities. There are some goods that can, at present, be produced only in the industrialised countries. Producer durables for modern industry or modern consumer durables are some of such goods; so are the modern instruments of warfare. If the non-industrialised countries want them, they have to import them from the industrialised countries, and to pay for them they must export. If they have taken any aid or loan for their development from industrialised country, the repayment of the principal and interest will be in the form of export commodities; if they want to develop and/or defend themselves, exports are a must for all developing countries. Once the country is indebted, debt repayment becomes obligatory under the existing international economic order.

Being non-industrialised developing countries, most have to depend mainly on the exports of natural resource-based products. Let us assume that due to the strong demand for imports in these countries, there will be a tendency to generate capacity faster than the increase in demand. In such circumstances, competition among these countries is likely to bring down the price of these commodities to the level of the minimum necessary cost. This also implies that wage rates will be squeezed until the minimum supply price of labour prevails. Thus, as envisaged by Kravis *et al.* (1983), wage rate will depend on the export price of the traded goods. And when the increase in the capacity of these commodities lags behind the increase in demand, we can expect an increase in real wages for the workers in these countries. This fortunate state of affairs is expected to be reversed as soon as supply catches up demand. This scenario will go a long way to explain the sudden reversal of the trend of rising wages in Latin America in the 1980s.

WAGE RATE DETERMINATION IN COMMODITY EXPORTING COUNTRIES

Let the price of the export commodity be p_c in international currency, say $(fob). To understand its factor intensities we shall use a simplifying procedure, given among others by Samuelson (1965: 50–2). 'To discuss the role of intermediate goods and durable machinery in factor price equalization, we can often employ the net production function giving each final good in terms of *total* primary inputs needed for it alone'. So let the production of one unit of export commodity require in total (directly or indirectly) m_c imported intermediate goods measured in international currency (cif). Then, the direct and indirect value added generated by the production of that unit within the economy is

$$y_c = p_c - m_c \tag{18.1}$$

Let direct and indirect labour used in the production of that unit of the export commodity be l_c. Then,

$$p_c - m_c = w l_c [1 + \lambda_c] \tag{18.2}$$

Where λ_c is the proportion of non-wage income to wage income in the direct and indirect value added by its production. Then the wage rate in the international currency is given by

$$w = [p_c - m_c] / \{ l_c [1 + \lambda_c] \} \tag{18.3}$$

As it will be similar in all the industries, this gives us the current wage rate in the economy. With falling commodity prices, this formula gives the necessary reduction in national wage rates. As this is mostly achieved through the instrument of local inflation, the adjustment throughout the economy is instantaneous.

THE LEVEL AND STRUCTURE OF PRICES

To keep the algebra simple, we shall approximate the technology of production with input–ouput assumptions of constant returns to scale, no joint production, etc. Let A be the domestic flow coefficient input–ouput matrix, M and L be import and labour coefficient row vectors respectively. Further, let P be the price row vectors. Then,

$$P = (w L[I + \lambda] + M)[I - A]^{-1} \tag{18.4}$$

Here, λ is the diagonal matrix giving the industry-wise proportion of the non-wage income to the wage income.

This equation system gives only $n-1$ independent equations, and thus gives the internal price structure for given value added industry-wise. Equation

(18.3) gives this, for the value added in the production of the export commodity, and sets the standard for the rest of the economy. The price of the export commodity connects these with international prices. These n independent equations together will determine the purchasing power parity commodity-wise. If there is more than one export commodity, the one giving the lowest wage rate will be the effective equation, while the export of others will generate pure profits for the exporters.

Let p'_c be the price of the exported commodity at the receiving country's ports, and m'_c is the value at the exporting port of the total imported inputs required for the production of a unit of that commodity. And let $p'_c t_c$ and $m'_c t'_c$ be trade and transport cost of moving between the countries a unit of commodity c and its imported inputs respectively. Then the equation (18.3) will give

$$w = [p'_c - p'_c t_c - m'_c - m'_c t'_c] / \{1 . [i + \lambda_c]\} \tag{18.5}$$

Let T' be a vector $\{t'_c\}$ and M' the vector $\{m'_c\}$ then, equation (18.4) may be written as

$$P = wL[1+\lambda]\{(I-A)^{-1} + M'(I+T')(I-A)^{-1} \tag{18.6}$$

Taking equation (18.6) together with (18.5), we see that the price of the commodity exporting country has two components. One is proportional to wages; the second one is proportional to the direct and indirect (total) inputs of imports in the commodity. From equation (18.5) the wages in the country should be less than and the value of imported commodity more than those in the partner developed country to which the commodities are exported and from which the necessary goods are imported. Naturally, the goods having the higher import content will be proportionately more costly. Services (non-tradeables) are likely to have a small commodity input, and so are likely to be on the cheap side. At the other end of the scale, transport equipment, producers durables, etc. are likely to have a large direct and indirect import content, and thus should be proportionately much more costly. A spectrum of purchasing power parity, as shown in Table 18.1 is to be expected.

This structure of prices will be linked to the international price level by the price of the export commodity, giving us the level of prices within the country. To get a feel of the dimensions involved, let c be a commodity also produced in the country to which our country exports. And let it import its imported inputs also from the same country. Let the techniques of production be identical in the two countries making $l_c = l'_c$, and $\lambda_c = \lambda'_c$, and let t and t' be both 33% and the imported commodity inputs be 40% of the cost of production in the partner country, viz $m'_c = 0.40$. Then the above formula gives the wage rate in the developing country as only 22% of that in the partner country. In this case, the purchasing power parity for different goods in this country will range from 21% to 133% in terms of the prices in the partner country. It can be further skewed by the tariff and subsidy policy pursued by the country.

It may be noted that this order of difference in wage and price levels and variations in the structure of prices can reasonably be expected without any difference in the productivities between the two countries; where developing countries are still using the traditional or 'appropriate' techniques of production in some sectors, the order of difference may be larger still. Similarly, if the commodity is not produced in the partner country at all, this link is broken and the wage rate can be substantially less.

IMPLICATIONS OF CHANGES IN COMMODITY PRICE FOR INTERNAL PRICES

Differentiating equation (18.2), we get,

$$dp_c - dm_c = d\{l_c w[1+\lambda_c]\} \tag{18.7}$$

To isolate the effect of changes in the export prices, we may assume that prices of imports have not changed. Then,

$$dp_c = l_c d\{w[1+\lambda_c]\} \tag{18.8}$$

Further, differentiating equation (18.4), we get,

$$dP = L\,d[w\{1+\lambda\}]\cdot(I-A)^{-1} + dM\cdot(I-A)^{-1} \tag{18.9}$$

Assuming that the ratio of non-wage income to wage income changes in the same proportion in all the sectors, and that dM is equal to zero, we get,

$$dP = dp_c \cdot L(I-A)^{-1}/l_c$$

giving changes in prices of different commodities as proportional to the changes in the price of the export commodity. However, the existence of the second term $M(I-A)^{-1}$ in equation (18.4) implies that the proportionate changes in price will be unequal. This leads us to the obvious conclusion that higher the *total* imported input in the production of a commodity, the less its price in the international units will be affected by changes in the world price of the country's export commodity.

THE PRODUCTION POSSIBILITY FRONTIER

Let X and F be the column vectors of total output and final demand of the economy. 'Final demand' is the commodity-wise sum of consumption, investment, net stock changes, and exports. The total import requirements will be given by MX or $M(I-A)^{-1}F$. Total foreign exchange availability is given by $PE + Z - D$, where Z is the amount of the transfer of funds to the country as loans or aid, and D is the debt servicing charges. E is the vector giving the amount of the export of various commodities.

The production set must satisfy the following inequality

$$PE + Z - D >= MX = M(I-A)^{-1}\cdot F \tag{18.10}$$

Equation (18.10) gives the production possibility frontier for the economy as a whole; the actual production pattern will depend on the demand pattern in the economy. It is clear that any reduction in the price of the export commodity will result in a commensurate reduction in the size of the economy. Similar effects will result from the debt servicing activities and the opposite will be the effect of any transfer of resources to the country. Total employment will be equal to LX, where X is constrained by equation (18.10). So the decrease of P or Z or the increase of D will reduce employment in the economy pari passu.

The changes in the income and the price structure will have a twofold effect on the production structure, and these changes will be qualitatively different in cases of rising or falling export commodity prices. In the former, not only will the total demand increase but the demand pattern will also change to favour the commodities with higher import content. There is likely to be a surge of new investment to meet the new demand and the choice of technique will hardly tend to be import saving.

In the case of falling world commodity prices, not only will the total demand decrease, but it will decrease more for the commodities having a higher import content. The technique of production is likely to change towards less import intensity in commodities requiring a negligible amount of fixed capital to help in their production process. In industries where quite a bit of new capital equipment is necessary to effect a changeover to an import-saving technique of production, the process may take a long time indeed. It is difficult to attract new capital in an industry facing decreasing demand and lots of unutilised capacity; in such a case total capital investment should be able to be serviced by the net savings in imported inputs after paying for the substituted factor, rather than by total non-wage income. The existence of such an import saving which was not profitable before is rather unlikely.

In view of the above we can assume for practical purposes that the changes in the production possibility frontier and employment level, etc. as indicated by the formulae above can be fruitfully used for short- to medium-period analysis with decreasing world export prices.

CONCLUSION

We have seen above that the world price of the export commodity determines the wage rate in the developing country and that, together with the production technology and the extent of the direct and indirect imported inputs, determines the price structure. The availability of foreign exchange also determines the production possibility frontier of the economy.

A formula for such a production possibility frontier has been given; in the case of a reduction in the foreign exchange availability this can be used approximately to plan the required reduction systematically rather than being forced into reducing necessary production unduly in an haphazard manner. It will also be useful in delineating the implications of the extent of the current debt servicing as well as the effects of foreign aid and loans for the economies of the countries involved.

The neoclassical theory of international trade assumes that both trading partners can produce all the commodities; they trade because their factor endowments make them use different techniques of production, thus making the cost of production of various commodities different in the two countries: both countries can increase their economic welfare if they concentrate on the production of the commodities that they can produce comparatively cheaply expensively costly and then exchange them for the rest, provided that transport and trade cost does not negate the economic advantage.

The above theory is based on comparative static analysis, as well as on the Say's Law assumption that the goods are exchanged for goods in the same period, while prices are just a convenience for an essentially barter economy. Obviously, this theory requires modification when applied to the dynamics of the development process. Developing countries cannot produce all the commodities; they do not have either the know-how or the capital equipment to be able to produce most modern goods. They are involved in complicated monetary transactions – taking long-term loans in one year, servicing them in other years, etc. All these are done in some monetary unit whose value in terms of commodities goes on changing over years. A theory based on a barter in a static framework has hardly any chance of being useful under these circumstances. An outline of an alternative more suitable approach has been given above; predictions about the differences in the price structures of developing and developed countries based on it are confirmed by the 1980 UN study on purchasing power parity. Kravis *et al.* (1982)

Notes

1 The Development Dilemma

1. Arnold Toynbee in his monumental *A Study of History* (1934–54) has shown that most of the successful creative efforts of mankind resulting in a civilisation not only results in the establishment of a 'creative-cum-dominant' minority, but also of two types of proletariats – internal and external. The internal proletariat consists of the elements who work for the new order in the same locale, but in a subordinate position and comparatively gaining little fruits of it, like slaves in classical society, or serfs in a feudal one. The external proletariat are the elements who are outside the locale of the civilisation but who become formally or informally attached to it through technological, political or economic contacts.

2. Naoroji's concept of 'external drain' or 'unrequited exports' from the developing country deals with the material balances in the international trade. It is related to the balance of payment concept in the same way as the concept of Net Material Product used by the USSR is related to the concept of Net Domestic Product of mainstream economics. As will be shown, while discussing appropriate macroeconomic theory, this concept, combined with the scarcity of land, determines the economics of colonial development (see Naoroji, 1901; 1888).

6 Determination of International Commodity Prices

1. We can conceive of these equations as the reduced form of an equilibrium model of the market for primary commodities, which sees price as being determined by market clearing where the quantities demanded depend on the scale of world industrial production (M) and prices of raw materials (P); while supply is determined by prices and the new capacity created a few years before. Let structural equations be,

$$D = a - bP + cM$$
$$S = d + fP + gL$$

and

$$D = S$$

where, D and S are demand and supply of primary raw materials respectively, and L is investment with suitable lags. Coefficients b, c, f, and g are expected to be positive. Then one reduced-form equation will be

$$P = h + jM - kL$$

In this,

$$j = c/(b+f)$$

and

$$k = g/(b+f)$$

and therefore both are expected to be positive. b would be small, as in the short period raw material demand would be hardly affected by price changes. c will hardly change in the two periods, therefore a proportionate change in j in two periods should give, approximately, the reciprocal of the proportionate change in f.

10 The Wage Goods Constraint for Employment and Development

1. Out of these 34 countries, ten were developed countries having a 'real' per capita income more than 60% of that of the USA. They were the UK, Japan, Austria, the Netherlands, Belgium, France, Luxembourg, Denmark, Germany, and the USA. Four countries were European countries at the periphery of the developed world having 'real' per capita income between 45% to 60% of that of the USA. They were Hungary, Poland, Italy and Spain. Each of them is a part of one of the European developed countries' economic common market groupings – the EC or Soviet Comecon bloc.

The remaining 20 developing countries are divided into three groups according to their 'real' per capita income. Of these the lowest, having per capita income of less than 15% of that of the USA, consisted of eight countries: Malawi, Kenya, India, Pakistan, Sri Lanka, Zambia, Thailand and the Philippines. The next group consisted of six countries having 'real' per capita income between 15% to 30% of that of the USA: Korea, Malaysia, Columbia, Jamaica, Syria and Brazil. The remaining six countries of the study had 'real' per capita income between 30% and 45% of the USA: Romania, Mexico, Yugoslavia, Iran, Uruguay and Ireland. Of these, Ireland is a part of the European Economic Community and therefore is not a part of the developing world; the manner of its economic development will be different from that of the developing countries. Therefore, our understanding of the problems of developing countries will be better focused if we do not include it in our discussions. The economy of the other five has been badly affected by the collapse of prices and the debt crisis of the early 1980s; though in 1975 they were in this higher group, they had been pushed back into the equivalent of the second group with respect to wage rates, etc. by 1986. In view of this we have discussed only the first two groups as representative of the normal conditions in the developing world.

2. Let g and E represent the rate of growth of per capita consumption and income elasticity of demand respectively, then by definition,

$$\log C_t = \log C_0 + gt$$
$$\log C_0 = \log A + E \log Y_0 \text{ and,}$$
$$\log C_t = \log A + E \log Y_t$$

This gives, $\log Y_t = (g/E) t + \log Y_0$ where C_0, Y_0, C_t, and Y_t are per capita consumption and per capita income in the base and the tth year. This gives the rate of growth of per capita income as (g/E). This should be considered as an approximate value as the above equation describes the reality only approximately.

12 The Role of Scarcity Value and Market Price

1. The mathematics involved in deriving this value structure is somewhat arduous. Von Neumann has shown how theoretically it helps in selecting the best techniques of production, even when joint products are present. However, he makes an unnatural assumption of no distinction between the stock and the flow of commodities. He assumes that 'flow' is just a stock kept for one period, and dates stock so that stock of period t becomes an input of the tth period while that of year $t+1$ is the output of that period. (von Neumann, 1945). The value structure derived thus has been termed as a 'von Neumann price ray'. Sraffa (1963) has developed a non-mathematical construct of the problem, and found that the capital–output ratio thus achieved is the maximum rate of possible return on the capital. A method of calculation based on the usual assumptions of input–output analysis of no joint production and distinction between stock and flow has been given by Mathur (1967). As input–output tables are easily available for most of the countries, this method makes the calculation of scarcity values according to this system widely practicable.

14 The Economics of Technology Transfer

1. The coefficient of variation is the standard deviation divided by the average; its modal value would be about 0.185. We can take the difference of the best and average technology to be about 2 s.d. and the same between the worst and the average technology (this assumes that 5% of the cases on both sides were in some sense abnormal).

The data necessary for this research were specially tabulated by the

Census Bureau from its database. Our research is based on data from the 1982 Census of Manufactures. Individual establishment data in the file were sorted at both three-digit and four-digit levels according to the following scheme. First the cost per unit of output for every establishment in every industry was computed. Output was defined as shipments plus the change in finished goods and half of goods-in-progress inventories between 1981 and 1982. Total cost was defined as the sum of the purchased materials, fuels, electricity, communication services, and building and machinery repairs plus worker payroll and supplemental labour cost. Thus, the information gathered at this stage pertained to the average variable cost of each establishment. Disclosure rules prevent the Census Bureau from releasing information on any single establishment. Therefore, the unit of observation had to be changed from an establishment to a group of establishments. This was done by first arranging these in order of rising unit variable costs, both within each four-digit industry and its parent three-digit industry as a whole. Then groups of establishments were formed in such a way that the unit cost of each establishment within a group was less than that of any establishment in the subsequent group. The number of establishments that fell within a group was determined in such a way that this number was equal for all groups within an industry.

Once these groups were formed information was collected for variables like output, employment, material and energy inputs, wages etc. In fact most of the data available on the short file of Census was collected. We did not collect the data regarding individual material input as that would have led to tabulating data from the comprehensive files themselves. This would have been not only very much time consuming but also quite costly in terms of resources. Further, it would have been much beyond our aim to have a preliminary understanding of the dimensions and hence practical importance of the problem of the layers of techniques in US manufacturing industry.

The table below reports on the coefficient of variation of unit output costs for 442 four-digit industries. Coefficient of variation is defined as standard deviation divided by the mean value. From the first column, it can be seen that the coefficient of variation of unit variable costs ranges

Table 1   The dispersion in costs per unit of output in 4-digit industries

Coefficient of variation of unit costs	No of 4-digit industries
0.042 – 0.099	15
0.102 – 0.150	80
0.151 – 0.200	178
0.201 – 0.250	124
0.251 – 0.299	33
0.301 – 0.347	11
.446	1

from a low 0.042 (Creamery Butter, SIC Code 2021) to a high of 0.446 (Industrial Gases, SIC Code 2813). The vast majority of industries (68%) have a coefficient of variation ranging from 0.151 to 0.245. To gain a feel for these numbers, consider the Screw and Machine Products Industry (SIC Code 3451). This industry has three five-digit product classes and a diversification index equal to 0.079. Thus it is a fairly homogeneous industry. Yet, unit variable costs in this industry range from 0.367 to 1.105 across 49 groups of establishments (omitting the last 50th one), with the mean value of 0.769. The coefficient of variation of unit variable costs in this industry equals 0.198. Thus the values reported in the table below are evidence of significant dispersion in unit variable costs across establishments within large number of four digit industries.

For manufacturing as a whole, the most efficient techniques have been found to be 41 per cent cheaper than the average techniques. This also implies that the overall least efficient techniques are about two and a half times more costly than the most efficient techniques. This is a huge figure. If what is apparent is simply true, we are almost shocked to realise that the average input–output tables that we are accustomed to use, can be so inaccurate when dealing with the results of the incremental increase or decrease of economic activity in a country. Even if some of the large variation observed is due to industry mix or differential product specification of products from different establishments, the variation is substantial. The large variation seems to be a result of the continuous embodiment of technical improvements in new investments. This preliminary study indicates the necessity of in-depth probing of these issues so that we may have a more precise idea of the spread of the cost of production through its various technological layers of various industries.

An issue of interest is whether the wide dispersion in unit costs at the four-digit level is concentrated in any particular parent two-digit industry. The evidence on this point is given below in Table 2. The last column in this table shows the average value of the coefficient of variation across four-digit industries within a given two-digit industry. The table shows that the phenomenon of unit cost dispersion is significant, widespread and cuts across all two-digit manufacturing sectors.

Table 2   The dispersion in costs per unit of output in 4-digit industries
arranged by their parent 2-digit industry

SIC Code	Industry Name	No. of 4-digit Industries	Coef. of Var Average
20	Food & Kindred Products	46	0.165
21	Tobacco Products	3	0.210
22	Textile Mill Products	30	0.163
23	Apparel & Other Textile Prod.	33	0.204
24	Lumber & Wood Products	17	0.190
25	Furniture & Fixtures	13	0.162
26	Paper & Allied Products	17	0.140

Table 2   continued

SIC Code	Industry Name	No. of 4-digit Industries	Coef. of Var Average
27	Printing & Publishing	16	0.225
28	Chemical & Allied Products	27	0.218
29	Petroleum & Coal Products	5	0.187
30	Rubber & Misc. Plastic Prod.	5	0.205
31	Leather & Leather Products	11	0.206
32	Stone, Clay, Glass Products	27	0.212
33	Primary Metal Industries	24	0.169
34	Fabricated Metal Products	36	0.184
35	Machinery, except Electrical	44	0.203
36	Electric and Electronic Equip.	37	0.187
37	Transportation Equipment	18	0.137
38	Instruments and related Prod.	13	0.221
39	Misc. Manufacturing Industries	20	0.192
	All Manufacturing	442	0.191

This shows that technical progress has been across the board during the last decade or so. It has not been confined to the so-called high rise industries only.

15 The Role of Subsidies and Import Controls in Modernising Low-income Countries

1. Not only do exporters of manufactured goods in market-oriented developing countries have to have low wage rates in terms of international currency (dollars), but centrally-planned developing economies have to follow suit as and when they choose to have trade relations with industrialised countries. Thus the average nominal wage rate in the USSR reduced from 20 to 14 per cent of that of the US between 1980 and 1985. Similar changes of nominal wage rate as a percentage of the US wage rate for the German Democratic Republic were from 39% to 23%; for Czechoslovakia from 18% to 14%; for Bulgaria from 16% to 12%; for Hungary from 13% to 6%; for Poland from 13% to 7%; and Yugoslavia from 22% to 8%. (UNIDO, 1987). This clearly shows that the erstwhile centrally-planned economies also fell into the category of developing economies and their development is subject to similar constraints as that of the market-oriented developing countries.
2. However, the least costly way to increase the production of foodgrains in the country is not to increase the subsidy on fertilisers; modern technology in agriculture has still not fully spread over the whole of the country. As is well known, the diffusion of a new technology follows the

logistic or learning curve over time (for a survey of diffusion research for an innovation see Rogers (1962 and 1986). But for modern agriculture it is not that simple; it requires a package of complementary inputs such as irrigation and the development of a suitable variety for each climate – soil – crop complex. It has been found that the marginal gains of extra expenditure on such inputs are greater than the expenditure in further subsidising fertilisers. Due to the diminishing returns on the intensity of fertiliser use, increasing its area of use is more cost effective until there is scope (see in this connection Desai, 1986: pp. 248–70).

3. It is interesting to note that Brown (1978) found a similar level of subsidy in Pakistan. He writes,

'The 2 billion rupees of government budget subsidies to lower wheat prices in 1976 amounted to one-half the value of all marketed wheat, including imported wheat. For fiscal year 1975, subsidies to consumers for wheat and for farmers for purchased inputs at provincial and national levels were budgeted to equal about 60% of all current and capital expenditures on agriculture, irrigation and water development projects. The cost of subsidies was drastically under-estimated, however, actual payments amounted to about 90 per cent of the budgeted levels of the type of expenditures noted.'

This level of subsidies for food is not only found in the exporters of manufactures in the market-oriented developing economies but also in centrally planned command economies. The latter have not been treated in detail in this book. Suffice it to note that the efforts to make those economies more market-oriented led to sharp increases in food prices resulting in general inflationary pressures. In 1988 the open inflation in Hungary was 15%, in China 30%, in Poland 60%, and in Yugoslavia 100%. The prospects of removing huge food subsidies have created quite a volatile political situation in the USSR in 1990. It is estimated that there the removal of food subsidies would treble the price of bread and double that of other foodstuffs. The situation is similar in other centrally planned economies. These subsidies thus seem to be of the same order as those in India and Pakistan.

18 Why International Price Structures Differ

1. For instance, the average real industrial wage in 1983 as a percentage of that in 1980 was 71% in Brazil, 93% in Chile, 91% in Columbia, 82% in the Dominican Republic, 57% in Mexico, 76% in Panama, 78% in Peru, and 53% in Uruguay. (From $ value in UNIDO, 1987, adjusted by the US consumer price index.)

Bibliography

Baer, Werner (1972) 'Import Substitution and Industrialization in Latin America: Experiences and Interpretations', *Latin American Research Review*, vol. 7/1.

Baily, M.N. (1983) 'The labour market in the 1930s' in Tobin, J. (ed), *Macroeconomics Prices and Quantities*, (Washington D.C.: Brookings Institution).

Barker, R. (1977) 'Economic Aspects of High Yielding Varieties of Rice', *FAO Studies in Agricultural Economics and Statistics, 1952–77* (Rome: FAO).

Bhagwati, J. (1967) 'The Tying of Aid', reprinted in Bhagwati, J. and Eckaus, R.S. (eds), *Foreign Aid* (Penguin edn, 1970).

Bhagwati, J. (1984) 'Why services are cheaper in poorer countries', *Economic Journal*, vol. 94, pp. 278–86.

Bhalla, G.S. (1979) 'Transfer of Technology and Agricultural Development in India', *Economic and Political Weekly* (Bombay) (December).

Bhalla, G.S. and Chadha, G.K. (1982) 'Green Revolution and Small Peasant', *Economic and Political Weekly* (Bombay) (May).

Brown, G.T. (1978) 'Agricultural Pricing Policies in Developing Countries', in Schultz, T.W. (ed), *Distortions of Agricultural Incentives* (Bloomington: Indiana University Press, 1978).

Brown, L.R. (1985) 'Reducing Hunger', in *State of World 1985* (New York: Worldwatch Institute, Norton).

Crouzet, F. (1972) *Capital Formation in the Industrial Revolution* (London: Methuen): 173.

CSO (various years) *Input–output Tables for the UK*.

Desai, G.M. (1986) 'Fertiliser Use in India: The Next Stage in Policy', *Indian Journal of Agricultural Economics*, vol. 41/3, pp. 248–70.

Edgeworth, F.Y. (1881) *Mathematical Psychics* (London: Routledge).

FAO (1979) *Agriculture: Towards 2000* (Rome: FAO).

FAO (1986) *Inter-Country Comparisons of Agricultural Production Aggregates*, FAO Economic and Social Development Paper, 61 (Rome: FAO).

Frank, A.G. (1978) *Dependent Accumulation and Under-Development* (London: Macmillan).

Galbraith, J.K. (1952) *American Capitalism: The Concept of Countervailing Power* (London: Hamish Hamilton).

Galbraith, J.K. (1958) *The Affluent Society* (London: Hamish Hamilton).

Genazzini, Luigi and Horhager, Alex (1987) 'Food Self-Sufficiency in the Southern Mediterranean Countries', *European Investment Bank Papers* (September).

Gerschenkron, A. (1962) *Economic Backwardness in Historical Perspective* (Cambridge, Mass.: Harvard University Press).

Ghai, D. and Radwan, S. (eds) (1983) *Policies and Rural Poverty in Africa* (Geneva: International Labour Office).

Ghosh, D. (1983) 'Marketed Surplus for Foodgrains in India' in *Scandinavian Journal of Development Alternatives*, vol. 3/4, pp. 89–106.

Government of India (1985–6) *Annual Report*, Department of Food and Civil Supplies (Government of India: New Delhi).

Grilli, Enzo and Yang, Maw Cheng (1988) 'Primary Commodity Prices, Manufactured Goods Prices, and Terms of Trade of Developing Countries: What the Long Run Shows', *The World Bank Economic Review* (January).

Gulati, A. (1987) *Effective Protection and Subsidies in Indian Agriculture* (Delhi: University of Delhi, mimeographed).

Haberler, G. (1936) *The Theory of International Trade* (London: Growse).

Hicks, J. (1969) *A Theory of Economic History* (Oxford: Oxford University Press).

Hicks, J. (1974) *The Crisis in Keynesian Economics* (Oxford: Basil Blackwell).

HMSO (various years) *Studies in Official Statistics*, 16 (1970); 12 (1973) (London: HMSO).

HMSO (various years) *Business Monitor*, DA 1004 (1980, 1983, 1988) (London: HMSO).

IMF (1986) *International Financial Statistics Yearbook* (Washington: IMF).

Kaldor, N. (1983) 'The Role of Commodity Prices in Economic Recovery', *Lloyds Bank Review* (July).

Kothari, V.N. and Dadi, M.N. (1975) 'Economic benefits of Rural Electrification in Gujarat' (University of Baroda).

Kravis, I., Heston, A. and Summers, R. (1982) *World Product and Income: International Comparisons of Real Gross Product* (Baltimore: Johns Hopkins University Press, for the United Nations).

Kravis, I., Heston, A. and Summers, R. (1983) 'The Share of Services in Economic Growth', in Adams, F.G. and Hickman, B.G. (eds), *Global Econometrics: Essays in Honor of Lawrence R. Klein* (Cambridge, Mass: MIT Press) pp. 188–218.

Krishnan, T.N. (1965) 'The Role of Agriculture in Economic Development: An Econometric Study of Price Relationship in India, 1950–62'. Ph.D. Thesis, (Cambridge, Mass: MIT).

Lele, Uma (1985) 'Terms of Trade, Agricultural Growth and Rural Poverty in Africa', in Mellor, J.W. and Desai, G.M. (eds), *Agricultural Change and Rural Poverty* (Baltimore: Johns Hopkins University Press).

Leontief, Wassily (1936) 'Quantitative Input–Output Relations in the Economic System of the United States', *Review of Economics and Statistics*, vol. 18, p. 456.

Leontief, Wassily (1951) *The Structure of the American Economy 1919–39* (New York: Oxford University Press).

Lewis, W.A. (1952) 'World Production, Prices, and Trade, 1870–1960', Manchester School of Economics and Social Studies, vol 20, pp. 105–37.

Lewis, W.A. (1954) 'Economic Development with Unlimited Supply of Labour', *The Manchester School*, vol. 22, pp. 139–91.

Lewis, W.A. (1955) *Theory of Economic Growth* (London: Allen and Unwin).

Mahabubul Haq (1965) 'Tied Credits: A Quantitative Analysis', reprinted in Adler, J. and Kuznets, P. (eds), (1967) *Capital Movements and Economic Development* (London: Macmillan).

Mahdi, M. (1988) 'Determination of International Commodity Prices'. Paper Presented at Seminar on 'Collapse of Commodity Prices and Debt Problems' (Aberystwyth: University of Wales).

Mathur, P.N. (1956) 'Income Elasticity of Foodgrain Consumption of Agricultural Labour in India', Gokhale Institute of Politics and Economics Discussion Paper, Pune, India.

Mathur, P.N. (1959) 'Marketable Surplus and Food Problem', Gokhale Institute of Politics and Economics Discussion Paper, Pune, India.

Mathur, P.N. (1962) 'Two Concepts of Capital–Output Ratios and Their Relevance for Economic Development', Artha Vijnana, vol. IV/4, Pune, India.

Mathur, P.N. (1967) 'An Appropriate System of Deflation of Sectoral Incomes in a Developing Economy', *Industry and Wealth*, XII/1.

Mathur, P.N. (1977) 'A Study of Sectoral Prices and Their Movements in the British Economy in an Input–Output Framework', in Leontief, W. (ed), *Structure, System and Economic Policy* (Cambridge: Cambridge University Press).

Mathur, P.N. (1978) 'Some notes on Labour in Guyana', mimeographed.

Mathur, P.N. (1987) 'Price Behaviour With Vintage Capital', discussion paper, 87–20, Department of Economics, University College London.

Mathur, P.N. (1989) 'Cost Variability Within US Manufacturing, Returns to Scale, Product Mix etc.', ninth international conference on input–output techniques (Keszthely, Hungary) (September).

Mathur, P.N. and Ezekiel, H. (1961) 'Marketable Surplus of Food and Price Fluctuations in a Developing Country', *Kyklos*, vol. 14.

Mathur, P.N. and Hashim, S.R. (1979) 'Quantification of Gains in Manufacturing Imports of Interregional Cooperation among Developing Countries', in Breheny, M. (ed), *Developments in Urban and Regional Analysis* (London: Pion).

Mathur, P.N. and Prakash, S. (1980) 'Inventory Behaviour of Indian Agriculture and its Effect on General Price Level', Proceedings of First International Symposium on Inventories (Budapest: Akademiai Kiado).

Mukherjee, P.K. and Sivasubramonian, S. (1958) 'Agricultural Output and National Income in India', in Bhattacharjee, J.P. (ed), *Studies in Indian Agricultural Economics* (Bombay: The Indian Society of Agricultural Economics).

Myint H. (1958) 'The Classical Theory of Trade and Underdeveloped Countries', *Economic Journal*, vol. 68/2.

Naoroji, Dada Bhai (1888) *Poverty of India – Papers and Statistics* (London: W. Foulger & Co.).

Naoroji, Dada Bhai (1901) *Poverty and Un-British Rule of Britain in India* (London: Sonnenschein & Co.)

Nath, S.K. (1969) *A Reappraisal of Welfare Economics* (London: Routledge and Kegan Paul).

Neumann, J. von (1945) 'A model of general economic equilibrium', *Review of Economic Studies*, vol. 13, pp. 1–9.

OAS (1987) *Trade and Financing: Evolution of Approaches to Solve the External Debt Problem*, Organisation of American States, Informative Document (Washington: OAS).

Orne, W.A. Jr (1987) 'End of Mexico's Oil-Boom Era has meant hardship for Citizens', *Washington Post*, 16 August 1987, pp. 1–13.

Papanek, G.V. (1977) 'Economic Development Theory: The Earnest Search for a Mirage', in Nash and Manning (eds), *Essays on Economic Development and Cultural Change* (Chicago: University of Chicago Press).

Parry, J.H. (1971) *Trade and Dominion – European Overseas Empires in the Eighteenth Century* (London: Weidenfeld and Nicolson).

Patel, S.J. (1961) 'Rates of Industrial Growth in the last century, 1860–1958', *Economic Development and Cultural Change* (April).

Popkin, J. and Mathur, P.N. (1989) 'A Study of Embodied Technical Change in US Manufacturing Based on 1982 Census Data', ninth international conference on input–output techniques (Keszthely, Hungary) (September).

Poston, M.M. 'Recent Trends in the accumulation of Capital', *Economic History Review*, vol. VI/11.

Prakash, S. (1986) 'Econometric Modelling of Price Formation Processes in Indian Economy, etc.', Eighth International Conference in Input Output Techniques, Japan.

Prebish, Raoul (1950) *The Economic Development of Latin America and its Principal Problems*' (New York: UN Sales no: 50.73.9.62). Reprinted in *Economic Bulletin for Latin America*, vol. VII, no. 1, 1962.

Radhakrishna, R. and Indrakant, S. (1987) *Effects of Rice Market Intervention Policies*, Center for Economic and Social Studies (Hyderabad).

Robbins, L.C. (1935) *An Essay on the Nature and Significance of Economic Science* (London: Macmillan).

Robinson, J. (1956) *The Accumulation of Capital* (London: Macmillan).

Rogers, E.M. (1962) *Diffusion of Innovations* (New York: Free Press).

Rogers, E.M. (1986) 'Three decades of research on the diffusion of innovations: progress, problems, prospects', paper presented to the DAEST Conference (Venice).

Rostow, W.W. (1960) *The Stages of Economic Growth* (Cambridge: Cambridge University Press).

Salter, W.E.G. (1960) *Productivity and Technical Change* (Cambridge: Cambridge University Press).

Samuelson, P. (1965) 'Equalization by Trade of the Interest Rate along with the Real Wage', in Baldwin, R.E. *et al.*, *Trade, Growth, and The Balance of Payments: Essays in honor of Gottfried Haberler* (Chicago: Rand Mc Nally).

Samuelson, P. (1984) 'Second Thoughts on Analytical Income Comparisons', *Economic Journal*, 94, pp. 267–78.

Santos, T.D. (1970) 'The Structure of Dependence', *American Economic Review*, vol. 60/2, pp. 231–6.

Sapsford, D. (1987) 'A Simple Model of Primary Commodity Price Determination: 1900–1980', *The Journal of Development Studies*, vol. 23/2.

Schumpeter, J.A. (1934) *The Theory of Economic Development* (English Translation) (New York: Oxford University Press, 1961).

Seers, D. (1962) 'Why Visiting Economists Fail', *Journal of Political Economy*, 70/4, pp. 325–38.

Seers, D. (1963) 'The Limitations of the Special Case', *Oxford University Institute of Economics and Statistics Bulletin*, 25/2.

Shankar, U. and Hema, R. (1984) 'Optimum Rate Structure for Electricity', University of Madras discussion paper.

Singer, H. (1950) 'The distribution of gains between investing and borrowing countries', *American Economic Review, Papers and Proceedings*, vol. 40, pp. 473–85.

Sirohi, A.S. (1984) 'Impact of Agricultural Subsidies', *Indian Journal of Agricultural Economics*, vol. 39, pp. 563–85.

Smith, Adam (1776) *An Inquiry into the Nature and Causes of the Wealth of Nations* (New York: Random House, 1937).

Solow, R.M. (1957) 'Technical Change and the Aggregate Production Function', *Review of Economics and Statistics*, vol. 39, pp. 312–20.

Spraos, J. (1980) 'The Statistical Debate on the Net Barter Terms of Trade Between Primary Commodities and Manufactures', *The Economic Journal*, vol. 90, pp. 107–28.

Sraffa, P. (1963) *Production of Commodities by Means of Commodities* (Cambridge: Cambridge University Press).

Sukhatme, P.V. (ed) (1982), *Newer Concepts in Nutrition and Their Implications for Policy* (India: Pune, Maharashtra Association for Cultivation of Science, Pune, India).

Sulaiman, M. (1989) 'A Study of Prices and Inflation in North-East Africa', Ph.D. Thesis, University of Wales, Aberystwyth, 1989.

Toynbee, A. (1934–54) *A Study of History* (Oxford: Oxford University Press).

Weintraub, E.R. (1979) *Microfoundations: The Compatibility of Microeconomics and Macroeconomics* (Cambridge: Cambridge University Press).

UNIDO (1986) *Global Report 1986* (Vienna: United Nations Industrial Development Organisation).

UNIDO (1987) *Global Report 1987* (Vienna: United Nations Industrial Development Organisation).

Wicksell, K. (1934) *Lectures on Political Economy* (London: Routledge).

Wierer, W. and Abbot, J.C. (1978) 'Fertiliser Marketing', *FAO Economic and Social Development Series*, 12 (Rome: FAO).

Williams, E. (1966) *Capitalism and Slavery* (New York: Capricorn Books) (1966 edn of a book first published in 1944).

Wittfogal, K.A. (1956) 'The Hydraulic Civilisations', Proceedings, Princeton Symposium. Reprinted in Kasperson, A. and Mingli, J. (1969) (eds), *The Structure of Political Geography* (Chicago: Aldine).

World Bank (1980) *World Development Report 1980* (Washington D.C.: World Bank).

World Bank (1981a) *World Development Report 1981* (Washington D.C.: World Bank).

World Bank (1981b) *Accelerated Development in Sub-Saharan Africa – An Agenda for Action* (Washington: World Bank).

World Bank (1987) *World Development Report 1987* (Washington: World Bank).

World Bank (1988) *World Development Report 1988* (Washington: World Bank).

World Resource Institute (1986) *World Resources 1986* (Washington D.C.: World Resource Institute).

Index